The Herndons

The Herndons

An Atlanta Family

CAROLE MERRITT

The University of Georgia Press   *Athens*

Paperback edition, 2017
Published by the University of Georgia Press
Athens, Georgia 30602
© 2002 by the Alonzo F. and Norris B. Herndon Foundation
All rights reserved
Set in 10.5 on 17 New Baskerville

Most University of Georgia Press titles
are available from popular e-book vendors.

Printed digitally

The Library of Congress has cataloged
the hardcover edition of this book as follows:
Merritt, Carole.
    The Herndons : an Atlanta family / Carole Merritt.
xii, 258 p. : ill. ; 26 cm.
    Includes bibliographical references and index.
    ISBN 0-8203-2309-8 (alk. paper)
    1. Herndon, Alonzo, b. 1858. 2. Herndon, Alonzo, b. 1858—Family.
3. Herndon family. 4. African American families—Georgia—Atlanta—Biography.
5. Upper class families—Georgia—Atlanta—Biography. 6. African American
businesspeople—Georgia—Atlanta—Biography. 7. Atlanta (Ga.)—Biography.
8. Atlanta (Ga.)—Social conditions. 9. Atlanta (Ga.)—Race relations. I. Title
F294.A853 H476 2002
975.8´23104´092396073—dc21
[B]   2001045117

Frontispiece: The Herndon mansion.
Paperback ISBN 978-0-8203-5182-7

Contents

Acknowledgments   *ix*

ONE. Homecoming   *1*

TWO. Adrienne's Debut   *16*

THREE. Alonzo's Debut   *32*

FOUR. Diamond Hill   *46*

FIVE. Unity in Division   *67*

SIX. All Hell   *85*

SEVEN. A New Home in the Rock   *101*

EIGHT. An Untimely Death   *125*

NINE. The Dearest Sweetheart   *133*

TEN. To the Top   *155*

ELEVEN. A Home of Her Own   *171*

TWELVE. The Next Generation   *184*

THIRTEEN. Bearing the Cross   *197*

Epilogue   *212*

APPENDIX. Family Trees   *215*

Notes   *221*

Selected Bibliography   *243*

Index   *251*

For Magnolia and Erica

and in memory of Earl and Melba.

Acknowledgments

This book was originally planned in 1990 as a publication in conjunction with a major exhibition called "The Herndons: Style and Substance of the Black Upper Class in Atlanta, 1880–1930." That exhibition of a multiyear project sponsored by the Herndon Foundation was installed in 1993 at the Atlanta History Center and ran for two and a half years. What had been envisioned as a complement to the exhibition became a work that would stand on its own—not only as an elaboration on the exhibition themes of race and class in a southern city but also as a more definitive narrative on an extraordinary African American family.

The 1910 mansion of the Herndon family has since 1984 been a house museum and is now a National Historic Landmark that interprets the family's significance and historical context to a broad public. It is an elegant symbol of Black achievement, a fine example of Black design and craftsmanship, and a stunning exhibition of the family's original furnishings. It is the repository of the family's papers, a rich collection of correspondence, school materials, business records, drama notes and programs, books and photographs. Conscious of their historical significance, the Herndons left a phenomenal collection of materials that document nearly a century of Black leadership in Atlanta. The story presented here is based largely on these papers.

That Alonzo Herndon, an uneducated slave-born man, could become through barbering and the founding of the Atlanta Life

Insurance Company one of the richest Blacks in the country is a wonder of hard work and determination that beat the odds of race and class. That his wife, Adrienne McNeil Herndon, could achieve significant acclaim in education and drama and that her design of her mansion would produce a landmark structure is an uncommon tale of a woman ahead of her time and outside of her assigned place. For two generations the Herndon family, through the son, Norris Herndon, and the second wife, Jessie Gillespie Herndon, held its place among Atlanta's leadership in business and philanthropy.

As the third generation, the Alonzo F. and Norris B. Herndon Foundation seeks to sustain the Herndon legacy. Its operation of The Herndon Home, its charitable contributions, and this book are dedicated to that legacy. I have chosen to leave the Herndons' words as written out of respect for them and for the authenticity of their statements as historical documents. To edit spelling and grammar would compromise the record and moreover would discredit their very remarkable educational achievement. The Foundation has supported and encouraged this book from beginning to end. I am particularly grateful to Dr. James Palmer, formerly the medical director of Atlanta Life and a Foundation trustee, for pushing me to finish the book and helping to arrange for the time and materials to do so. Dr. Edward Irons, the president and chairman of the Foundation, has steered the book through the publication process, confident that the importance of the story would find an appreciative press. Norris Connally, who is Alonzo Herndon's great-nephew, a retired Atlanta Life auditor and a Foundation trustee, has shared the Herndon family history and supported the Home at every turn. Perhaps no one had a more serious appreciation for the work of this project than did Henry Brown, a retired vice president of Atlanta Life and a Foundation trustee, who himself is a repository of information on nearly sixty years of the history of the Herndon family and Atlanta Life. Roswell Sutton, a former Foundation trustee and a key informant on the development of Auburn Avenue's businesses, continues to support the Home and its mission. I thank trustees Herman Russell, Felker Ward, and Nancy

Boxill for their wise counsel. I wish that Helen Collins, the first woman to serve as Atlanta Life Chair and as Foundation trustee, were alive to read this book. She was my mentor and hopefully would take pride in its publication. Former trustees, Johnnetta Cole and Elridge McMillan, set standards for trustee guidance and continue their support of the Home. I am grateful to The Herndon Home staff who have operated the museum while I attended to the exhibition project and the book: Davia Brown, Ernestine Brown, Victor Brown, Shauna Collier, Tonja Evans, Stephen Glass, Ernestine Hardge, Gerald Kemp, Jeffrey Leak, Joann Martin, Chris Mitchell, Keri Norris, and Karcheik Sims-Alvarado. The Herndon Home has depended on scores of volunteers. I am grateful to all of them, but make special note of those who furthered our work by going beyond the call of duty: Joanne Carruthers, Jacqueline James, Shirley Johnson, Joyce Jones, Rose Palmer, Roberta Phillips, and Joann Walker.

I am particularly grateful to Richard Long, Emory University professor, and Rose Palmer, who were the first to read the manuscript and to encourage its publication.

The National Endowment for the Humanities supported the exhibition project as did the Georgia Humanities Council, the Southern Education Foundation, and the Atlanta History Center, whose director, Rick Beard, generously made many resources available to us. Jesse Hill, then president of Atlanta Life, committed the company's substantial support of the exhibition project, including its publication. We are indebted to Kathryn Dixson, the exhibition curator, who was a delight to work with and whose skill and persistence were critical in the production of a major interpretive statement. We commend Staples and Charles for the elegance of their design. We thank Murphy & Orr, who fabricated a beautiful and richly crafted exhibition that is planned for permanent installation.

Oral informants, persons who had known the family or its work and associates, were among the most valuable sources of information. They are listed in the selected bibliography, but special mention must be made of those whose information was essential to understanding the Herndon story: Kathleen Redding Adams, Norris Connally, Adrienne Bailey Edwards, Norris Edwards, Lessie Herndon Hill, Wallace and Serena Jefferson, Florence McGehee, Eloise Milton, Rose Palmer, Girtha Cooper Patrick, Homer Perry, Bessie Rodd, and Bazoline Usher. Marion Porter, former housekeeper for Norris Herndon, was in a sense the first curator of the mansion and became a key informant on Norris's life.

I am indebted to Alexa Henderson for her fine scholarship on Atlanta Life. She has done the pioneering research on the company and has provided a model and guide for my work. A'Lelia Bundles, Adele Alexander, Adelaide Cromwell, and Willard Gatewood, who have published important scholarship on elite Black families, were sources not only of information but also of inspiration. I thank Beverly Guy Sheftall, who consulted on the exhibition project and has given critical guidance in matters of interpretation. Kelly Caudle, my editor, was a critical support and a delight to work with.

I thank my family: my mother, Magnolia Sleet, our family's historian, who inspired my life's work and who as a native of Social Circle, Georgia, provided important context to Alonzo Herndon's story; my sister and brother-in-law, Melba and Alonzo Fields, who though distant in California were a supportive presence; and my daughter, Erica Shani, who has kept up with every step of this venture and has lovingly urged me on. Finally, for everyone and everything that contributed to this book, I thank God.

The Herndons

CHAPTER 1

Homecoming

Alonzo Herndon missed the train that Sunday afternoon. He had seated his six-year-old son, Norris, in the coach at the Atlanta terminal and left momentarily, perhaps to check on tickets or baggage. But before he could return, the train pulled off with Norris left traveling by himself to Social Circle, the little town forty miles away in Walton County, Georgia, where his father had been born.[1] It must have been a frightful journey for the boy, but perhaps his fellow passengers in the Jim Crow coach were of some comfort. Someone on the train would have known his father, perhaps even the conductor. Alonzo Herndon was Atlanta's premier barber, proprietor of its finest shop, and the city's wealthiest Black.

Alonzo Franklin Herndon, early 1900s. No Black man stood higher in Atlanta than Alonzo Herndon at the turn of the twentieth century.

In about an hour the train reached Social Circle, a town of about twelve hundred people in the red clay farmland of Georgia's piedmont. Alonzo had telegraphed the stationmaster there and asked that he take Norris from the train and send for Emory Herndon to care for the boy until he could arrive. Norris would not have known this Herndon and may have been puzzled that a young White man came for him at the little depot. Emory took the boy the few blocks to his house on Monroe Street, where in a warm bedroom that winter evening in January 1904 Norris had supper with Emory's wife, Cora, who was tending their baby son. Cora would recall nearly seventy years later a polite and friendly child, bravely and calmly waiting for his father to come on the next train. She remembered that Norris had a chicken drumstick for supper and had thanked her for the meal, saying that he enjoyed it. He spoke of his mother, who was in Boston studying drama. After a while, Alice Newsome came to their house. She was the cook of Emory's father, Elisha Herndon, who lived across the street. In spite of the Herndons' protest, Aunt Alice, as they called her, swept Norris to her home nearby to wait for his father. One of the first to learn of Norris's arrival, she had moved quickly to claim the child on Alonzo's behalf.[2]

In one evening, Norris was introduced to his father's divided origins: on one side, the Whites who politely hosted his solo visit, and on the other side, the Blacks who seized hold of him as if by divine right. Aunt Alice was of the old homeplace, the community of families where Alonzo had been born a slave and had spent the first twenty years of his life. The Emory Herndons were of the same place, but of a separate kinship. When Alonzo arrived on the next train about two in the morning, he was directed to Aunt Alice's, where he rested till after daybreak. In a horse and buggy borrowed from Elisha Herndon, he and Norris rode the four miles to the little farm settlement around Fellowship Baptist Church.[3]

Homecoming was a frequent journey for Alonzo. Though his mother had been dead for more than ten years, a tight net of kin and near-kin still held him. It was a generation ago that he had first left Social Circle. Now, the former slave and ex-sharecropper was Atlanta's leading Black businessman, who was coming home this time to introduce his only child.

The reception would have been royal. Any of several households would have offered its best in homage to an illustrious son. On this visit, the hosts may well have been McHenry (Mack) and Alice Brown, leading members of the Fellowship Church community. Their farm was within walking distance of the church and was favored with a spring that ran pretty and clear. Alonzo's gourd would have hung among many others on the old tree nearby.[4] Perhaps it was here that Norris first tasted spring water. Like Uncle Mack's spring, the source of Alonzo's life issued directly and steadily from the ground, forever nourishing, but deep enough to drown in.

In 1858 a slave
I was born on a farm in Walton County Ga. near
the little town of Social Circle. I
(I remained on the farm until nearly)?
20 years old.

My mother was
Emancipated when I was seven years old
and my brother Tom five years old. She was
sent adrift in the world with her two
children & a corded bed & few quilts.
She hired her self out immediately for
by the day and as there was no money
in the country she received as pay
potatoes molasses and peas enough
to keep us from starving. Our
former master finally allowed us
to take shelter in a one room log
cabin with four other families. My
mother had only her bed space under
which she stored the her daily earnings up potatoes or peas or molasses
At seven and a half years old my
mother gave me all my grandfather take to help

Watered by the Alcovy and Apalachee rivers, the rolling foothills
of Herndon's birthplace had yielded a respectable cotton crop. But
it had offered Alonzo nothing except hard labor on land he would
never own. He had to leave Walton County and begin anew. "I was
some twenty years old," Alonzo wrote later, "and decided to seek my
fortune in a broader field. I managed to save up eleven dollars."[5] For
three years of sharecropping with his mother, that was an incredible
feat. Most sharecroppers ended each year owing not only half the
crop but also the money the landlord claimed had been advanced for
food and supplies. By hook and crook, Blacks were kept just a short
step from slavery. Alonzo had avoided this pitfall, however. Somehow

Alonzo, Sophenie, and Thomas Herndon, c. 1890. Alonzo wrote, "My mother was emancipated when I was seven years old and my brother Tom five years old. She was sent adrift in the world with her two children and a corded bed and [a] few quilts. . . . She hired herself out by the day and as there was no money in the country, she received as pay potatoes, molasses, and peas enough to keep us from starving."

keeping reign over his own accounts and living a life at very low subsistence, he had carefully saved, penny by penny, more than he had spent. Even as a boy, he had demonstrated his skill in nurturing the dollar by selling peanuts, axle grease, and molasses to supplement the family's earnings. Moreover, he had discovered the power, the promise, of entrepreneurship. "I had in mind going into business for myself," he said of his plans to escape the dependency of sharecropping. He left Social Circle on foot and got as far as Coweta County, seventy-five miles away, where he continued at field labor for a few months more. He eventually backtracked to a town not far from Atlanta. "I went to Jonesborough," he recounted, "and hired myself to a barber for six dollars a month and learned the barbers trade."[6] Having been born a slave on July 26, 1858, and having remained a sharecropper till 1878, Alonzo could not have made a more profitable choice. He was capitalizing on a trade traditionally reserved for Blacks in the South. Black men could make good money in service to Whites, particularly in cutting White men's hair. Herndon found in barbering a small window of opportunity, a narrow path to wealth and prestige.

Though the journey to riches had not always been steady, Alonzo Herndon became in just thirty years after slavery a wealthy man at the top of his trade. By the time of his visit to Social Circle that winter of early 1904, the Herndon Barbershop at 66 Peachtree Street had been operating for about two years. It had been a crowning achievement. At the midpoint of what would become a fifty-year career in barbering, Alonzo had established himself in a three-story building on the major commercial street in the heart of downtown Atlanta. No Black man stood higher in Atlanta than Alonzo Herndon at the turn of the twentieth century. He had assumed his position gradually, held it quietly, and secured it shrewdly with real estate, acquiring more property than any other Black Atlantan. Moreover, Alonzo was less than two years away

Alonzo stands in front of the log house where he lived after Emancipation. "Our former master finally allowed us to take shelter in a one room log cabin with four other families. My mother had only her bed space under which she stowed her daily earnings," Alonzo wrote.

Alonzo Herndon, c. 1915. The home people called him "Lonza."

from launching his greatest business venture: a life insurance company that would become one of the largest Black financial institutions in the country. Atlanta had proved to be fertile economic ground for the former slave. And it had offered him, a country migrant, a young and relatively open urban society within which he could climb, introducing him to his wife Adrienne McNeil, a teacher from Savannah, and presenting to him the company of other upwardly mobile Blacks like himself.

Each homecoming was a celebration of Alonzo's success, the home folk applauding every step. But surely each visit was also a bitter reminder of his harsh beginnings. He would confide to a business associate years later how, as a child in slavery, he was beaten so badly that when he urinated, "his little privates hurt and burned." Herndon spoke of the experience to demonstrate how the system sought to break the spirit of Black boys. The abject poverty that his family experienced was surely no less painful. When the Civil War ended, his family was homeless. "My mother was emancipated," he wrote, "when I was seven years old and my brother Tom five years old. She was sent adrift in the world with her two children and a corded bed and [a] few quilts." Kicked off the farm she had called home for thirty-four years, his mother, Sophenie, faced freedom with fewer material comforts than she had known in slavery. Her only option was field labor. "She hired herself out by the day," Alonzo recalled, "and as there was no money in the country, she received as pay potatoes, molasses, and peas enough to keep us from starving. Our former master finally allowed us to take shelter in a one room log cabin with four other families. My mother had only her bed space under which she stowed her daily earnings."[7]

The former master, Frank Herndon, was Alonzo's father, a farmer who at the time of Alonzo's birth owned five slaves and a hundred and fifty acres of land outside of Social Circle. He and his wife, Mary, though better situated than most Whites who owned no slaves, were far from wealthy. As the firstborn of Merriman and Annie Herndon, however, Frank would soon have control of a plantation-size holding:

"[Herndon] always was plain. He was tall, very light, and could pass for White easily. He wore glasses with no rims [and] . . . always wore dark clothes. He was common. You wouldn't think he had a penny," said his cousin, Bessie Rodd.

the twenty-five slaves and the nearly one thousand acres of land of his aging parents.[8] Among his slave children, however, as for most of the slave children of White masters, none of this wealth was to be shared. When upon emancipation Sophenie was "sent adrift" with her bed and two children (perhaps at the insistence of Frank's wife), the father was freeing himself from slavery's most intimate ties. Never to acknowledge his slave children publicly, he left Alonzo without place and property, a Black boy who looked like a White boy.

The home people called him "Lonza." Forever the country boy, he knew and loved the life well, returning again and again to its fountain. "He liked to go through the hogs and the chickens," recalled a

Charles T. Herndon, Alonzo's half brother, who was the son of Alonzo's father Frank and Harriet Herndon, sister of Alonzo's mother Sophenie. (Courtesy of Florence Jane Johnson-Gilmore-McGehee)

cousin, Bessie Vaughn Rodd. "He always *was* plain. He was tall, very light, and could pass for White easily. He wore glasses with no rims [and] . . . always wore dark clothes. He was common. You wouldn't think he had a penny."[9] Often coming in the fall to hunt for rabbits with Uncle Mack's son Lonnie, Herndon readapted with ease and humility to country life. The Browns fondly recalled Alonzo washing in the bowl and pitcher just like everyone else: "He never got above that."[10]

According to Girtha Cooper Patrick, Uncle Mack's granddaughter, "He would come to Fellowship Church Homecoming every third Sunday in August, . . . sit under the big tree in [her grandfather's] yard, drink water from the spring, and eat his dinner there." He knew all the old families, and when children passed by, he'd ask them, "What family do you come out of?" And then, "Tell your mother to come here."[11]

Radiating through the community was an extensive network of families related by blood and marriage. The Browns, who hosted many of Alonzo's homecomings, were linked to the Coopers, the Patricks, and the Hills, who were in turn tied by blood and marriage to the Whites, Baccuses, Clemmonses, Fambroughs, and Malcoms. The Herndons' direct kinship was to the Vaughns and to the Berrys, and indirectly by association to all the rest.[12]

Social Circle kinship was like a large cloth blanketing the entire community. Few if any families would have had no ties to others in the area. And significantly, the fabric of kinship was interwoven White with Black. Men like Frank Herndon had sex with slave women, by some degree of force or consent, in brief or extended unions, generating blood ties with a race they despised. These men, their wives and families, indeed the entire community of Whites, denied or ignored such blood ties, ripping apart for all concerned the foundation of marriage and family, and structuring a community that could never become whole.

Sophenie had only two children, Alonzo and Thomas, both of them sired by Frank. Frank, however, apparently had other illegal mates and children clustered around his household. He had a son, Charles, by Sophenie's younger sister, Harriet, and at least two children, William and Henry, by another slave, Febe Mayo. These, along with Sophenie and her sons, were among Frank's back-porch families, close by but in the unacknowledged recesses of southern kinship. The Black kin spoke of their situation only in secret, after children had been sent out of the room. They were afraid the White man would hear. One of Febe's descendants explained that Whites "didn't want Niggers half in their race no where."[13] Mixed blood, nevertheless, made for a colorful, albeit divided, society that ranged in skin shades from black to white, and was ordered by race, White over Black. Virtually never did Whites admit anyone with Black ancestry to their families. And without exception they allowed no one with Black blood in their race, no matter how white the skin. Flying viciously in the face of family, fathers enslaved their own children and discarded them upon Emancipation. Alonzo, therefore, could claim only his Black ancestry—just half of his lineage. And though he had three sets of siblings, he could fully acknowledge only Thomas. Of his half sisters and half brothers, Black and White, with whom he shared the same father, only those with Black mothers would have been part of his informal kinship, a network bound more tightly by association and mutual respect than by blood.

Alonzo Herndon, c. 1920. He "would come to Fellowship Church Homecoming every third Sunday in August."

On the trip with Norris that winter, Alonzo may also have visited Bill Knox, his old chum from Fellowship. Knox and his wife, Ida, owned a fourteen-horse farm in Whitney, a few miles from the church between Social Circle and Monroe. The Knoxes were the only family out their way. Anybody they saw in the distance on the road was headed, they knew, for their house. They would have spread a great feast for Herndon and his child. Knox, a prosperous farmer and a carpenter with a sawmill, was the wealthy son of Fellowship who had cut a path close to home.[14]

Bill Knox, Alonzo's old chum from Fellowship Baptist Church, owned a fourteen-horse farm in Whitney, a few miles from the church between Social Circle and Monroe. (Courtesy of Michael Syphoe)

Life converged in Herndonville, a small unincorporated area at the crossroads to Social Circle and Whitney. Fellowship Church was to the west on a one-acre tract of land purchased from Frank Herndon and his father, Merriman.[15] Not a mile away off the main road was the Annie Mary Church, named, respectively, for Frank's mother and wife. Across the road and about one hundred yards back on a slight rise of land surrounded by cotton fields sat the Herndon Cemetery, where in a clearing rested the Whites, and adjacent to them behind a wire fence in a larger area of untended plots, the Blacks. Alonzo may have shown Norris his mother's grave there. The four-foot-high granite headstone that towered above the other markers was inscribed, "None knew her but to love her." Little else documents her life. The only known photograph of her shows a light-skinned woman about sixty years old, standing sternly between Alonzo and Thomas, their jaws as broad as hers. Rather than face his mother's disapproval, Herndon had left home without telling her. He recalled later, "I knew my mother would never consent to my leaving the farm, so I took my little hand trunk on my shoulder and stole silently away in the darkness of night." Once established in Jonesboro, he bought a little three-room cottage and sent for her and his brother.[16] Singularly devoted, Alonzo did not marry until the year after his mother died.

Sophenie's parents, Carter and Tama Herndon, were probably buried in Herndon Cemetery also. They were mulattoes who had been born in the early 1800s, perhaps the children of Herndon slave masters whose surname they assumed and passed on to their children. Alonzo had lived in his grandparents' household after Emancipation.

The road to Whitney.

Alonzo Herndon at Herndon Cemetery, which sat across the road at Herndonville and about one hundred yards back on a slight rise of land.

He explained later, "At seven and a half years old, my master gave me alone to my grandfather to take to help me for my board and keep until I was thirteen, at which time I was pulling a crosscut saw with a full-grown man." So, under the tutelage of his grandparents, Lonza learned to labor. Frank Herndon then bound Alonzo in a three-year apprenticeship, a legal agreement he made with Sophenie to obtain his son's labor, paying twenty-five dollars the first year, thirty dollars the second, and forty dollars the third. Such apprenticeships were often thinly disguised arrangements to exploit Black children, keeping them nearly in slavery, obligating their labor for pennies a day. That his former master continued to control Alonzo's life after Emancipation is a measure of Frank Herndon's power, if not of his fatherly concern.[17]

What would Alonzo have told Norris on that visit about his father? Probably nothing. Miscegenation was too advanced a subject, too complicated a lesson for a six-year-old. Moreover, a child could not be told what was taboo to acknowledge publicly, what generally remained unspoken in private. Surely Norris had asked about Emory and Cora Herndon, and may have inquired about Elisha Herndon, who had loaned them the horse and buggy. But it is unlikely that Norris was told at that time that Elisha was Alonzo's half brother and Emory his half nephew. Norris would not have understood why to Cora and Emory he was a guest and not a cousin. On the one hand, the White Herndons were cordial and respectful, implicitly acknowledging a special relationship with Alonzo. But on the other hand, they insisted on a separate and superior rank and ignored or denied any blood ties. Black and White mixed in sex but not in family. When Alice Newsome, who was not blood kin to Alonzo, swept Norris to her home across the street, she was asserting that race is thicker than blood. For all his White ancestry, Alonzo Herndon was nevertheless Black.

At the heart of Alonzo's home community was Fellowship Baptist Church—a congregation organized just three years after the war, when a council of two ministers and eight members gathered under an oak tree. Less than forty years later, at the time of Alonzo's visit, a membership of about two hundred and fifty under the leadership of the Reverend Wyatt Rome was meeting in a thirty-by-fifty-foot frame building. Few Herndons by then were still on the church roll: Hannah, William, Homer, Henry, and Larkin.[18] Thomas, Alonzo's only sibling, had long since moved to McDonough, in Henry County, not far from Jonesboro; and the Berrys had migrated to Flippen in the same county.

Had Alonzo and Norris arrived a day earlier, they might have worshipped at Fellowship. Since their host, Mack Brown, had also become an ordained minister several years before and was one of the pillars of Fellowship, church would have been the main event. Alonzo had been raised in a strictly disciplined religious community, where on the third Saturday afternoon of each month, the men met in conference and presided over church affairs, struggling to keep the building in good repair and the membership in gospel order. Any breach of church rules that threatened the "call for peace and fellowship" was reported to the men. At one January conference some time before

At the heart of Alonzo's home community was Fellowship Baptist Church. The Reverend Harrison Vincent is on the steps. (Courtesy of Lena Williams)

Alonzo's visit, Larkin Herndon was excluded from membership for "picking a gittaur for worldly people to dance." The same sentence was passed for drinking, cursing, living in adultery, and giving birth to a child outside marriage.[19] Alonzo's church in Atlanta had no less strict a moral code. But in joining First Congregational, where many of the city's prominent Blacks belonged, he had selected a circle of friends and a culture of worship that were a far cry from his home church. In time, Alonzo seldom attended Fellowship, but he held fast to its people for the rest of his life.

It is unknown whether Alonzo visited his father before leaving Social Circle in early 1904. Frank Herndon may have been ill at the time, for he died the next August at the age of 82. He left nothing for Alonzo. In his will he carefully identified his heirs: "In referring to my children, I mean E. M. Herndon, John T. Herndon, Samantha Aycock and Martha E. Whatley." This exclusion was of no material consequence to his unnamed son, however. By then, Alonzo Herndon had amassed a fortune that far surpassed his father's.[20] If Alonzo returned in August to attend his father's funeral, it is certain he would have sat apart from the White Herndons. If he had come to their house to pay his respects, he could have been acknowledged only as a member of the Black community, and he surely would have entered by the back door. One can only speculate about the grief or bitterness Alonzo carried at his father's death. But had he gone to the cemetery for the burial, he most certainly would have felt sharply the irony of the distance that separated his parents' graves.

CHAPTER 2

Adrienne's Debut

Adrienne McNeil Herndon,
1904. "It is simply inevitable that
I shall end up on the stage. The
footlights have beckoned me since
I was a little child, and
I simply must respond."

Back in Atlanta father and son returned home to the Bumstead Cot-
tage, a large, rambling house on the campus of Atlanta University.
Adrienne Herndon was away in Boston preparing for her dramatic
debut later that month. After several summers of study there at the
School of Expression and in the midst of teaching elocution at Atlanta
University, her chance to perform professionally had finally come.
During an extended absence from the university, Adrienne rehearsed
for a recital of Shakespeare's *Antony and Cleopatra*.

As a condition of their marriage, Alonzo had promised to support Adrienne's drama pursuits.[1] "It is simply inevitable that I shall
end up on the stage," she confessed. "The footlights have beckoned
me since I was a little child, and I simply must respond. It has always been my dream to portray all the heroic feminine characters of
Shakespeare . . . first on the platform and later on the stage."[2] Henry
Clapp, drama critic of the *Boston Herald,* had introduced her to David
Belasco, America's leading theater manager, who had seen her work
in New York and confirmed her talent. "You will undoubtedly make a
fine character actress," he wrote to her several days before the debut.[3]
Such acclaim was critical encouragement to a beginner preparing for
a superhuman undertaking: the recital from memory of twenty-two
characters of a difficult Shakespearean work. Without scenery, costumes, or supporting readers, Adrienne engaged an audience of about
three hundred in Steinert Hall that Thursday afternoon, January 28,

1904. She began the recital nervously, according to one critic, but then calling upon her training and instinct, she gave voice to a complicated play, ending each of fifteen scenes to loud applause. When it was over, the same enthusiasm called her back to the stage several times.[4] "She has a remarkable gift and unusual aptitude," concluded the critic from the *Boston Herald,* citing her "fine voice [and] excellent stage manner, entirely free from pretence and self-consciousness." The impersonation of an angry Cleopatra, he said, was "brilliantly well done." He saw Adrienne as "a young lady of decided personal attractions, with a fine presence, a handsome face and a very graceful figure, who carries herself easily, [and] enunciates well with a fine voice."[5] The *Boston Daily Advertiser* noted her "delicately rounded throat, and a wealth of dark brown tresses," describing her as "at once self assertive and enduring."[6] More than ten newspapers in the Boston area reviewed the debut, the result of Adrienne's thoroughly executed promotion: circulars, announcements, advertisements, and the references of well-placed persons.[7]

It was as if all of Boston had been awaiting this "notable event in the Shakespearean forecast."[8] The flaws in Adrienne's performance were also duly noted, one reviewer claiming that the techniques of her training often hampered her delivery. "As of nearly all popular elocutionists there is a great need of better instruction on points of emphasis and proportion," wrote the *Herald.* The *Journal* also claimed that "too much conventional teaching and too much deliberate effort is over all her work." They concluded, however, that Adrienne had great potential, citing her "large possibilities of uncommon range, sensibility and effectiveness" and predicting that "only [on the stage] could she find a fitting scene for her unusual capabilities."[9]

Boston obviously had no idea who this promising young talent was. Adrienne Herndon made her debut under the stage name of Anne Du Bignon, having told the press that she was from an old South Carolina family of colonial French and Creole ancestry, an identification that came as close to the truth as she dared.[10] As a "Creole," a racially ambiguous term, Adrienne was neither admitting nor denying that

Playbill for Antony and Cleopatra.

First Impersonation in Boston
of
SHAKESPEARE'S

Antony and Cleopatra

BY

ANNE DU BIGNON

STEINERT HALL

Thursday, January 28, 1904
at three o'clock

TICKETS ONE DOLLAR

Management

Geo. W. Britt, Boston.

David Belasco confirms that Adrienne has dramatic talent.

BELASCO THEATRE

BROADWAY & 42d STREET
New York City

Under the sole management of DAVID BELASCO.

N. Y., Jan. 8th, 04.

My Dear Miss Du Bignon:

        In consequence of the terrible Chicago disaster, I was unable to go to Boston as I intended to do. The Fire Commissioners have kept us all busy. I don't know when I shall be in Boston again, but I want you to understand how pleased I was with your work. You will undoubtedly make a fine character actress. Remember, anything I can do at any time, I shall be only too happy.

        Faithfully,

David Belasco

Miss Eleanor Du Bignon,
    Boston, Mass.

she was Black. The theater audience saw her as a White woman whose coloring hinted of Latin origins. They sensed her ancestry without knowing her race.

They would not have known that Adrienne was born Elizabeth A. Stephens (they called her "Addie") on July 22, 1869, in Augusta, Georgia, to an unmarried ex-slave, Martha (Mattie) Fleming. Adrienne indeed had South Carolina ties. Her maternal grandmother, Harriet Hankerson, had come from Barnwell, a rural community across the Savannah River from Augusta. At Adrienne's birth in 1869 in Augusta, her mother, Martha, was about seventeen years old and presumably a house servant like her grandmother Harriet. Martha was the daughter of William R. Fleming, a prominent White merchant of Augusta and Savannah. His paternity was documented in Adrienne's family Bible, the notation "grandfather" recorded over his name by

Adrienne's mother, Martha Fleming, c. 1868.

Adrienne's sister Jennie. In the yellowed 1884 obituary pasted on an adjacent page, Fleming is described as "an exceedingly popular citizen of Augusta." At one time a board director of the Central Railroad, he possessed, according to the obituary, a "fine intelligence, rare conversational power, and a warm heart that sunned a geneal nature." There was no mention in the obituary of family, other than his sister, a Mrs. Tutt, at whose home in nearby Lincoln County he died. Martha's brother, Thomas, who was apparently William Fleming's other child by Harriet, eventually moved to Indiana, where it is presumed he passed for White. Years later he sent Harriet a photograph of himself as an elderly man and inscribed it, "To my mother."[11]

If Martha's father had no constant presence in her life, Adrienne's father was even more distant. Martha had never married Adrienne's

father, a Black man by the name of George Stephens, whose family came from Edgefield, South Carolina, and Augusta. Extremely light-skinned, Stephens ultimately forsook his family to pass for White. A Stephens family descendant stated that George vowed he would kick the red clay of Georgia off his feet and make a new life for himself. Though presents from him arrived occasionally from Wanamaker's in Philadelphia, none of his family ever saw him again.[12] In 1871, when Adrienne was two years old, Martha married Archibald McNeil, a Savannah butcher, and had two more children, a daughter, Jennie Olive, and a son, Willie.[13]

The Boston audience in Steinert Hall that January afternoon was also unaware that they were applauding the wife of one of the richest Black men in the country. Alonzo himself was very likely at the debut, perhaps clapping the loudest and offering one of the several floral tributes Adrienne received after her performance.[14] He would boast later of her accomplishment: "She knew [Shakespeare's] life from babyhood up. When she came before the public in the great city of Boston she gave the whole twenty two characters and never missed a line."[15]

That afternoon at the debut, however, Alonzo could not have acknowledged his own accomplishments. He was implicitly the husband of Anne Du Bignon. Even if he had been introduced as Alonzo Herndon, few in the theater would have known of his business success

Adrienne, right, with her half sister Jennie Olive and half brother Willie, c. 1885.

or of his racial background. Horace Bumstead, the White president of Atlanta University, was in the audience with his family, but apparently Adrienne had forewarned them, lest her racial identity be discovered. "We shall caution our friends on the point that you mention," Bumstead had written just before the recital in a letter of thanks for the box seat tickets she had sent.[16]

The recital may have been Alonzo's first chance to meet Samuel and Anna Curry, founders of the School of Expression, where Adrienne had studied and under whose auspices the debut had been arranged. For several years, the Currys had interceded with Alonzo on Adrienne's behalf. "She needs to study until she is ready to perform as a platform artist," Anna Curry had written to him a few years before. Their initial plan, which seemed to address racial restrictions in the American theater, was that Adrienne first establish a reputation in London before making a debut in the United States. "Please help her financially," Anna Curry pleaded. "There will be only limited separation from her family."[17]

Samuel Curry, founder of the School of Expression.

But the separations became extended. After receiving a degree in general culture in 1902, Adrienne enrolled for the September term of 1903 to study for the public reader's diploma. Alonzo and Norris very likely spent that Christmas without Adrienne, who, rather than return to Atlanta for a brief stay before the debut in January, apparently remained in Boston.[18] It was during this absence of nearly six months that father and son made their winter trip to Social Circle.

After the Steinert Hall debut, Adrienne engaged the George Britt Company, a lecture and musical agency, to arrange for platform appearances. "I think I have procured a $75 engagement for you . . . at Lynn, [Massachusetts]," Britt wrote to Adrienne about two weeks after the debut.[19] The engagement seemed a promising beginning. The seventy-five-dollar fee may have impressed even Alonzo, but the high cost of launching his wife's platform career also must have attacked his frugal heart. Adrienne's weekly salary as a teacher would barely have covered her twenty-four-dollar printing bill for the circulars, announcements, and programs.[20]

Standing only about five feet tall, Adrienne was nevertheless commanding.

To Alonzo, whose formal schooling totaled only a year at a country school in Georgia, the forty-dollar tuition for a two-month term of elocution studies would have seemed mighty steep.[21] The debut incurred other costs: private lessons from the Currys at three to six dollars per session, the twelve-dollar rental of Steinert Hall, and room and board for several months, presumably a substantial amount at Franklin Square House. Alonzo paid for it all. Adrienne's record of his support from August to January totaled nearly six hundred dollars.[22] That most Black families earned only half of that in a year was surely not lost on Alonzo.[23]

When Adrienne returned to her family later that winter, Alonzo would have seen a woman still aglow from the rave reviews and the prospects of a platform career. Surely he was struck again with the beauty and presence that had first attracted him to her when she was a senior student at Atlanta University.

Standing only about five feet tall, Adrienne was nevertheless commanding. Her talent was driven by a will to succeed that matched her husband's. The Herndons, after all, were two of a kind: extremely talented and powerfully ambitious. No wonder Adrienne had obtained Alonzo's prenuptial permission to pursue her drama studies, hoping to ensure that marriage would not undermine her plans.

They became one of Atlanta's most attractive couples when they married on Halloween of 1893 at Adrienne's home church, Mount Zion Baptist in Savannah. She at twenty-four years old and he at thirty-five were marrying late, both well along on their intended paths. Adrienne had finished Atlanta University Normal School three years before and had begun teaching at the city's Gray Street Public School. For three years Alonzo had been the proprietor of the barbershop at the Markham House, Atlanta's second-largest hotel. Here were two people at the top of their class. Few Atlantans at that time, Black or White, had Alonzo's money or Adrienne's professional status.

Of all the women Alonzo could have chosen for a wife, Adrienne was perhaps the one whose identity depended least on his. She stood not as Mrs. Alonzo Herndon, but on her own as Adrienne Herndon,

Adrienne and Alonzo married on
Halloween of 1893 at Adrienne's
home church, Mount Zion Baptist
in Savannah.

the teacher, or preferably as Anne Du Bignon, the aspiring dramatic artist, setting her own course and developing a distinctive style in a society that for the most part rejected such independence in women. "The South has not yet accustomed itself to the thought of its women adopting professional careers or appearing in any other than simply social ways," she explained to a Boston newspaper before her debut. Identifying as a southern woman, Adrienne could speak to the burden of gender, but not of race: "All these prejudices have yet to be overcome, so you see when Southern women do these things they do it in the face of all tradition and trying opposition."[24]

Joseph Bryan Cumming, half brother of Martha Fleming.

She had felt keenly the restrictions her own family placed on her aspirations. "I was born of an old Southern family," she recalled for the press, referring to her White ancestors, "that counts for each of five generations a brilliant orator and it was a great disappointment to my parents that this family gift of oratory was wasted in me."[25] Adrienne may have been alluding primarily to Major Joseph B. Cumming, widely known as a gifted speaker. The *Atlanta Journal* at his death in 1922 described him as "a public speaker of great ability whose superior could not be found in this country for eloquence, grace of expression and poetic beauty of thought." Cumming, a Confederate veteran and a prominent attorney who had graduated from the University of Georgia and Harvard Law School, served for nearly fifty years as the general counsel for the Georgia Railroad and Banking Company. Adrienne claimed him through her mother's half brother Joseph B. Cumming, who was the son Harriet had had apparently by this leading citizen of Augusta.[26] Adrienne lamented her family's failure to appreciate her oratorical skills. "When as a girl I gained honors at school for my work in expression, instead of hearing praise at home for these distinctions my mother would exclaim 'Why could you not have been born a boy? . . . Then you could make us proud by your oratory.'" Adrienne confessed that "many hours of my childhood were spent in trying to kiss my elbow, for I was told by my mates at school that by such a [feat] I might be transformed into the coveted boy. . . . It never occurred to my parents that I might use this gift of oratory in any way professionally."[27]

It was probably Alonzo, however, to whom she referred when she admitted to the Boston newspaper that she had been "forbidden the stage." The paper reported that she was contenting herself with the platform, "believing that it will pave the way to the stage by gradually accustoming family and friends to the thought of her appearing as an actress."[28]

Alonzo most certainly knew that his marriage to Adrienne would not be a conventional one, and he was awed by her talent and drive and proud of her accomplishments. Moreover, he no doubt saw her intelligence and style as significant supports to his own ambitions. He probably had no realistic idea during their courtship how much time, energy, and money a career in drama would demand, so probably in deference to Alonzo's wishes, Adrienne altered her career plans, hoping the compromise would be temporary.

By summer of 1904, however, Adrienne was trying desperately from Atlanta to pick up the momentum of the debut. The engagements had not come as expected. Finally, a booking was made in Bellows Falls, Vermont, for December 13. "So there, my dear," wrote Janet Owen, who served as her press agent in Boston, "is a definite engagement made at last, and even if it is quite a ride from Boston, you will clear all the profit yourself." Owen had compiled a list of women's organizations for potential recitals. "I do wish those other clubs would answer my letters!" she complained.[29]

What a comedown the Vermont engagement must have seemed to Adrienne! Nearly one year after the heady triumph of *Antony and Cleopatra,* she would be performing before a small audience hours away from the liberal and cultured Boston. It would not have been the size of the profit that concerned Adrienne, but rather the scale to which her dreams had been reduced.

Even David Belasco had become inaccessible. She may never have seen him again after her first reading in his theater in New York the month before her debut. In answer to her invitation to the Steinert Hall recital, his assistant wrote that "owing to illness Mr. Belasco has

She stood not as Mrs. Alonzo Herndon, but as Adrienne Herndon, the teacher, or preferably as Anne Du Bignon, the aspiring dramatic artist.

Atlanta University's first Shakespeare production, The Merchant of Venice, *1905.*

been obliged to go South, and he will not return for some months." Nearly a year passed before there was another response to her appeals, the assistant explaining in a letter that "Mr. Belasco is in Washington at present for the production of his new play. When he returns in January, I will endeavor to make an appointment for you."[30]

Something had gone dreadfully wrong. The great promise of even a platform career was evaporating. Had Belasco changed his mind about her talent? Or had he or others discovered her race? Someone at the School of Expression, where she had enrolled as Adrienne Herndon, could have told on her. Or maybe a drama critic had investigated her background. So well publicized a performance and so intriguing a performer had to have aroused the interest, indeed the suspicion, of a relatively small theater world.

Adrienne was thrown back on herself. The stage beckoned, she insisted, but save for vaudeville and minstrelsy and all-Black productions, it admitted no one with Black blood, no matter how few the drops. She could look the part, know and interpret it effectively, but she could not have the part. Child of a slave-born house servant, she was prepared nevertheless for Shakespearean drama, but the closest she would get to its stage would be the training for it. She would be in constant preparation for a performance that would never take place.

Her fate may have been dawning on her slowly that summer, for she altered her course somewhat. During the 1904–5 school year, she prepared for Atlanta University's first Shakespearean production, *The Merchant of Venice*. Having done as much as she could with Shakespeare in the Northeast, she would bring him south. The senior classes of the normal school and the college presented the comedy during their class night exercises that next June of 1905. The month before, the William Gillette Theater Company from New York had come for a performance of *Sherlock Holmes in the Adventure of the Second Stain* in Bumstead Cottage.[31] Gillette's appearance meant that Adrienne was no longer keeping her background a secret from the theater community. Perhaps Adrienne was beginning to realize that the elocution and drama department she directed was her best opportunity for professional fulfillment, at least for the time being. She would make Atlanta University a regional center for the dramatic arts. In the process she would allay some of Alonzo's concerns about the expenditures of time and money in pursuit of a dream that had begun to fade.

Her childhood on Duffy Street in Savannah may not have seemed so distant to Adrienne that summer of 1905. She had gone an incredibly long way to Steinert Hall, but it was as though she were back where she started, frustrated by gender and excluded by race. Adrienne, however, was tenacious, and her dreams faded slowly. Throwing herself into her work at the university, she nevertheless held on to her ties to the legitimate theater. Late that year she sent a wreath and card to Belasco upon the death of a family member. Belasco himself responded with a letter of thanks, but there was no mention of another meeting.[32]

CHAPTER 3

Alonzo's Debut

"I kept reaching out for a greater world, a broader field. . . . I thought that Atlanta would give me the better opportunity," said Alonzo.

About a year before Adrienne's debut in Boston, Alonzo had had a debut of his own in Atlanta. Abruptly and with a small advertisement in the classified section of the *Atlanta Constitution* on December 13, 1902, Herndon opened the barbershop at 66 Peachtree Street that would ensure his leadership in the trade for the rest of his life. In the heart of downtown Atlanta at the turn of the century, Herndon was operating the city's leading Black business. It was the ultimate accomplishment for a man who had started in a little one-chair shop in Jonesboro about twenty miles away. That first shop in Clayton County with its "white-washed board walls [and] its tiny cheap-looking glass and crude homemade chair" was the lowly start of the glory to come. When Alonzo arrived in Jonesboro around 1878, the town's population was about one thousand, almost twice the size of Social Circle at the time.[1] His first barbershop may have been located somewhere in the block of storehouses situated on Main Street diagonally from the depot and directly across the railroad tracks from the courthouse. Anthony Battle, the barber (probably Black) who operated a basement barbershop in the area, may have been the one to whom Alonzo hired himself for six dollars a month to learn the trade. Or Nelson Smith, a mulatto barber in the town, may have been the one to give the Social Circle native his start. In any event, Alonzo learned quickly, for he soon set up his own shop, perhaps in the same area of town, and gained years of experience before his next move. "I kept reaching out for a greater world, a broader field," Herndon recalled, "and so after five years in Jonesboro, I started for Rome, [Georgia], having heard that it was five or six times as large. I worked there two months and decided to go to Chattanooga as it was a new and booming town. I found that both Rome and Chattanooga did not come up to the graphic descriptions I had heard of their opportunity, and so after looking over the field I thought that Atlanta would give me the better opportunity." Indeed, Atlanta did. In time, Herndon could confidently claim that his Peachtree Street shop, the Crystal Palace, was the finest in the world.[2]

The way up had been neither steady nor certain. At times he became so discouraged that he had considered leaving the trade. "I started to quit the barber business and go to work in a plow factory," he admitted. He did, in fact, work there for a time, but, advised by the factory owner to stick with barbering, he "went back and made a success."[3] It took, however, twenty years to get to Peachtree Street.

Atlanta was barely forty years old when Herndon arrived in 1882. There were less than forty thousand residents, nearly half of them Black.[4] The city had rebounded quickly after the devastation of the Civil War to become the region's commercial and financial center.

In the heart of downtown at the turn of the century, Herndon began operating Atlanta's leading Black business. Herndon's barbershop at 66 Peachtree Street, fourth building from the left. (Courtesy of the Atlanta History Center)

Moreover, Atlanta had no economic ties to the plantation past, no firmly entrenched planter elite. It was a young city and relatively open to new business, Black and White. Just twenty-four years old himself, Alonzo Herndon grew up with the city. "I began . . . as a journeyman in one of the first-class shops," he wrote, referring to his work as an experienced barber in the Marietta Street shop of William Dougherty Hutchins. Hutchins was of the first generation of barbers in Atlanta, having been one of a handful of free Blacks in the trade before the Civil War.[5] In the South barbering for the most part was the work of Black men. The barber, after all, was the consummate body servant, courteous and accommodating in deference to a master. In the city the barbershop became a high-status domestic service gone public and could be a very lucrative enterprise.

By the time of Herndon's arrival, Atlanta had twenty-five barber-shop proprietors listed in its business directory, most of them Blacks who catered exclusively to Whites in the downtown area.[6] As the new barber in town, Herndon was in line to become a master in one of Atlanta's most prosperous Black trades. "I came to Atlanta with the determination to succeed," he said, "and by careful, conscientious work and tactful, polite conduct, I succeeded so well that [Hutchins] urged me to buy half interest in the business and thus became a partner with him."[7] Herndon admitted that his success depended not only on management but also on the manner in which he served his patrons. Herndon cut the hair of White men who under any circumstances could assert their superiority over him, a Black man. He served only at their pleasure. Were Herndon not polite and tactful, even when a customer's racism was most offensive, he could not have stayed in business, much less have made good money. There was a growing market of White men in post-Emancipation Atlanta who were accustomed to service by Blacks; Herndon was eager to capitalize on it.

The partnership with Hutchins lasted only two years. "I eventually sold my interest in this shop," Herndon explained, "and went into business for myself."[8] It would take about five more years before Herndon reached that next milestone. After the partnership ended,

Herndon remained for about a year with Hutchins at the Marietta Street shop, which curiously had come under the ownership of Noble P. Beall, a White clerk at the Muse, Swift and Gregg clothing store on Whitehall Street.[9] The circumstances under which Herndon and Hutchins sold their interests to Beall are unknown, but obviously there had been some difficulty in the partnership. Had Hutchins, who was Atlanta's senior barber, experienced some financial reversals? Perhaps that had been one of the reasons he had urged Herndon into the partnership. Hutchins had been one of Atlanta's most prosperous Blacks, owning real estate assessed at $2,400 about the time Alonzo arrived in Atlanta. Only one person in the Black community owned more property: James Tate, a grocer.[10]

Though Herndon had great skill in managing money, he probably had not yet accumulated enough to be on his own. Barbering in downtown Atlanta incurred substantial costs for rent and fixtures.

Whatever the reason, the partnership with Hutchins was dissolved in what seemed to be a step backward for both men. After a year, Beall returned to clerking, and Hutchins apparently regained ownership of the shop on Marietta, where he continued for another year. Herndon barbered across the street at 18 Marietta Street in the shop of James R. Steele, a Black man.[11] Ironically, Hutchins ended his career a couple of years later as owner of a shop at 60 Peachtree Street, just three doors down from where his former partner would reach the heights of barbering.[12] It was as though the elder barber had run the distance to Peachtree Street, but had to pass the baton to Herndon for the second generation.

In the meantime, Herndon entered a two-year partnership with William R. Betts, a Black barber, locating first at 6 Whitehall Street. The partnership then moved to 24 Loyd Street, the same address of the Markham House, where Herndon the next year became the sole barbershop proprietor.[13] "I started out alone with a five-chair shop," he recalled.[14] The Markham was second only to the Kimball House and claimed at its construction in 1875 to be "the most comfortably arranged house in the South . . . [with] every modern improvement."[15]

Within the hotel district and adjacent to the Union Depot, the barbershop catered to both locals and travelers.

Herndon had fallen heir to the tradition of Black hotel barbers. On the very site of the Markham House had stood Washington Hall, the city's first hotel, where as early as 1859 Erasmus Cobb, a free Black, had been the barber.[16]

The Markham House shop was at street level, adjacent to the hotel's drug store, dining room, bakery, laundry, saloon, and billiards room. At the curb in front of the barbershop stood a wooden barber pole more than seven feet tall, painted red, white, and blue, symbolizing the bloodletting arts that barbers had practiced centuries before. The shop was large enough to accommodate five barber chairs in the main room and presumably a few baths in a small rear extension.[17] A two-year lease specified that there would be "water for said baths and barbershop whenever the same runs and there is heat upon the building sufficient, but they are not to run the heat for that especial purpose." Herndon agreed to pay seventy-five dollars a month, a substantial amount in 1890, and was required to have the guarantee of John Silvey, a wholesale dry goods merchant who owned a quarter interest in the Markham. Herndon had apparently found in Silvey an influen-tial supporter in Atlanta's White business community. On the next two-year lease, Silvey's signature was not required, but the monthly charge increased to eighty-three dollars.[18]

In 1890 the Markham House barbershop was still a relatively new establishment. Each barber tended a large upholstered barber chair that swiveled on a wooden frame. He worked at dark wood cabinets with a built-in porcelain sink. From a high ceiling hung electric lights and fans and underfoot lay an elaborately patterned tile floor. Wood paneling with a gingerbread trim screened the main part of the shop in the front from the back room that led to the baths.[19]

"I started out alone with a five-chair shop." Alonzo Herndon, center, with his barbers, Charles Faison, left, and others, c. 1895, at the Markham House, Atlanta's second largest hotel.

Georgia
Fulton County} This Agreement made and Entered into this 22nd day of August 1889 between Charles Beermann and Company, a partnership composed of Chas Beermann and Joseph Thompson as first parties, and A. F. Herndon party of the second part all of said County Witnesseth; That the first parties have this day leased the party of the second part for a period of two years, beginning the first of September 1889, and ending the first of September 1891, the Barber shop and Bath tubs situated in the Markham House in the City of Atlanta, said county, at and for the price of Seventy five ($75.00) Dollars per month, payable in advance on the first day of each month beginning September 1st 1889 Said first parties are to furnish said second party water for said baths and barber shop whenever the same runs and there is heat upon the building sufficient, but they are not to run the heat for that especial purpose. Said second party is to return said premises at the end of this lease in as good condition as now, natural wear and tear excepted and they shall not sub-let the same without the written consent of the said first parties. All needed repairs and improvements will be made by the second party at his own expense. In case said second party fails to pay any monthly

instalment of rent, as herein provided, on the first day of the month then first parties shall have the right to terminate this lease and re-take possession of said premises

In case said premises are destroyed by fire this lease is thereupon to terminate.

Witness said parties hands in duplicate the day and date aforesaid

Charles Beermann & Co
A. F. Herndon

For value received, I hereby guarantee the payment of the rent as herein agreed to be paid by the said A. F. Herndon, and in case he should fail to pay the same promptly, I will pay the amount as they become due to the expiration of this lease.

John Silvey

Markham House Lease, 1889.

The shop operated about twelve hours a day, from eight in the morning to eight at night during the week and until about midnight on Saturday.[20] As owner and manager of the business, Herndon probably did not cut hair full time. The front chair would eventually belong to Charles A. Faison, a native of North Carolina, who had begun at the shop as a fifteen-year-old shoeshine boy, but who after an apprenticeship under Herndon become a barber.[21] In addition to Herndon and Faison were four other barbers and two porters who shined shoes and attended the baths.[22]

Just north of the Markham around lower Ivy and Decatur streets was a Black commercial district where small hotels and boardinghouses were served by restaurants, barber shops, blacksmiths, shoemakers, and billiard halls, all in the midst of livery stables and a lumber mill. Also on Ivy Street was the Good Samaritan Building, a four-story brick structure that was owned by one of the state's Black fraternal orders and that may have been the city's first Black office building.[23] Herndon at the Markham serving Whites, and the Good Samaritans not far away in service to their own community, symbolized the split economy of racial segregation. Though Blacks could not have gotten their hair cut in Herndon's shop, the community claimed his success, proud that one of its own made good money. Little did Herndon know at the time that the Black economic cooperation fostered by the Good Samaritans and other Black mutual-aid groups was laying the foundation for what would be his next great enterprise.

About the time he opened at the Markham, Herndon became interested in Adrienne, who was in her senior year at Atlanta University.[24] With his barbering finally on sound footing he was prepared to take the long-delayed step to marriage.

First Congregational Church on Houston Street was probably where Adrienne and Alonzo met. Affiliated with Atlanta University, the church attracted many of the city's Black upper class. On May 11, 1884, just a couple of years after his arrival in Atlanta, Alonzo joined the church. He would eventually become church treasurer.[25] When Adrienne came to the city about three years later to attend Atlanta

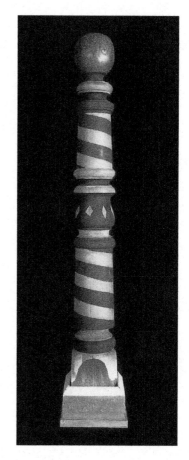

Herndon barbershop pole, c. 1890. (Courtesy of the Atlanta History Center)

University, she boarded with the family of George White, one of the church's first deacons.[26] The Whites' small frame house was a few doors down from the church.

"First Church," as the members called it, was not yet a generation old. It was the child of the American Missionary Association of the Congregational Church, which gave rise to Atlanta University and which would supply most of Georgia's teachers from the North.[27] Alonzo began courting Adrienne under the watchful eye of this church community that no doubt believed their union would find God's favor. Moreover, the match seemed beneficial for worldly reasons. Alonzo was handsome and rich; Adrienne, beautiful and talented. The community may have seen Alonzo as its most eligible bachelor, but there were surely other promising men in Adrienne's sight. At Atlanta University she would have known James Weldon Johnson, destined for prominence as a writer, composer, and civil rights activist; Loring Palmer, who would receive a medical degree from the University of Pennsylvania and practice on Whitehall Street; William Matthews, future principal of the Houston Street School; and George Towns, soon to be her colleague on the university faculty.

Alonzo had none of their educational qualifications, and he openly acknowledged his deficiencies. He remembered clearly his journey on foot from Social Circle, arriving in the little town of Conyers and becoming terrified at the sound of telegraph wires humming overhead: "My knees quaked with fear for I thought I was being telegraphed. For my knowledge of books and the world was gleaned during these twenty years of my life in twelve months schooling, which constitutes all the schooling I have ever had. I received this twelve months teaching in doses of five weeks a year." Herndon, however, was a literate man and well spoken.[28] Though his spelling was sometimes phonetic and his punctuation often lacking, his letters and speeches were fluent, effective, and indeed eloquent. Adrienne may have polished some of his manners, but by the time they met, Alonzo was self-taught and self-made. His own drive and intelligence had advanced his learning far beyond his schooling.

If Adrienne had reservations about his educational background, she had no doubts about his financial future. Not only was he at the top of his trade but he had also begun to invest his savings in real estate that by 1890 was assessed at $3,875. He was some distance from becoming Atlanta's richest Black man. Roderick Badger, the dentist, for example, owned nearly three times the amount of property and probably earned a higher income from his practice.[29]

Just ten years out of sharecropping, Alonzo probably still had mud on his shoes. And though he was sporting a thick handlebar mustache and a gold-headed walking stick, he was far from fashionable. Adrienne, however, would certainly have appreciated his good looks. Moreover, Alonzo was charming and fun. "He was always telling jokes, always having you laughing," a cousin remembered.[30] One evening Alonzo was courting Adrienne at the White family house. George White, who was one of the city's first Black postal clerks and a very dignified man, thought he had found a tactful way to suggest that it was late and time for Herndon to leave. "I'll have to be turning the lights off soon," he said. Alonzo responded, "I don't mind. I like it better that way."[31]

Alonzo would not have had far to go home that night. He lived at 181 Harris Street, where he had been renting for several years. He would someday own a number of properties on that street and elsewhere in the Fourth Ward, the political division on the east side of town where most of Atlanta's upper-class Blacks lived.[32]

After nearly three years of courtship, Alonzo and Adrienne married. At the time there seemed to be no limits to the couple's climb to the top, Alonzo advancing in barbering and Adrienne in teaching. Herndon's days at the Markham House, however, were numbered. By the middle of 1896 the hotel was gone and the barbershop with it.

One Sunday night, May 17, a huge fire destroyed the square block on which the hotel stood. Starting from a gasoline stove in a small frame restaurant on Decatur Street, the fire spread quickly to the hay racks of a livery stable and for a time leaped over the barbershop to

On May 17, 1896, Herndon lost his barbershop in the Markham House fire. (Courtesy of the Atlanta History Center)

Within a year, Alonzo had set up shop in the Norcross Building on Marietta near Peachtree Street. (Courtesy of the Atlanta–Fulton County Public Library System)

the upper story of the Markham. Frame structures that were bone-dry from a rainless spring fueled a fire that burned for about two hours.[33]

Herndon was probably at home that Sunday night. He and Adrienne lived at 70 Ivy Street, just three blocks up from the hotel. They would have seen the sky lit up by the fire as bright as day. They were virtually in the midst of the commotion as all the city's fire engines galloped to the site and furiously pumped water on roaring walls of fire. Herndon was likely among the throng of thousands who clogged the intersections to witness one of Atlanta's worst fires. He would have stood helplessly as the flames gutted his shop. The crowd let up a cheer as each of several horses escaped the burning stables. By early morning, in the ruins of the livery, the one human casualty was discovered: Gilbert Zachary, a Black stable attendant, "his body burned to a crisp."[34]

With a gross income from his barbershop averaging $1,500 monthly, Herndon was by any standards in Atlanta's upper income class. Only a handful of Blacks, perhaps 1 to 2 percent, belonged to Atlanta's African American elite. But far richer than any Black and alienated from Whites of comparable income, Herndon was virtually in a class by himself.

After the fire, Herndon moved temporarily across the street, setting up shop in what had been the Gridiron Restaurant at the corner of Wall and Loyd. "I will be glad to serve my regular patrons and the public," said Herndon in an advertisement that appeared that Wednesday, May 21, in the *Atlanta Constitution*. He soon moved to the corner of Decatur and Peachtree streets. About a year from the date of the fire, he moved again, this time to the ground level of the Norcross Building at 4 Marietta Street, just west of Peachtree Street. In agreement with Robert Dohme, a White grocer, he leased the space of what had been the Columbian Barbershop for ninety-three dollars a month, and purchased its fixtures and furniture for a thousand dollars.[35] He had come almost full circle from his start with Dougherty Hutchins fourteen years before, but now he was on his own and in command of a larger shop.

Within a few years, the Marietta Street operation grew to thirteen barbers and four porters. Like the Markham barbershop, it was a full-service operation, offering haircuts, shaves, shoeshines, baths, and pressing to White men only.[36]

Herndon's barbershop was an extremely dignified place for both barber and customer. "The atmosphere was very genteel," Albert

Daniel, a customer, recalled. "The barbershop clientele was a better class . . . [and there was] not much frivolity among the barbers . . . [who] were all considered real high class gentlemen in their community."[37] Barbering created a distinctive relationship between two separate and unequal orders of gentlemen. The barber was the confidant of men who had knowledge of the inner workings of business, law, and society. Herndon very likely paid close attention to the privileged information that would serve his business interests time and time again.

The gross income of the shop climbed to an average of $1,500 a month. After paying the barbers and other expenses, Herndon netted about half that amount, giving him an annual income of more than $8,000 from barbering alone, and by any standards, placing him in

Fire struck again in December 1902, destroying the entire block of the Norcross Building and Herndon's barbershop with it. By week's end Herndon had reestablished his barbershop at 66 Peachtree Street, which would be its final and finest location.

Lease for 66 Peachtree Street, 1907.

Atlanta's upper income class.[38] Within the Black community he had become the most affluent, and would acquire the most real estate, his holdings to surpass those of every Black college in the city except Atlanta University. By 1910, having purchased mostly small rental units on the west side of town, he had amassed real and personal property with an assessed value of more than $37,540.[39] Far richer than any other Black and alienated by race from Whites of comparable income, Herndon was virtually in a class by himself.

Fire struck central Atlanta again, early on a Tuesday morning, December 9, 1902, starting in the basement of the Snook and Austin Furniture Company on Peachtree Street, just around the corner from Herndon's barbershop in the Norcross Building. The square block was destroyed, at an estimated loss of about $325,000. Herndon claimed damages of $2,000, but by Saturday was in operation again, having relocated to 66 Peachtree Street, his final and finest location.[40]

CHAPTER 4

Diamond Hill

Owning more real estate than any Black Atlantan and living in the largest house available to Blacks in the city, Herndon was king of the hill.

Curiously, although Alonzo was Atlanta's wealthiest Black, rich in real estate and poised on Peachtree for a yet higher ascent in business, the Herndons were without a house of their own. For about the first three years of their marriage, they boarded at 70 Ivy Street (Peachtree Center Avenue) with Frances Norris, an older Black woman. Norris, a white-skinned ex-slave from Rome, Georgia, was the daughter of her slave master, who had provided for her education. Entering Oberlin College a slave, she graduated a free woman in 1864 with a bachelor of arts degree. After coming to Atlanta in the late 1870s, she taught for a few years at Storrs, the early Black school from which First Congregational Church and Atlanta University evolved. Subsequently, with a small inheritance from her White father, she invested in real estate.[1]

Norris's large two-story home and carriage house were located across from the Franklin Publishing Company in a district of small hotels and boardinghouses. Joining the Herndons in the boardinghouse were Adrienne's mother, Martha, who had moved from Savannah with her daughter Jennie, age twelve. Her husband, Archibald, had been dead about eight years, and having struggled during that time working as a seamstress, laundress, and maid while also caring for her children, Martha was now dependent on Adrienne and Alonzo. Norris and the Herndons were probably the only Blacks on the block. Although some Blacks were scattered throughout the area in small frame dwellings for servants on back alleys and although many were concentrated near Decatur Street, no other Blacks resided on Ivy Street north of Gilmer.

The city directory's list of Ivy Street residents did not identify Norris as Black. Very likely neither her neighbors nor perhaps her other boarders were aware of her race. And like Alonzo, she derived a significant income from service to Whites not only as a landlord but also as a caterer. Her boardinghouse was an enclave where she and the Herndons lived within the margins of race, neither fully Black nor fully White. But looking White, living among Whites, and making their living from Whites, they nevertheless by the insane demands of racism belonged to Blacks. Adrienne's family had long been in similar circumstances. In Augusta they had lived in or close to White households, serving as maids, laundresses, and nurses. And in Savannah, no other Blacks lived on the block of Duffy Street where they resided.[2] Living separately from their race, these urban dwellers were at times as close as Blacks could come to passing for White in their own community without totally renouncing Black blood. Martha McNeil would have found a kindred spirit in Frances Norris. Both were the daughters of White men and the granddaughters of White men. At least two generations of such unions had bred very light-skinned individuals. Emancipation may have undercut the opportunity for interracial matings, but since by choice or circumstance these light-skinned persons generally married others of their color, they perpetuated a class of Blacks with predominantly White ancestry. An urban neighborhood of transients afforded some anonymity, some freedom from the technicalities of race.

The Herndons and Norris may have lived in the midst of Whites unrecognized as Blacks, but they stood out among their race as a white-skinned subcaste. At one extreme was Norris, whose White ancestry had brought education and money. At the other extreme was Alonzo Herndon, whose ancestry had gained no material or educational advantages. Save for his hard work and exceptional talent, Alonzo would have been a light-skinned nobody, like most of the children of White slave masters. But Alonzo, gifted and full of grit, had earned a place among Atlanta's Black elite, that handful of privileged, mostly light-skinned Blacks who by force of money, property, education, or skills stood far above the masses. Light skin became their badge of

Frances Norris, in whose boardinghouse the Herndons lived before moving to Diamond Hill.

material and social privilege, their mark of beauty and goodness, intelligence and power. Moreover, their color reflected a virtually universal preference for light over dark. With racism firmly rooted within and without the Black community, light skin assumed superiority over dark skin just as White assumed superiority over Black.[3]

Norris's boardinghouse was an ideal location in many respects for the Herndons. It was near the Markham, the Union Depot, and the commercial activity along Peachtree and Marietta streets. First Congregational Church and the Fourth Ward community of up-and-coming Blacks, who at that time had begun to settle along Auburn Avenue east of Piedmont, were within a few blocks. But the downtown area was inconvenient for Adrienne, because she worked on the west side of town. Some time after the Markham House fire, and about a year after Adrienne began teaching at Atlanta University, the Herndons moved to the university campus.

In 1867, with funds largely from the Freedman's Bureau, the trustees of Atlanta University purchased about sixty acres situated on the city's highest ridge, popularly known as "Diamond Hill."[4] The land, though not far from the bottoms, where much of Atlanta's Black population in the area lived, was high ground, symbolic of education's noble purpose and the elite class that developed around it. With Adrienne's influence and Alonzo's resources, it was inevitable that the Herndons would live on the hill.

In a sense, Diamond Hill was another enclave, an exclusive reservation. Its White inhabitants were the Congregationalist teachers and administrators from the Northeast who, through the American Missionary Association, had committed their lives to the education of former slaves. Its Black students ranged from the advantaged descendants of White fathers and Black mothers to the struggling children of upwardly mobile Blacks. The Herndons had progressed from their marginal life on Ivy Street to the very core of another White community where they, however, could openly acknowledge their race. Diamond Hill was like a missionary outpost on the western frontier of Atlanta. It was the first society of its kind in the city. Here in the Deep South, Blacks and Whites were living and working together for the uplift of a race. Teachers at Atlanta University, unlike those at other Black schools of higher education during the period, shared dormitories with students, ate at their tables, attended their chapel, and socialized with them at school functions. For a time, a handful of White faculty children had attended Atlanta University classes. This singular "co-education of the races" caught the eye of the state in 1887, and when the university insisted on offering education "to all of either sex

Atlanta University college graduates, 1903: front row, left to right, George White, Louie Delphia Davis, Emma White, Annie Mack, and Harry Pace; back row, left to right, Edward Overstreet, Samuel Grant, Emanuel Houstoun, and Charles Westmoreland.

Horace Bumstead, president of Atlanta University from 1885 to 1906.

without regard to sect, race, color, or nationality," the state of Georgia discontinued its annual allocation of $8,000.[5]

Ironically, a school for the higher education of Blacks had been organized in Atlanta before the city's present-day historically White colleges were founded and before public education in Georgia was mandated. By the time of the Herndons' move to the university, five other Black institutions of higher education had been established in the city. Atlanta Baptist College (later known as Morehouse) and Atlanta Baptist Female Seminary (later known as Spelman) were adjacent to Atlanta University. Clark University and Gammon Theological Seminary had located in the Black suburb of Brownsville, southeast of Atlanta, while Morris Brown College was established east of downtown in the Fourth Ward. Atlanta had become a center for Black higher education. No other city in the world had this concentration of Black colleges. Atlanta University, however, would be the leader among them in preparing Black teachers and educating the "talented tenth," that minority of Blacks who by virtue of intelligence and ability were destined to be teachers, ministers, and other professionals in service to the masses. Most of the students in Atlanta's Black colleges would for several decades be in elementary and secondary courses. But as early as 1876, Atlanta University was awarding Georgia's first bachelor of arts degrees to Blacks.

Long after the university's founding, the earthworks of Confederate defenses could still be seen along the ridgelines of Diamond Hill. Like Atlanta, the university rose from the ashes of the Civil War, but unlike the city, it became a bastion of racial integration.

For a while the Herndons stayed in South Hall, the boys' dormitory, but soon moved to the Bumstead Cottage, nearby at 169 Vine Street.[6] Bumstead was hardly a makeshift arrangement for the Herndons. It was a cottage in the New England sense—a huge Shingle-Style house that was simply the only mansion available to Blacks in Atlanta. Horace Bumstead, the White Atlanta University president, had built the house by the mid-1880s, but spending most of his time on fundraising in the North, found it necessary to vacate the house.[7]

Adrienne's scholarship and drive had paved the Herndons' way to the university. She had always been a bright student at the West Broad Street public grade school in Savannah and had become the protégé of her teacher Alice Miller, a half sister of Frances Norris.[8] After completing the eighth grade, Adrienne enrolled in 1886 for the four-year program at Atlanta University's normal school with substantial aid from the university. Archibald McNeil, a butcher with a stall at the Savannah City Market, had provided well for his family. Though not a part of Savannah's old Black elite, the McNeils had been comfortably middle class. But upon Archibald's death from tuberculosis in 1885 at the age of forty-one, the family lost ground. Martha struggled to take care of the family while working as a seamstress, laundress, and domestic servant. She could pay only forty dollars of the sixty-four-dollar tuition for two semesters at Atlanta University. Each month from September through May, she forwarded a five-dollar money order to Atlanta University through James H. C. Butler, the principal of the West Broad Street School. Additional aid would have been necessary for the twenty-three dollars per month in room and board if Adrienne lived on campus. For at least part of her time at the university, she boarded presumably at less cost with the George White family on Houston Street. As a scholarship student, Adrienne would have performed extra duties on campus.[9]

West Broad Street School in Savannah, where Adrienne McNeil completed the eighth grade before enrolling in 1886 at Atlanta University's normal school.

Adrienne McNeil, the normal school student, second from right, with classmates, c. 1890.

OPPOSITE PAGE
TOP: *Adrienne Herndon, front row, standing right, with her Atlanta University graduating class, 1890. (Courtesy of Atlanta University Center, Robert W. Woodruff Library)*
BOTTOM: *Adrienne McNeil Herndon, the elocution teacher, seated front row center with her students, c. 1895.*

For Adrienne, education was an escape from a family tradition of domestic service. Household servants in prominent White families had been a relatively advantaged class among Blacks during slavery and immediately following. But with business and education offering greater opportunities for income and professional status, domestic service was no longer a route to the Black upper class.

Education, however, was more than a means to social security and status. It was also a mission, spiritual as well as temporal. Atlanta University in large measure was a religious community, established for the moral and educational salvation of the masses. "I am doing all I can to hold up a high standard for dear old A.U. and for my race," wrote Adrienne from Greensboro, Georgia, where she was teaching the summer before her senior year in the Normal School. She confessed that her summer assignment in a rural area had not been easy. "I thought once that I would have to give up the struggle," she wrote to President Bumstead, "but the Lord has been very kind to me and has strengthened me so that I have held out thus far." Although the dual mission of education and moral enlightenment had at times seemed overwhelming, the young students proved promising. "I find a great source of comfort in my little Friday afternoon prayer meetings," she

As a student of Adrienne's remembered, "She was so pretty, we thought she could teach anything. She had blue eyes and the skin was a creamy type. Her hair was not exactly straight, but had a kind of wave or crink in it. . . . Mrs. Herndon's clothing was always soft."

wrote. "Several of my pupils have accepted the Savior since I have been among them."[10]

Following her graduation in 1890, Adrienne's first full-time position was apparently at the Gray Street Public School, northeast of Diamond Hill, one of four grade schools serving the city's Black community. That summer she taught at the first session of the state's Black branch of the University of Georgia in Athens. Subsequently established in Savannah as the State College of Industry for Colored Youth, it became known as Georgia College for Negroes, and finally as Savannah State. Two other Atlanta University graduates joined Adrienne that summer: Loring Palmer, who would become Adrienne's physician, and Richard R. Wright, destined to become president of the Savannah college.[11] Returning in the fall to the Gray Street School, her tenure would be limited. Her marriage in 1893 disqualified her from teaching in the system, but by 1895 Adrienne had returned to her alma mater to teach elocution in the high school and college departments.[12]

"She was so pretty, we thought she could teach anything," remembered Kathleen Redding Adams, one of her students. "She had blue eyes and the skin was a creamy type. Her hair was not exactly straight, but had a kind of wave or crink in it. It stood a little bit; it fluffed. . . . Mrs. Herndon's clothing was always soft. . . . If your voice was off key, she worked on you. . . . She thought your voice should be trained."[13]

Adrienne herself was thoroughly trained. Seven summers and a school year of elocution in Boston made her one of the most professionally trained women in the city.

On July 15, 1897, the Herndons' first and only child, Norris Bumstead, was born, named after Frances Norris and the university's second president. Attending the birth was Dr. J. G. Earnest, a White physician who had an office in his home on Houston Street. The baby was welcomed with gifts fit for a prince: gold buttons from Frances Norris, who became known to the child as "Auntie Nor"; a silver cup from great-grandmother Harriet Hankerson; and another silver cup with saucer from the dentist Dr. Roderick Badger.[14]

On July 15, 1897, the Herndons' first and only child, Norris Bumstead, was born, named after Frances Norris and the university's second president.

"His lordship crowed when three weeks old and ever since has been using his vocal organs for the purpose of showing how his young ideas were shooting," Adrienne wrote in Norris's baby book. On one of his first outings with his grandmother, Norris was remembered wearing a long white baby dress, his face "just as red as a little piece of beef."[15]

Adrienne probably taught at least the first semester of her second school year at the university before Norris's birth the following summer, and probably returned to teaching by the fall of 1898. For when Norris was eleven months old and still on the breast, Adrienne took him with her to Boston, where apparently she resumed her summer studies at the School of Expression. The child took his first steps in that city, and when, on the same day, he pursued the newsboy down Camden Street, a friend captured it on camera.[16] For fourteen months Adrienne nursed her baby. "Then it was thought advisable to wean

Martha McNeil, Adrienne's mother, lived with the Herndons and cared for Norris.

Norris Herndon takes his first steps in Boston as his grandmother Martha and a newsboy look on, 1898.

baby," Adrienne wrote. A little before the fall session at the university, Adrienne and Alonzo traveled to Lithia Springs, a resort town nearby where Blacks sometimes vacationed. "After being away two days," Adrienne reported, "mama returned to see how baby was getting on and she can never forget the look of reproach baby gave as he threw his little arms around her and cried."[17]

The expectations, indeed, the demands of husband, son, and society very likely nurtured in Adrienne an abiding guilt for her absences from home and family. Fortunately, her mother was living with them in the Bumstead Cottage and offered considerable help with the care of her child. Mattie was the attending nurse at her grandson's birth and became a constant presence in his young life. Norris called her "Mama." "When you look too dirty," Adrienne once wrote to her young son, "go to grandma and ask her [to] please put some clean clothes on you so you'll look like mama's sweet yitte boy." A family friend reminded Norris when he was a teenager that "your grandma

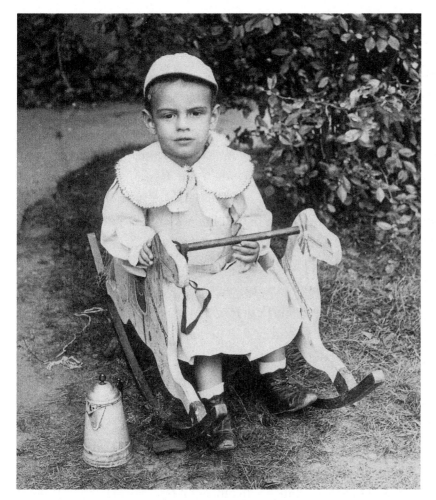

used to carry coffee pots around in a basket for you to play with." Norris had called them his "corky pots."[18]

Mattie, a heavyset woman with gray eyes, was probably unschooled, but she could read and write. She had probably become literate following Emancipation. With her skills and her carriage, she was considered "the cultured woman of that day."[19] House servants were exposed to the manners of privileged families, and since they were in line to receive their masters' cast-off clothing and household goods, they often bore the trappings of upper-class life.

Without Mattie, it would have been impossible for Adrienne to carry her load as wife, mother, teacher, and rising dramatic artist. Because of her frequent absences, Adrienne tried to keep in constant touch with her child by mail. In a postcard from Boston, she complained to the little boy, "No letter yet. Have you forgotten Little Mama?" It was not only her studies but also her travels with Alonzo that often kept her from Norris and left the child in Mattie's care. In 1900 Adrienne and Alonzo attended the Paris Exposition, spending three months in Europe. "Mama's Darling," Adrienne wrote Norris from Venice on his third birthday, "this morning Mama was thinking how sweet you looked one day when she dressed you to go out with Auntie Nor and she made you tip your hat to us when you were leaving. Today Mama went bathing in the blue Adriatic Sea and a lady was carrying her little baby in and it was crying just as you did at Tybee [near Savannah, Georgia] when Mama and Papa went in. . . . Mama talks to every little baby she sees cause she hasn't got any little boy here. This is your birthday. You must not forget Mama."[20]

In spite of the absences, and perhaps partly because of them, an intense affection and loyalty developed between mother and child. Norris was once asked teasingly if he would like to have been the son of one of his father's old girlfriends. "Not at all," the little boy answered. "I had rather not been born if Little Mama couldn't be my mama."[21]

"He was a very quiet type of little boy," recalled Kathleen Adams. "He was always at his mother's or his father's side. And as he grew up, he didn't mingle too much with other children—kept to himself, more or less." Adams remembered him in his flowing tie and jacket with the Buster Brown collar, "always smiling, but not venturing out."[22]

In those days Norris Herndon's world was for the most part within walking distance of Bumstead. At seven years of age, Norris was among the first to attend Oglethorpe, Atlanta University's practice school, which opened in October 1904. But for the rest of grammar school, he went to Mitchell Street Public School, which was only a little further away, but considerably distant in class. Perhaps for the first time in his life, this son of wealth rubbed shoulders with children of poverty.[23]

For ten years, until the Herndons began construction of their

own mansion next door, Bumstead was, as they referred to it, their "home in the rock." The cottage was the only house on the block, and it faced University Place at the northern fringe of the campus. With two stories and at least ten rooms and four porches, the house was about five thousand square feet.[24]

In the "Big Parlor," as they called it, a large wall mirror reflected a room full of tufted armchairs and matching settees, capped with lace, all against a backdrop of floral wallpaper and dark wood trim. At one end was the Kimball upright piano Alonzo had given Adrienne as a wedding gift, a small portrait of himself on the Chinese rosewood table beside it. At the other end was the fireplace, where on the mantel was a photograph of Samuel Curry of the Boston School of Expression.[25]

Not given to waste, the Herndons shared Bumstead for a while with the family of Howard Pitts, one of Alonzo's barbers. With Pitts's wife, Ammina, daughter India, and three sisters-in-law, the number of residents in Bumstead climbed to ten. It was like an exclusive board-inghouse with separate bedroom wings and parlors. Bazoline Usher, who at the age of thirteen was a student in the Atlanta University high

*Bumstead Cottage at 169 Vine
Street.*

*The "Big Parlor" in Bumstead
Cottage.*

school and who tutored India Pitts in math, recalled that Adrienne and Ammina were good friends and that they often took trips to downtown Atlanta, where she supposed the two women passed for White. As Black women they could not have tried on clothing in Rich's department store nor could they have entered the De Give Opera House through the front door or sat on the first floor. Adrienne attended the theater in Atlanta frequently; Ammina may often have been her companion. Usher remembered India Pitts's constant comparison of the two families: "The Herndons are rich but we are poor."[26]

Late in 1897, the same year Norris was born, William E. B. Du Bois arrived on campus to teach history and economics and took residence in South Hall with his wife, Nina Gomer, and infant son, Burghardt. Du Bois, Herndon, and George Towns, who as instructor of literature and pedagogy had begun his tenure in 1895, made up the university's

Adrienne Herndon, right, with Ammina Pitts at Bumstead Cottage, c. 1905.

LEFT: *Late in 1897, the same year Norris was born, William E. B. Du Bois arrived on campus to teach history and economics and took residence in South Hall with his wife, Nina Gomer, and infant son, Burghardt.*

MIDDLE: *George Towns, Atlanta University professor of literature and pedagogy.*

RIGHT: *John Hope, who in 1906 became the first Black faculty member of Atlanta Baptist College (later, Morehouse). In 1929 he became the first Black president of Atlanta University.*

entire Black faculty—not the first, but certainly among the most illustrious. All three had begun their higher education at leading Black institutions, Herndon and Towns at Atlanta University, and Du Bois at Fisk. Each had studied further at White institutions in Boston: the School of Expression, where Herndon received diplomas in general culture and public reading; and Harvard University, where Du Bois became the first of his race to receive a doctorate and where Towns obtained a second bachelor's degree. John Hope, an Augusta native, would also become a leading member of Atlanta's Black educational elite. Having graduated from Brown University, he arrived in Atlanta in 1898 with his wife Lugenia, becoming the first Black faculty member at Morehouse College. These four teachers were at the heart of Atlanta's Black educational elite at the turn of the century. They were colleagues, companions, and neighbors, uplifting the race through learning. Remarkably, this noble venture in Black education on the Hill enlisted in the beginning very few Black faculty. All of the Black institutions of higher learning in Atlanta, except Morris Brown, which was founded by the African Methodist Episcopal Church, began with White founders, teachers, and administrators. "The time was not ripe," Edmund Ware, the first president of Atlanta University, insisted in the 1870s, for the introduction of Blacks to the Atlanta University faculty.

"The trustees would not agree to such an appointment." And Atlanta University resisted longer than any other Atlanta Black institution in the hiring of Black teachers in large numbers. Well into the twentieth century, the university's faculty was largely White. By comparison, John Hope became the first Black president of Morehouse College in 1906, when the faculty had become, in a few years, virtually all-Black.[27]

How ironic that Alonzo, who had so little schooling, should marry one of the most educated women in the city and live on the campus of one of the leading institutions for higher education in the region. Although Adrienne had gotten them there, Alonzo made it possible for them to stay in fine style. Without him, Adrienne would have been far less prepared for her work as head of one of the university's strongest departments, and little exposed to the theater world of the Northeast.

Unevenly matched to Adrienne in education, Alonzo nevertheless was her social equal. In late-nineteenth-century Black Atlanta, when

Atlanta University faculty with family members, c. 1905. Adrienne Herndon, seated at farthest left; Alonzo Herndon, standing at farthest left behind her; Norris Herndon, in front row, second child from the right; W. E. B. Du Bois, standing in back, first man from the right; Nina Du Bois, standing in back, sixth woman from the right.

Vine City in the valley below Diamond Hill.

few had education or property, ownership of the Markham House barbershop placed Herndon at the top of a business elite comparable to the city's educational elite. Alonzo had less schooling than many Black businessmen of his generation, but his entrepreneurial skills were second to none. And he moved with confidence within the university community. His financial success had propelled him into a select class of people, among whom his intelligence and drive stood out nonetheless. Herndon may not have been able to discuss intellectual history with Du Bois, but he could certainly have enlightened America's leading social scientist on Black business and rural life. Recognizing Herndon's wealth and importance, the university eventually appointed him to its trustee board, where he served as secretary and treasurer for many years. Surely no Black in the city donated more to Black education than Alonzo Herndon, who contributed as much as a thousand dollars a year.[28]

To the north and west of Diamond Hill was the rest of Vine City, a mostly working-class, African American community, that was often rough and disreputable and that bordered two of the worst Black slums in Atlanta: Lightning, to the northeast, and Beaver Slide, to the south. Although this western arc of the city had its share of Black success, it was on the east side of downtown in the Fourth Ward, where most of the city's middle- and upper-income Blacks lived at the time. The Herndons, however, remained on the Hill, committed to the young college community and awaiting a new day in Black neighborhood building on the west side.

However high he climbed on Diamond Hill, Alonzo Herndon never lost sight of the valley where he started and where most of his people still lived. He had no illusions that the Atlanta University community allowed him to escape the realities of race and class in the rest of the world. His business success demanded that every moment he be sharply aware that he was a Black man in a city controlled by Whites. Though Adrienne may have been counting for a time on the remote possibility that she could be both Anne Du Bignon and Adrienne Herndon, Alonzo embraced a single identity. "I have always been proud of my race," he would say.[29] Within its restrictions he found opportunities and attainable goals. Transcending race and class, Alonzo crossed back and forth between Black and White worlds, upper and lower. He lived on Diamond Hill, but he was still tied to family and friends in Vine City. Many of his people from Social Circle had migrated to Atlanta, and settled near him. Julia Fambrough, a domestic, lived down the hill on Walnut Street, her daughter Mattie Lou Wilborn, at the corner of Vine and Carter streets, where next door would live Uncle Mack's grandchild Girtha Cooper. For a time his cousins, Florence and Archer Berry, lived with him and later on Carter Street. And his brother Tom's daughter, Carrie Hennie, and her husband, Herbert Connally, would move to a large house with their children, Norris and Calvin, a few blocks south of Hunter Street (later called Martin Luther King Jr. Drive).[30]

By 1915, Herndon owned nearly one hundred rental properties in the city, more than any other Black Atlantan. Some of his properties were in the Fourth Ward, but most of them in Vine City concentrated on Maple, Davis (eventually, Northside Drive), Delbridge, Carter, and Rhodes streets. All were within walking distance of Bumstead.[31] These small one- and two-family frame dwellings yielded an income each month that helped support the gracious life in a university community. The rental income and the proceeds from barbering made Herndon's next great business venture possible. Herndon's residence may have been rented, but no Black lived in a larger one. He was the richest of them all and owned the most property. In turn-of-the-century Black Atlanta, Herndon was king of the hill.

CHAPTER 5

Unity in Division

Alonzo Herndon as featured on front page of Atlanta Age, *30 September 1905.*

The Hunter Street trolley ran from the city limits at Ashby Street to downtown Atlanta about two miles away, carrying Alonzo back and forth between the two worlds of a racially divided city. Making its way east through the corridor that had been cut through the Atlanta University campus, the streetcar veered southeast along Tatnall Street, and at West Mitchell Street passed the diamond-shaped parcel that gave the area its name. Continuing on Nelson Street, the car crossed the viaduct over the railway gulch and followed Mitchell Street until it turned northeast on Peachtree Street toward the center of town. "The car runs so convenient for me," Herndon would boast. It took him to his barbershop, to Auburn Avenue, and to within a block of his church, First Congregational.[1]

But he could take no pride in his ride in the back of the car, where all Blacks were forced to sit. Herndon's barbering success belied the ever-tightening grip of Jim Crow in all areas of city life. What had once been understood in custom was made legally explicit in a 1900 city ordinance requiring barbershops to serve either Blacks or Whites. Though Herndon would remain the region's premier barber, Blacks would soon lose hold of a profession they had once dominated. Herndon and his peers were clearly the targets of Whites seeking to take over the lucrative trade. "Skilled White Artists," proclaimed the advertisement of Klein's Barbershop at 25 Marietta Street.[2] What had been desirable in slavery was becoming intolerable after Emancipa-

The Hunter Street Trolley on Diamond Hill.

tion. As slaves, Blacks had served in all areas of domestic life, but as free persons, they were competing in the city for the better jobs and living space with Whites who, like themselves, were poor migrants from the country. Segregation took the place of slavery to keep Blacks underfoot.

In spite of their color and money, the Herndons were in the same subordinate position. Had Alonzo wanted to buy a meal in downtown Atlanta, he would have had to go to one of the Black lunchrooms on lower Ivy or Decatur Street. No White restaurant or saloon would have seated him. Nor would the Carnegie Library have admitted him. When the Terminal Station celebrated its opening in May 1905, it is certain that Herndon and other Blacks were not among the crowd that marched through the main entrance to the tune of "Dixie."[3] For the next several decades, Blacks would be subjected to a separate entrance, separate waiting room, and separate ticket counter. From the most ordinary pleasures to the most fundamental human rights, racial segregation ruled. Blacks followed a separate path through Grant Park, swore on a separate Bible in the city courthouse, and of the handful of men like Herndon who were eligible, cast votes in separate ballot boxes for candidates chosen in White-only primaries.[4]

In response to the divisions and exclusions, Blacks struggled for unity. To survive, they had to cooperate. To meet their needs, they had to found their own institutions. Forced to seek a market among their own people, Black businessmen had already begun to move to another avenue for the next stage of development in the new century. From the door of his barbershop on Peachtree Street, Herndon could look down Auburn Avenue, which in a couple of decades would be the spine of the most significant Black business district in the country. At the turn of the twentieth century, he stood at the center of Black enterprise in Atlanta, straddling two eras. He would engage two worlds of business, two separate markets, turning the deep and constant racial divide to his own advantage. On Peachtree Street he was pushing the tradition of Black domestic service to its profitable extreme. On Auburn Avenue he would transform the tradition of Black mutual

Alonzo Herndon's barbershop at 100 Pryor Street in the Candler Building annex.

The Herndons gathered at Bumstead for portraits in the snow, 1905; left to right, Alonzo, unidentified man, Clara Simkins, unidentified woman, Norris, Adrienne, John Henry Bailey, and Thomas Herndon.

aid into one of the most successful Black insurance companies in the world.

In 1905, just three years after coming to Peachtree Street and in spite of deteriorating race relations, Herndon moved decisively on two fronts. In partnership with Charles Faison, his associate since the Markham House days, he opened a second barbershop, located at 100 Pryor Street in the annex adjacent to the new Candler Building. And for the first time, he invested in something other than real estate, acquiring a little church burial association, which with other similar purchases would establish the Atlanta Mutual Insurance Association.

The year 1905 had been an exceptional one, beginning with Atlanta's worst winter storm to date. Sleet and snow hit twice, paralyzing the city for a few days in early February. As power was cut off, trolleys came to a stop, and blacksmiths were kept busy rough-shodding horses to keep them from slipping on the ice. The freeze did not close the barbershop, however. Herndon, his twelve barbers, and four porters were on duty the morning after the first freezing rain and did a brisk business, as was usual for a Saturday.[5]

Apparently, Alonzo and Adrienne found this episode of ice and snow so novel that they gathered kinfolk for photographs in the front yard of Bumstead. Among them was Adrienne's first cousin Clara Simkins, a seven-year-old who was visiting from Augusta, and Thomas, Alonzo's younger brother—and also a barber—who lived with his wife and children in McDonough, about thirty miles away. Tom had been in poor health for several months, suffering from Bright's disease, a kidney ailment. He had spent much time bathing in the mineral waters at Indian Springs in Butts County and had sought medical help in Atlanta and elsewhere. This trip to Atlanta would have been one of his last. A few weeks after the winter storm, he wrote to Alonzo, "Brother, I will drop you a few lines to let you know how I am [getting] along. I am improving I think. I will go to the shop today." His barbershop was located in a building he owned near the town square on Griffin Street. But if Tom's health improved, it was not for long. On Wednesday morning, June 7, at five o'clock, according to the county newspaper, "McDonough's well-known and popular colored

Thomas Herndon, c. 1900.

Thomas Herndon's house in McDonough, Georgia.

Alonzo Herndon II, son of
Thomas Herndon.

Carrie Hennie Herndon,
daughter of Thomas Herndon.

barber breathed his last." He died at the age of forty-five, leaving his
thirty-four-year-old wife, Emma Woodward, a son, Alonzo Franklin II,
age sixteen, and a daughter, Carrie Hennie, age fifteen. Tom apparently died at home in his large frame house, also on Griffin Street, a
few blocks from his barbershop. The *Henry County Weekly* praised Tom
as "an exemplary citizen, perfectly inoffensive, courteous & worthy in
his habits in every way." But although, as the obituary stated, "he was
held in the highest esteem by both white & colored people," the paper
could not afford him the title of "Mr.," as was its custom in referring
to White men.[6]

With Tom gone, Alonzo was the only survivor of his immediate
family, his mother having died the year before his marriage, and his
father, just ten months before his brother's death. None of them were
alive for the two significant events occurring later in 1905, one that
briefly pushed Alonzo into the national politics of race, and the other
that directed his public and private strategy for racial uplift for the
rest of his life.

Alonzo Herndon seemed out of place in the gathering of twenty-nine
men on July 11 at the Erie Beach Hotel in Fort Erie, Ontario. At forty-

seven, he was older than most of the men at the founding meeting of the Niagara Movement, the century's first organized effort of African Americans to demand full citizenship. Nothing in his background as slave, sharecropper, or barber explained his presence at the historic meeting. The Niagaraites were for the most part an educational and professional elite, eager for first-class citizenship and sorely disenchanted with the leadership of Booker T. Washington.[7]

Ten years earlier, Washington, the thirty-nine-year-old principal of Tuskegee Normal School, had spoken on opening day at the Cotton States and International Exposition in Atlanta. He had captured the fears and hopes of most Blacks and Whites, effectively stating the case for Black accommodation to social and political inequality in exchange for economic advancement. Even Du Bois, who would become the organizing force behind Niagara, had praised the address in a telegram to Washington: "Let me heartily congratulate you upon your phenomenal success at Atlanta—it was a word fitly spoken."[8]

Alonzo Herndon was very likely among the crowd of twenty-five thousand at Piedmont Park that Wednesday evening on September 18 to hear the speech that thrust Washington to national leadership. He, too, would have been in full agreement with the compromise. Had not Alonzo Herndon's profession been compromise for the sake of economic progress? Did not his wealth rest on his accommodation to Whites? Yes, and at times it must have been a difficult bargain. However accomplished and wealthy, Herndon was nevertheless considered inferior to Whites of any station. Though he was the owner of the city's finest barbershop and was richer than most of his customers, Herndon could not have sat beside them to get his hair cut in his own shop. He described his business demeanor as "tactful, but I hope manly, conduct toward my southern patrons, with whom I am happy to say I have always [had] the most pleasant relations and in whose esteem I have every reason to believe my business is held."[9]

So why was he at Niagara? Undoubtedly, Herndon fully understood the historical significance of the meeting, and apparently accepted, if not welcomed, its political necessity. Conveniently, Niagara Falls was out of earshot of his Peachtree Street customers. But it could well have

Attendees at the founding meeting of the Niagara Movement in July 1905; Alonzo Herndon, back row, second from left; Norris, second row, second from left; and W. E. B. Du Bois, second row, second from right.

been Adrienne's prodding that got Alonzo to the meeting. A radical woman for her day, Adrienne felt painfully the social and professional exclusions of the White world. She would easily have caught the spirit of Niagara and championed its objectives. Her most cherished goal—performing on the American stage—could not be achieved with social and political accommodations to racism. As colleagues and friends, she and Du Bois admired and supported each other's work. Du Bois had just served as Adrienne's stage carpenter for the William Gillette production of *Sherlock Holmes in the Adventure of the Second Stain*.[10] She would have been in close touch with his ideas and his projects. Adrienne herself was at Fort Erie, as was Norris. Niagara was a family affair for the Herndons. Though women were not allowed at its founding meeting, Adrienne played an indirect role, very likely having encouraged Alonzo's attendance and perhaps having urged that Norris be included in the famous portrait of Niagaraites superimposed on a view of the falls. The boy, who in a few days would celebrate his eighth birthday, was in the second row, held by Frederick L. McGhee, a slave-born Minnesota attorney seated next to Max Barber, editor of *Voice of the Negro*. Norris's hand was resting on the shoulder of Clement Morgan, another slave-born lawyer and former barber.[11] In the third row behind Du Bois stood Alonzo, looking dapper in his derby. The portrait had been carefully staged. Could it have been Adrienne herself in the wings directing the play of heads and hands for this very serious drama?

Following Niagara, the Herndons remained in the area, vacationing. "Hello there, Mama!" Alonzo wrote to Martha from the Canadian falls the day after the meeting adjourned. "We are all well." And from Toronto the next week another postcard was sent: "We have had a fine time here. Mr. H. leaves for home Thursday or Friday. Love to all, Addie."[12]

About the time the Herndons were preparing for Niagara, a little church burial association in their community was reorganizing in a last-ditch struggle to survive. The Atlanta Benevolent and Protective Association, which was founded and led by the Reverend Peter James

Bryant, pastor of Wheat Street Baptist Church, had been in operation for about a year. A member paid five to twenty-five cents each week in dues and in the event of sickness or death received a benefit of one to fifty dollars. This was primitive insurance, small organizations pooling their money for life's catastrophes. The association was one of the numerous small self-help groups that had sprung up in African American church communities everywhere since Emancipation. They were part of an old tradition of mutual aid that had developed in the late 1700s among free Blacks in cities. Even on some plantations, there had been networks among the slaves for supporting the sick.[13]

At the turn of the century, however, the Atlanta Benevolent and Protective Association found its mission in great difficulty. It was too young and too small to meet the needs of a Black population in Atlanta that had grown about twentyfold in the two generations since Emancipation. Bryant and his assistant, James Arthur Hopkins, were busy ministers with too little time to attend to the affairs of the new organization. On July 6, just a few days before the Niagara meeting opened, a bill was introduced in the Georgia legislature that threatened to deliver a fatal blow to such associations. The proposed legislation targeted Georgia's insurance industry, which, like that of other states, suffered from mismanagement and financial abuse. All organizations like Atlanta Benevolent that provided small benefits for low weekly payments would be defined under the proposed regulations as "industrial insurance" and would be required to deposit with the state five thousand dollars in security against all claims. Bryant and his associates knew they would never be able to meet the requirement. Though Whites made offers to purchase the association, Atlanta Benevolent agreed to find a buyer in the African American community. Surely, they did not have to search long before deciding to offer the organization for sale to Alonzo Herndon. By the time of the Niagara meeting, Herndon had bought the Association for $140.[14] While Herndon sat in the Niagara discussions on civil rights strategy, he must have also been thinking of this next business move. Political protest was clearly not his critical path. The Niagaraites were ready for full integration, politically and socially, but Herndon would continue to exploit the segregated markets created by political and social inequality. If Herndon participated in the discussions at Niagara, surely his views were conditioned by his circumstances. He shared Niagara's purpose, but not its priorities. From Du Bois's perspective, Herndon seemed limited in matters of "broad sympathies and knowledge of the world."[15] But what Herndon may have lacked in intellectual breadth, he made up for in depth of business experience. Seizing upon the opportunity to take mutual aid to the next step, he purchased not only the Reverend Bryant's association but also two others—the Royal Mutual Insurance Company and the National Laborers' Protective Union. He then reorganized them as the Atlanta Mutual Insurance Association.

So, Niagara and Atlanta Mutual were born the same summer. They were two different, but not mutually exclusive, paths to racial progress. While the Niagaraites were preparing their challenge to Booker T. Washington, Herndon was organizing what would become one of the most significant Black businesses in the country. The Georgia insurance bill became law on August 22. Herndon obtained his company's charter on September 6. On September 19, he deposited five thousand dollars with the state in bonds and securities acquired with his own money, making Atlanta Mutual the first company, Black or White, to qualify under the new state regulations.[16]

The Knights and Daughters of Tabor, one of the leading Black fraternal orders in the state, announced the founding of Atlanta Mutual on the front page of its publication *Atlanta Age*, hailing it as "The First To Comply With The New Insurance Law Of Georgia."[17] The news was of great interest to the Black mutual-aid community—the hundreds of orders, lodges, benevolent groups, and burial associations operating in Georgia and dealing more or less in insurance. Next to the church, they were the most important Black institutions, structuring a separate society and economy. They were for the most part local, independent brotherhoods steeped in values and memories that perhaps went even beyond slavery. The host of cooperative societies that had grown up in West Africa may also have generated in some sense Black self-help on American soil.[18]

Atlanta Mutual was the newest member of the community. The organization was neither lodge nor fraternal order, nor benevolent association, but its rituals, paraphernalia, and fellowship nevertheless would constitute a distinctive form of African American financial support. It was a different kind of brotherhood, also inspired by cooperation, but driven by personal gain. Its costs were only a few pennies a week, but unlike most of the aid groups, Atlanta Mutual could offer benefits protected by law.

Buying Atlanta Benevolent was seen by the community as an act of philanthropy; Herndon was viewed as the savior of Black enterprise, rescuing a race institution from possible takeover by Whites.[19] But of course philanthropy was not the purpose; the profit potential was considerable. White insurance companies for the most part refused to insure Blacks, who, they claimed, were poor risks.[20] Atlanta Mutual, therefore, was tapping a lucrative and virtually captive market. It was not the first Black insurance company in the state, but the capital behind it was a promising sign that it would become the biggest.

Entrepreneurship was Herndon's practical response to Niagara. Though private enterprise was an old strategy for racial uplift, to Herndon it was still the most viable. "The great need in America," he would say, is "more business and bigger and better business. . . . Without this the race [can] not hope to hold its own or advance."[21] Herndon would not have given that same endorsement to political action, but chose not to get caught in the debate between Du Bois and Washington.

In fact, Herndon had become quite adept at sidestepping organizations and their politics, whether inter- or intraracial. Herndon apparently never attended another meeting of the Niagara Movement. Nor was he to be actively involved in the organization that would fall heir to its purpose. The first meeting of the Atlanta Branch of the National Association for the Advancement of Colored People (NAACP) was held January 31, 1917, in the assembly room of Atlanta Mutual. But Herndon was not among the prominent Atlantans who signed the charter application. And although he paid his NAACP membership

dues, he would never become engaged in the workings of the association.[22] Even Washington became frustrated with Herndon's lack of participation in his National Negro Business League. Though Herndon was present at its founding in Boston in 1900, he did not attend regularly. There was perhaps no better example of Black business success than Herndon's, but he apparently never gave the testimonial that was a standard feature of league meetings. He let his barbering and Atlanta Mutual speak for him. Herndon was uncomfortable with self-promotion. Preferring to take a backseat, he reserved his boasts for private jests within the family circle. He invested few resources in organizational politics.

Soon insurance would take greater hold of his time and energy, demanding that he oversee a larger fraternity and lead a broader

Founding meeting of the National Negro Business League in Boston, 1900. Booker T. Washington, center front with hat. (Courtesy of the Tuskegee Archives at Tuskegee University)

community. To his barbershop clients Herndon served as a menial, but to the Black community that Atlanta Mutual served he was nevertheless a master, presiding over a newly formed brotherhood of white-collar workers.

He called upon men who had insurance experience, developing his first management team partly from the companies acquired in the organization of Atlanta Mutual. From Royal Mutual Insurance Association came his second vice president, W. L. G. Pound, and his assistant superintendent, Solomon Johnson. Johnson—who had served as secretary and manager—and Pound had organized Royal Mutual, and upon its acquisition by Atlanta Mutual, they brought all of Royal Mutual's members to the new company.

Herndon hired as his assistant general manager Edward Howell, who had been head of the National Laborers' Protective Association. However, his top managers came out of the Union Mutual Relief Association, the first Black insurance association chartered in Georgia, which presumably offered the most experienced Black insurance professionals: Wade Aderhold, his first vice president and treasurer, and John Crew, his general manager and secretary.

On its front page, the *Atlanta Age* featured the photographs of Herndon and his team, looking like a gallery of distinguished African American brothers. The publication described Crew as "the colored insurance man of Georgia," and W. H. Jackson, whom Herndon had appointed assistant superintendent, as "an insurance Napoleon." "President Herndon," it reported, "has decided to make his company the strongest in the state and is putting forth every possible effort to take hold of the smaller companies now in the field." In just five years Herndon would acquire a total of nine companies.[23]

Atlanta Mutual was born in one of Auburn Avenue's first Black office buildings, the 1904 structure developed by Henry A. Rucker, a prominent Republican Party operative and businessman whom President William McKinley had appointed as Internal Revenue Collector. The Atlanta Benevolent and Protective Association had leased a small room in that building at the corner of Piedmont Avenue. According to

Atlanta Age, *30 September 1905.*

an Atlanta Mutual history, the company began operations there with "an old-fashioned 'blind typewriter,' two second-hand desks, a table, [a] half dozen old chairs and a few other small things. Insurance in force," it reported, "was less than $100, with one full-time agent and one full-time clerk." Within weeks of opening, however, Herndon moved his operation two blocks east to his own property at 202 Auburn Avenue on the northeast corner at Bell Street.[24]

It was a large three-story frame building that had been known as the European Hotel, and a few years before had been the property of the Atlanta Loan and Trust Company. Herndon and a few business-men had founded the institution in 1891 for the purchase, sale, and development of real estate. But the building at 202 Auburn was one of only two properties the company would ever own—the other an improved parcel diagonally across the street on the southwest corner. When Atlanta Loan and Trust Company defaulted on the northeast property at 202 Auburn, Herndon purchased it for $825 at a sheriff's sale to protect his investment as the major stockholder, and would eventually buy the southwest corner property upon default. Herndon gave the stockholders two years to reimburse their share of the $825 so that they could reclaim the property for Atlanta Loan and Trust.

Officers and Executive Committee of the Atlanta Branch of the National Association for the Advancement of Colored People, 1917: Standing, left to right, Peyton Allen, George Towns, Benjamin Davis, the Rev. L. H. King, Dr. William F. Penn, John Hope, David H. Sims; seated, left to right, Harry Pace, Dr. Charles H. Johnson, Dr. Louis T. Wright, Walter F. White, President.

He never received the promised payment. Instead, Atlanta Loan and Trust filed a suit accusing him of thwarting the association's efforts to hold its property. The court documents reveal a negligent operation: unpaid stock subscriptions, incomplete minutes, uncollected rents, and meetings suspended for years. Most telling was the institution's failure to maintain its own property. Speaking in court on his own behalf, Herndon contended that Atlanta Loan and Trust "just depended upon just letting [matters] rock along without putting any more money into it . . . and if anything [came] up, it was up to me to go and borrow or bet or do the best I could." Many of the directors, from their perspective, distrusted Herndon's shrewd real estate dealings. Moreover, some were jealous of his power and money. He was the largest Black property holder in Atlanta; they were a resentful underdog. According to Henry Lincoln Johnson, the lawyer in the foreclosure of the property on the southwest corner, "The directors would rather anybody would have the property [other] than Herndon," even if it meant losing the property. The suit was ultimately settled in Herndon's favor, and so for fifteen years, 202 Auburn Avenue would be the home office of Atlanta Mutual.[25] Two doors down the street was a larger Black insurance company, Union Mutual, from which Herndon had drawn two of his officers and which Atlanta Mutual would acquire in the next ten years.

Black insurance, Herndon found, was a hard row to hoe. The turnover of managers was high. Within three years, Aderhold and Crew were gone and Herndon moved to take charge of the company's day-to-day operations.[26] Of his first team, only Sol Johnson would remain with the company for the rest of his career. Moreover, the search for competent and trustworthy managers and agents was never-ending. Since Black life insurance in Georgia was not yet ten years old, the pool of experienced workers was extremely small. "It is better that we select and train our own men," Herndon concluded, "than to go after the men of other institutions." His concern was not only to ensure competence but also to instill ethical business practices from the start. The "crookedness of certain other institutions," he feared, could infect the Atlanta Mutual force.[27]

The best agents were men and women who linked salesmanship to racial uplift. "We had to convince [Black people] that we were building for their children for tomorrow," recalled Robert Chamblee, an early agent and district manager. "We were trying to build up a business *with* Negroes, *for* Negroes, and to *employ* Negroes. . . . We had to build it ourselves." Working out of their own homes as independent agents on twenty per cent commission, they sold sick and death benefits of one to fifty dollars for a nickel to a quarter a week. For people who had no money in the bank, a two-dollar-a-week benefit during sickness or fifty dollars for a funeral meant a great deal. There was stiff competition, however, from White agents of companies like Industrial Life and Health Insurance Company that sold the same kind of door-to-door insurance in the Black community. Black agents had to convince a skeptical Black public that Atlanta Mutual, a Black company, would pay off. "Very few colored people believed in one another," Chamblee sadly admitted. "[Suspicion] was the general attitude of our people." The company would look back on those times as "the pioneer days, when the trails were rough and rugged and great clouds of ignorance and superstition beclouded the way."[28]

Traveling sometimes by bicycle or narrow gauge trains, agents spread Atlanta Mutual policies throughout Georgia. After three months of operation, the company had a sales force that covered the state from Rome to Bainbridge, serving more than six thousand policyholders with about $181,000 of insurance in force.[29]

But Atlanta Mutual had entered a developing market, and its future in Black insurance was uncertain. "Success," Herndon would say, "depended on generalship, the ability to get men to cooperate." Whether assembling a management team, energizing agents, or countering the suspicions of African Americans, Herndon and Atlanta Mutual were forever grappling with the problem of getting Blacks to work together.[30] Before the next year was out, however, it would be painfully clear that the need for Black cooperation had reached an all-time high. With racism at a peak, Black self-help out of necessity was on the rise. Atlanta Mutual would thrive on the crest of segregation.

CHAPTER 6

All Hell

The mob smashed the front windows of Herndon's barbershop on Peachtree Street that Saturday night. The shop had probably closed early, though business had been heavy as usual. By six o'clock that evening a group of White men had gathered at Pryor and Decatur streets, three blocks from the barbershop, enraged by newspaper reports of assaults by Black men on White women. As extra after extra hit the streets claiming new assaults, an hysteria of race and sex took over downtown Atlanta.[1]

How long the barbershop remained open that evening of September 22 is uncertain, but Herndon and his barbers probably saw enough of the angry mob that triggered the Atlanta Riot of 1906. The barbers may not have heard the self-appointed leader who mounted a dry goods box on Decatur Street and goaded the crowd to violence, but they would have heard reports of Blacks beaten unconscious by gangs of Whites. From the door of the barbershop, they could have seen Whites chasing Blacks on Peachtree.[2]

Before long, the barbers would have had to stop cutting hair and seek shelter in the basement or the upper stories of the building. Those who lived in the Fourth Ward several blocks east of Peachtree may have made a run for home while the mob was engaged on Decatur. Herndon, however, would have had to escape to Diamond Hill, not an easy run, but his color may have been his cover. He could have moved through many areas of the city unrecognized as Black. Or

Walter White recalled: "We saw a lame Negro bootblack from Herndon's barbershop pathe-tically trying to outrun the mob of whites. Less than a hundred yards from us the chase ended. We saw clubs and fists descending to the accompaniment of savage shouting and cursing. . . . Its work done, the mob went after new prey. The body with the withered foot lay dead in a pool of blood on the street."

perhaps Herndon left downtown in a cab or on one of the streetcars before they came under attack by the mob later that night. Whatever the route, it appears that all of Herndon's barbershop workers found safety that night, except one. A bootblack, apparently Fred Walton, was run down by the mob and killed. About seven-thirty that evening George White, a Black mailman light enough to pass for White, was on his evening rounds with his thirteen-year-old son Walter, and witnessed the murder. "We saw a lame Negro bootblack from Herndon's barbershop pathetically trying to outrun the mob of Whites," the son later wrote. "Less than a hundred yards from us the chase ended. We saw clubs and fists descending to the accompaniment of savage shouting and cursing. Suddenly a voice cried, 'There goes another nigger!' Its work done, the mob went after new prey. The body with the withered foot lay dead in a pool of blood on the street."[3]

It was no accident that the first battle of a race war was waged on Decatur Street, a couple of blocks from Peachtree. The area was Black turf, where boardinghouses, barbershops, restaurants, and saloons, some owned by Blacks, often sheltered illicit sex and gambling, some of it interracial. These activities on Decatur and Ivy streets were the shame of many Blacks and were, in the minds of most Whites, the symbol of Black crime, specifically rape. On Friday plainclothes police had torn pictures of nude White women from the walls of Black saloons, because, as they said, they "inflamed the minds of negro men."[4] The Saturday-night crowd of White men drinking and loitering in the area became crazed by erroneous reports of Black insults and rallied for an invasion of the district. "To Decatur Street," they cried. "Let's clean the Black devils out—teach them a lesson." Storming the street with a hail of stones and sticks, they wrecked barbershops and restaurants, routing several hundred Blacks. Taking refuge in a Black skating rink on Central Avenue just off Decatur, many Blacks eventually escaped to the area around the old train station.[5]

What had begun that evening as an angry crowd of young White men, jeering and shoving Blacks, grew into a mob of thousands of all ages and classes intent on wholesale lynching. White men came from Bellwood, Reynoldstown, Oakland, and all over the city. Mayor

Decatur Street, c. 1900. It was no accident that the first battle of a race war was waged on Decatur Street a couple of blocks from Peachtree. It was an area of Black boarding houses, barbershops, restaurants, and saloons that some Whites frequented. "To Decatur Street," the mob cried. "Let's clean the black devils out—teach them a lesson." The Saturday-night crowd of White men drinking and loitering in the area became crazed by erroneous reports of Black men assaulting White women. (Courtesy of the Atlanta History Center)

James Woodward mounted the same dry goods box on Decatur that earlier had been the rabble-rouser's podium. "For God's sake, men," he begged, "go to your home quietly and I promise you that every negro will receive justice. . . . I beseech you not to cause the blot on the fair name of our most beautiful city." But Woodward, a known carouser, had no moral authority, and the crowd was beyond control. In his later attempt to disperse the mob, one of the crowd responded, "Oh, go home yourself, Jim. We're after niggers."[6]

For the most part, the police stood by or joined in the attack. Blacks were on their own to defend themselves as best they could. It was better to run and hide than to stand and fight, outnumbered by a mob seeking blood.

Atlanta had to have known that race violence was coming. Rumors

James Woodward, mayor of Atlanta: "For God's sake, men, go to your home quietly and I promise you that every negro will receive justice. . . . I beseech you not to cause the blot on the fair name of our most beautiful city." (Courtesy of the Atlanta History Center)

The front page of the Atlanta Sunday News, 23 September 1906.

had circulated in the city for some time. Blacks and Whites were arming themselves, though Blacks had for months been refused the sale of weapons, and thus had them sent in from out of town. Some guns were shipped in caskets; others were delivered in dirty laundry. The newspapers had sensationalized racial conflicts all summer. In late July, a Black man was lynched in Atlanta for a rape that had not occurred. An attempted assault on a White woman dominated the front page of the *Constitution* the Saturday morning before the riot.[7] In an eighteen-month campaign for the governorship, Hoke Smith and Clark Howell had with racist rhetoric debated the merits of Black disfranchisement. For nearly two years, then, White Atlanta had been primed for a race riot.

By ten o'clock that September night, the mob had swelled to ten thousand. A run that evening on the pawnshops and hardware stores had armed the crowd with pistols, revolvers, and rifles. The mob broke up into smaller mobs, each pursuing separate targets. Barbershops were a favorite. The men who broke the windows of Herndon's shop were demonstrating how deeply they resented a Black man's success. Herndon had been wise to close his shop early. One barbershop that served Blacks, however, and was across from the post office on Marietta Street, became the scene of one of the most vicious attacks of the riot. Two barbers were still working at their chairs when rioters crashed through the windows and doors. As one barber threw up his hands in surrender, he was knocked in the face with a brick. Both men were shot dead. "Still unsatisfied," the newspaper reported, "the mob rushed into the barber shop, leaving the place a mass of ruins. The bodies of both barbers were first kicked and then dragged from the place. [The mob grabbed] at their clothing, [which] was soon torn from [the barbers], many of the crowd taking these rags of shirts and clothing home as souvenirs or waving them above their heads to invite to further riot. When dragged into the street, . . . [the bodies of] both barbers [showed faces that] were terribly mutilated, while the floor of the shop was [wet] with puddles of blood. On and on these bodies were dragged across the street to . . . the alleyway . . . and left there . . . [as] a ghastly monument to the work of the night and almost within the shadow of the monument of Henry W. Grady."[8] If this was the New South, Atlanta had nevertheless pushed to its violent extreme the racial repression of the Old South.

The mob did not limit itself to the central business district; several gangs poured down Auburn Avenue, where Black businesses like Atlanta Mutual were located. Finding the avenue deserted, however, they went elsewhere. "The negroes began to get scarcer and the mob restless," the *Constitution* reported. The hysterical crowd turned its attention to the trolleys arriving from outlying areas with unsuspecting Black passengers. "Take them off. Kill them. Lynch them," they cried when the car bound for Grant Park arrived at Marietta and Peachtree. Several Blacks were beaten on board, three of them to death. By eleven o'clock and after twelve more attacks, the streetcars stopped running.[9]

By that time Alonzo had escaped Peachtree Street, but the Herndons would have spent a fearful night in watch for the mob. No one knew how and where it would strike next. Blacks mobilized for what little protection and retaliation they could muster. Seventeen Black men shot at an Inman Park trolley car at the intersection of Butler Street and Edgewood Avenue. Though windows were shattered, no one was injured. The Black men, however, unlike most of the White mob, were arrested. Bands of angry young Black men roamed the streets in their neighborhoods shooting out lights to discourage invasion and firing at passing cars.[10] Other Blacks, many of them armed, kept guard inside their homes. One wonders how Alonzo was prepared that night to meet the mob.

Violence raged for nearly five hours before the riot call sounded around midnight. Fifteen slow strokes on the big bell at fire department headquarters summoned the state militia. According to the *Constitution*, Governor Joseph Terrell, who had retired early that night, was oblivious to the conditions until the paper informed him.[11]

The militia, however, were slow to respond. It was nearly two o'clock before several companies had been deployed. Mercifully, a

Le Petit Parisien

SUPPLÉMENT LITTÉRAIRE ILLUSTRÉ

Huit pages : CINQ centimes

DIRECTION: 18 rue d'Enghien (10e), PARIS

MASSACRE DE NÈGRES DANS LES RUES D'ATLANTA

A French weekly reported on the riot. By ten o'clock that Saturday night in September, the mob had swelled to ten thousand. "Take them off. Kill them. Lynch them!" Blacks arriving downtown on trolley cars were beaten and killed. (Courtesy of the Atlanta History Center)

hard burst of rain fell, breaking up the mob as each man sought shelter. By then there were virtually no Blacks on the street to lynch, and the rioters had begun to tire, their thirst for blood having for the moment been quenched.[12]

Alonzo would have learned quickly of the murder of his bootblack from George White, a friend of the family. However, he probably had to wait for the Sunday paper to read of the slaughter of the Marietta Street barbers. That it was a barbershop for Blacks would have given Herndon little comfort. The mob had also gone after the bootblacks of the Kimball Hotel, which had a first-class shop, like Herndon's, that served Whites only. Had Herndon and his barbers been available, the mob would have butchered them, too.

Many church bells were silent and pulpits and pews empty in the central city on Sunday. It is unlikely that the Herndons went across town to First Congregational Church, but perhaps they attended service on the Atlanta University campus in the chapel of Stone Hall. The congregants would have had much to address to the Lord that morning, grateful that they had survived the first round of the massacre and prayerful that they would withstand whatever was in store. Already, downtown Atlanta was filling again with Whites who roamed the streets in a mood of celebration, congratulating themselves for their work of the previous night. The streets were empty of Blacks, but the militia had to bar a gang from entering the Piedmont Hotel to lynch the Black waiters for fear they would damage the property of Hoke Smith, the governor-elect.[13]

The hysteria that continued to grip the White community was driven now by the fear of Black retaliation. Early Sunday morning a woman in the outlying area of Winship had reported a group of twenty-five Black men threatening to attack Whites. The *Constitution* reported that "a mob of nearly a thousand White men made with all haste to the spot."[14]

The militia had come to protect Whites from Black retaliation, not to protect Blacks from the mob. As more troops were summoned from Marietta, Cedartown, Rome, Griffin, and Macon, word spread that a

The state militia, who were slow to respond, keep guard on Sunday on Peachtree Street (top) and Marietta Street (center and bottom).

"Here we have worked and prayed and tried to make good men and women of our colored population, and at our very doorstep the whites kill these good men. But the lawless element in our population, the element we have condemned, fights back, and it is to these people that we owe our lives."—William Crogman, first Black president of Clark University.

mob would form after dark on Peachtree and march down Houston Street (later named John Wesley Dobbs Avenue) past First Congregational Church to the Black community called "Darktown." Knowing that the militia would not protect them, Blacks armed themselves and lay in wait. They shot out the street lamp at Houston and Piedmont Avenue. As the gang of Whites approached, some of them carrying torches, Black snipers stationed in a two-story brick building fired shots at them. The mob hesitated. After more shots rang out, the invaders retreated up Houston. George White, who lived on the fringe of Darktown, was again in the midst of the mob, but this time as witness to the invasion of his own neighborhood. Standing guard that Sunday night in their parlor, White and his son Walter heard a member of the mob cry out as they approached their house, "That's where that nigger mail carrier lives! Let's burn it down! It's too nice for a nigger to live in." They recognized the voice of their grocer's son.[15] The George White family, like most Blacks, lived and traded with Whites in a very uneasy alliance. The riot fanned the rage and resentment that smoldered in their midst under the cover of segregation. Young Walter, whom the riot so abruptly initiated to White violence, would grow up to face it again and again as executive secretary of the National Association for the Advancement of Colored People. On that Sunday evening, the sniper fire from the Black outlaws of Darktown had saved him and his family. Moreover, the defense of Darktown no doubt cut off the mob's advance to the Fourth Ward neighborhood further east, where Atlanta's most prosperous Blacks lived.

Some of Atlanta's Black elite questioned the contempt they had often held for their lower class. "Here we have worked and prayed," said Clark University's first Black president, William Crogman, "and tried to make good men and women of our colored population, and at our very doorstep the Whites kill these good men. But the lawless element in our population, the element we have condemned, fights back, and it is to these people that we owe our lives."[16]

By Monday morning, the first business day after the riot, Herndon's barbershop on Peachtree Street was open again.[17] Surely Hern-

don had heard of the attempted attack on Darktown from George White or others living in the area, but he was used to mobilizing after disasters, whether from fire, partnerships gone bad, or an angry mob. His response to worsening race relations had always been to forge ahead. With saloons closed by order of the mayor and with the presence of the military, Herndon apparently believed that the worst was over. Militia headquarters were just two blocks away at Peachtree and Marietta; since about one o'clock that morning, a company had been stationed around Atlanta University and the nearby colleges. More important, in opening his shop, Herndon was giving notice that he would not be driven from Peachtree Street.

The damage to the shop was apparently not as serious as Herndon may have feared. Perhaps it only required boarding up the windows until the glass could be replaced. Just five of Herndon's twelve barbers reported for work at Peachtree Street that Monday. By Wednesday the shop was operating fully, but without Fred Walton.[18]

George White, one of Atlanta's first Black mailmen, with unidentified woman and children.

James W. E. Bowen, president of Gammon Seminary, was among the 250 Blacks in Brownsville arrested for the possession of arms and for suspicion in the killing of James Heard, a White militiaman.

If the central city was calm that Monday evening, the outlying areas were not. Before Herndon would have retired for the night, Brownsville erupted. In this mostly Black suburb southeast of Atlanta, where a middle-class community had developed around Clark University and Gammon Theological Seminary, citizens feared an invasion by the mob. They had been calling the police for protection since the first day of the riot but to no avail. Arming themselves, they patrolled their campuses, and held meetings to plan for further defense. Word of their Monday night meeting reached the police.[19] In the minds of Whites, armed Blacks constituted rebellion. The county responded to the threat by sending an official mob of police and citizen deputies who proceeded to arrest any Blacks bearing arms. As prisoners were taken away, gunshot was exchanged. Blacks shot a White mounted officer, James Heard, out of his saddle. He died instantly, and five officers and citizen deputies were seriously wounded. Outgunned and unable to see in the dark, the county forces retreated.[20]

At daybreak on Tuesday, however, the militia advanced on Brownsville, arresting more than 250 Blacks for possession of arms and for suspicion of involvement in the death of Heard. Among them was James Bowen, president of Gammon Seminary, who had so earnestly sought police protection.[21]

Matters had taken a more dangerous turn. Blacks were no longer the only victims of the riot. Black armed retaliation was more subversive of the old order than was Black rape. That morning, out-of-town military companies that had been dismissed were recalled. Three hundred White men from all over the county were sworn into duty by the sheriff in front of the courthouse. The mayor and police chief had to intervene and disperse a crowd of about a thousand more who waited eagerly in the rain to be deputized. Because weapons were scarce, Governor Terrell ordered more by wire. The prospect of more gun battles between Black residents and White police and citizen militia was particularly frightening to the business leadership, who knew that continuing violence would undermine the city's booming economy. The city's White leaders could not afford to remain silent any longer. Brownsville brought them to the table.

Tuesday was full of meetings public and private. At noon, a few hours after Bowen and the others were marched to jail, Alonzo Herndon and six other Black leaders walked into city council chambers to meet with prominent White citizens, presumably businessmen, attorneys, and ministers. Blacks had requested the meeting, it was reported, but Mayor Woodward and law-enforcement officials had formally issued the call. It was an exclusive gathering. "Only those who have been asked to attend the meeting will be expected," the *Constitution* warned.[22]

Herndon qualified, as Atlanta's leading Black businessman and property owner. He very likely was already in communication with some of the city's most powerful men. They knew him as their barber and confidant and respected his high standing in the Black community. They were his White counterparts, as well as his financial advisors. As the races drifted further apart, Herndon and his patrons no doubt remained in a trusted relationship.

The newspaper did not identify the Whites who were invited to the meeting, but most of the Black representatives were ministers: Henry Hugh Proctor, Herndon's pastor at First Congregational Church; Bishop Henry McNeil Turner and Richard D. Stinson of the African Methodist Episcopal Church; and Bishop J. H. Holsey of the Colored Methodist Episcopal Church. Curiously, not one of this group identified in the newspaper was Baptist, the denomination of most Blacks. Representatives of Atlanta's Black college community were not expected to be present, either. John Hope, who had recently been appointed first Black president of Atlanta Baptist College (Morehouse College), and William H. Crogman, first Black president of Clark University, had apparently not been invited. And certainly Du Bois, who was now deep into his challenge of Booker Washington, and who had sat on the steps of South Hall with his shotgun in protection against the mob, would not have been welcome. The other two Blacks at the meeting were a physician, Dr. Thomas Heathe Slater, and a grocer, Willis Murphy. The *Constitution* described the select group as "leading conservative negroes."[23]

It is unknown what Herndon said at the meeting, but for a business-

"The dives must go. . . . [They] are foul nests where evil birds lay their poisonous eggs which hatch out into loafers, thieves, thugs, murderers and rapists."—The Reverend Hugh Proctor, minister of First Congregational Church.

"While there is no excuse for mob law, it cannot be denied that criminal idleness lies at the bottom of all the chaos and disorder."
—*Benjamin Davis, editor of the Black newspaper* Atlanta Independent

man whose bootblack had been killed, whose shop had been damaged, and whose fellow tradesmen had been slaughtered, police protection would have been of particular interest. By noon, however, it may have appeared that the perceived problem of White and Black lawlessness would be dealt with effectively. That morning a mass meeting of prominent Blacks and Whites proposed that all of the dives of the city, Black and White, Decatur Street and elsewhere, be closed down.[24] Herndon may have been at that meeting also and surely would have supported the resolution. Henry Lincoln Johnson, a Black attorney who also happened to be Herndon's lawyer, had already succeeded in getting the police to close down Black barbershops, restaurants, and other establishments and to prohibit Blacks from gathering on the street.[25] Pointedly, Herndon and his allies saw a Black curfew as the key to ending the riot.

Many Blacks were of one mind in their opposition to what they would have considered the riff-raff of their race—those lawless elements that frequented the pool halls, the saloons, and the mullet stands of the Decatur Street area. "The dives must go," the Reverend Proctor had preached the Sunday before the riot. "These dives are foul nests where evil birds lay their poisonous eggs which hatch out into loafers, thieves, thugs, murderers and rapists. . . . In the present critical racial situation the crime of one Black man can stir up all Atlanta."[26] Though some would have questioned his analysis of Black crime, the dire outcome he prophesied for Atlanta came to pass within a week. Atlanta's Black leadership for the most part was intent on keeping Black lawlessness under control. Benjamin Davis, editor of the *Atlanta Independent,* was convinced that Black criminal elements were primarily to blame for the disturbance. "While there is no excuse for mob law," he wrote in his paper, "it cannot be denied that criminal idleness lies at the bottom of all the chaos and disorder. . . . The law is the remedy and criminal idleness is the crime. Clean up the town."[27] With the problem of the dives now being resolved, the issue of Brownsville would have dominated the agenda of the noon meeting at city hall. The newspaper reported briefly that Black representatives agreed to cooperate with Whites "to keep down further trouble" and that both races "heartily approved of the action of the authorities in raiding Brownsville and jailing the negroes who were carrying firearms."[28] But had no one in the meeting made any distinction between Heard's killers and citizens bearing arms in defense? Maybe not. Did Herndon and the other Blacks know that the president of Gammon Seminary was among those herded to prison? Perhaps so. But probably no Black leader present would have pleaded for the right of Blacks to defend themselves. They may have claimed the right privately, but in session with Whites in the midst of a riot, they may have taken issue only with the failure of police protection. The Black leadership knew that they would remain a vulnerable people subject to the whims of Whites. They had no choice but to find what common ground they could with a White leadership that for now had had enough of lawlessness. And so the lower elements of both races were to assume responsibility for the cause and the cure of the violence. Du Bois was one of the few who publicly would place the responsibility for the violence at the feet of the city's business leadership. "Whenever an aristocracy allows the mob to rule," he wrote, "the fault is not with the mob."[29]

It seemed to make no difference to Blacks or Whites that the brutal assaults reported in the press were for the most part allegations of attempted assaults. One woman had claimed that a Black man who was "lurking under the brush," ran off when she got a gun. A second woman had alleged that a Black man "knocked her down" at the back door of her house and then "ran for the woods." The posse found a man who, according to the *Constitution*, could "furnish no good account of himself"; the group put him in the county jail. A third woman on Davis Street said that a Negro man grabbed her in the rear of her home and threw her to the ground. The posse was unable to find him. And finally, the fourth assault attempt was reported by a woman who said a Black man had peered through her blinds.[30] There had been no rapes after all, and in two incidents, not even physical contact had been reported. Instead, allegations, insinuations, and fears of assault

"I beg that you cease all violence and lawlessness. . . . Stay indoors at night; be peaceable, keep your tongues, subdue your passions, possess your soul in patience, divorce yourselves from criminals, obey and uphold the law and the good people will protect you."—The Reverend Peter James Bryant, pastor of Wheat Street Baptist Church. (Courtesy of Herman Mason Jr.)

"Whenever an aristocracy allows the mob to rule, the fault is not with the mob."—W. E. B. Du Bois, Atlanta University professor.

had generated a massacre in which countless people, mostly Blacks, had been killed.

In another mass meeting that Tuesday morning Black and White ministers pledged to do all in their power to control the lawless men within their respective communities. "As a member and leader of the race," the Reverend Peter Henry Bryant stated in his resolution to Blacks, "I beg that you cease all violence and lawlessness. We all, white and colored alike, deprecate the outbreak of violence . . . as well as the shameful cause of which it is the effect. And now it is the indispensable duty of the negro as well as the white man, to pour water on the flames. . . . Stay indoors at night; be peaceable, keep your tongues, subdue your passions, possess your soul in patience, divorce yourselves from criminals, obey and uphold the law and the good people will protect you."[31] Could the Black ministers have believed that the police would indeed protect Black residents? Were they assuming that the White leadership would now enforce the law on behalf of Blacks? Or were they bound and determined to urge Black lawfulness by any means necessary? In these most dangerous times, a conservative leadership wanted desperately to make peace. In the last mass meeting of Tuesday afternoon, White citizens deplored the crimes of the worst segments of both races, signaling the end of the violent episode. On Wednesday there were only scattered disturbances; by Thursday, the city had fallen into a gloomy calm. The official count, which was impossibly low and remains in dispute, was twenty-five Blacks and one White dead, and many times that number seriously injured among both races. But long after the last militia unit left town, the races would remain in contention. For the Herndons, the hell of violence had ended, but it broke loose their household. Uprooted from Bumstead, the family sought refuge elsewhere. Disrupted by the riot, the Herndons would never fully recover the well-being they had known before the mob began its terrible work that infamous Saturday night.

CHAPTER 7

A New Home in the Rock

"I feel we have never had a real home."—Adrienne Herndon

"The unsettled conditions here make us feel that we can never hope to have [a home] in this ungodly section," Adrienne wrote to Booker T. Washington. "Last year we broke up our home, took our little son to Philadelphia, put him in school there and since my return we have been occupying rooms in the Univ. dormitory. The house we occupied for ten years was Dr. Bumstead's home so that I feel we have never had a real home."[1]

Five months after the riot, Adrienne was responding to Washington's invitation to be featured among selected Black women in a forthcoming magazine article. She graciously declined. "I have come to feel," she wrote, "that I should like to hide from the eyes of the White man, or any rate the Southern White man the things I, as a Negro woman hold most sacred for fear they pause & look to jeer and ridicule."[2]

Alonzo was less pessimistic about the future. Business had resumed at both barbershops and at Atlanta Mutual. Although the riot may have confirmed that Black dominance in barbering was being undermined, Herndon remained confident of the profit still to be made in his trade. In another year he would open a third barbershop in partnership with William W. Williams at 34 North Forsyth across from the Grant Building.[3] He had not missed a step in his public affairs during the four-day upheaval in September. However, in his personal life over the next three and a half years, he and his family would at times lose their footing.

Before the riot week was out, the Herndons spirited Norris to the North. He and his grandmother were taken to Philadelphia to live at 1519 Cambridge Street with Mattie's younger sister Rachel Fleming Simkins and her eight-year-old daughter Clara. A third Atlanta refugee joined them: Auntie Nor, who was then about seventy years old. Norris enrolled in the third grade at a public school.[4]

The riot may have triggered other events in the Atlanta University community that helped to create the "unsettled conditions" Adrienne referred to in her letter to Washington.

It was probably no coincidence that only ten days after the riot started, Horace Bumstead sold the cottage to Atlanta University for six thousand dollars.[5] Although many of his colleagues may have been anticipating Bumstead's resignation as president long before it occurred that next July, the sale of the house was perhaps his first formal break with the institution he had served for more than thirty years.

The Herndons had to move from Bumstead to the dormitory so that the university could prepare the mansion for its next president. On what appeared to be short notice to vacate the house, the Herndons may have had to leave many of their possessions in the cottage for a while. Keeping watch in their absence was Alonzo's cousin, Archibald (Archer) Berry, a porter at the Peachtree Street barbershop, who for some time had been living with them in Bumstead.[6]

When the Atlanta University students returned for the fall term of 1906, Adrienne launched an ambitious program for her department, as though a rash of activity could supplant the desperation she felt about the riot. With the violence still fresh in mind, twelve students infused racial pride and nationalism in the competition that December for the Alumni Prize in speaking. Caroline Bond recited "Litany for Atlanta," an emotional piece that Du Bois composed about the riot as he rushed home on the train from Alabama to protect his family. Other contestants spoke of American independence and Haitian revolution; one celebrated Black valor with Paul Dunbar's "The Colored Soldiers."[7]

Program for the Alumni Prize in speaking.

Every month, Adrienne and the music teacher, Hattie Clifford, took charge of rhetoricals, which were student performances in music and oratory held on a Friday night in the chapel on the second floor of Stone Hall.[8]

At the end of the school year in April 1907, Adrienne went on the road, giving several benefit recitals for local charities. In Savannah, her program for the Men's Sunday Club drew upon her own writings, including selections from "The Shadow," an Indian play first performed by her students in Atlanta in 1903, and from "Vashti," a monologue based on the Bible story. With the Apollo Orchestra and other local talent performing between readings and with the refreshments that followed the program, the evening must have been one of the cultural and social highlights of her hometown that year.[9]

Lucy Laney, founder and principal of Augusta's Haines Institute, for which Adrienne performed a benefit drama recital.

Adrienne also sang at some of her recitals. A newspaper reported for the Savannah appearance that "Mrs. Herndon possesses a sweet soprano voice which was admirably displayed in the two songs which she sang as encores to the character impersonations." From Savannah, Adrienne went to Augusta, where she performed for the benefit of Lucy Laney's Haines Institute and then on to Aiken, South Carolina. Later that month in Chattanooga, her recital at First Baptist Church was a return engagement, this time for the benefit of the Masons in their effort to buy a home. The event was billed as "an intellectual treat"; Adrienne was described as "one of the most talented women of the race." Her recitals, like all of her work, were carefully staged, the Chattanooga program having been assisted by a pianist, musical director, and manager.[10]

Atlanta's theater offerings the spring before the riot inspired Adrienne and her work at Atlanta University that school year of 1906–7. Sarah Bernhardt had appeared in "Camille," a souvenir and farewell program at the Peachtree Auditorium in March. No one in the audience could have been more enthralled by the actress than Adrienne, whom probably no one suspected was Black. Bernhardt was her idol. Adrienne claimed that seeing the artist perform in her own theater in Paris in 1900 had inspired her to devote her life to drama.[11]

When the Ben Greet Company performed in *As You Like It* in the Atlanta area at a Brookwood theater in May 1906, Adrienne attended and penciled in a few notes on her program. That next spring of 1907, Atlanta University students presented *As You Like It* as the class night exercise. But unlike the Greet players, who skipped the first act, they did the whole play. The Atlanta University production may have been influenced by the Greet company costumes. Adrienne's program notes had recorded, perhaps for the part of Rosalind, a "white bridal gown made empire with . . . pleated fullness falling from [the] back shoulders [and] a veil of thin tissue silk."[12]

Significantly, the Black community in turn-of-the-century Atlanta had access to Shakespearean drama in costume splendor. All of Atlanta University's programs were open to the public and well attended, but the Shakespearean productions were the most popular.[13]

As the university's drama season ended, Adrienne must have felt relief and elation. Her students had performed Shakespeare worthy of any audience, and she was about to put dormitory life and Atlanta aside for a while. In a few days she would leave for New York City to study at the American Academy of Dramatic Arts. Life was indeed looking up; the prospects for a new home had brightened considerably.

On May 30, Alonzo bought the lot next door to Bumstead Cottage from Atlanta University for twenty-eight hundred dollars. It was a one-acre parcel that ran for three hundred feet along Walnut, from the new street (to be named University Place) all the way back to Carter Street.[14] The Herndons may have had their eye on this property for some time. But now, with the university's operating costs increasing and its accumulated deficit remaining high, the school was eager to sell the property for development by faculty families.[15]

Whatever the reason for the Herndons' delay in having a home of their own, acquiring this plot of land next door to Bumstead must have seemed well worth the wait. It was on the crest of Diamond Hill, one of the highest elevations in the city. To the east was a full view of downtown Atlanta; to the north, an overlook of the Vine City neighborhood; and to the west and south, the campus. There was perhaps no finer site in all of Atlanta to build a house. Adrienne could look forward to summer study with the assurance that her dream was becoming reality.

When Adrienne arrived at the academy in early June, she had already missed two months of the six-month junior year. At age thirty-seven, she was older than the recommended age for entrance. Her studies at the School of Expression and her fifteen years of teaching elocution and drama gave her perhaps far more formal training and experience than anyone in her class. That summer, Adrienne Herndon became Anne Du Bignon again, but no longer was she an unknown. William Gillette, whose company had performed at Bumstead, and David Belasco, who would have remembered her from Boston, were on the academy's advisory board.[16]

Adrienne was preparing this time not for platform performance

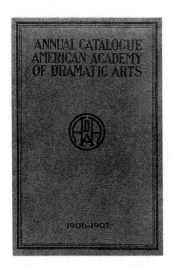

NEW EMPIRE THEATRE
40TH STREET & BROADWAY

CHARLES FROHMAN
MANAGER

1907-1908

American Academy of Dramatic Arts
AND
Empire Theatre Dramatic School

THE GRADUATION EXERCISES

OF THE TWENTY-FOURTH YEAR WILL
TAKE PLACE ON

THURSDAY AFTERNOON, MARCH 12
AT THREE O'CLOCK

YOU ARE INVITED TO BE PRESENT

but rather for the teaching and production of college dramatics. And perhaps in the back of her mind and deep in her heart was the hope that the American stage was still within her reach. In her junior year she would learn advanced techniques and practices. The senior year, however, would have had a greater appeal. Organized as the Academy Stock Company, the seniors were in constant rehearsals, appearing often before the public, critics, and other theater professionals. This would seem to be as close as Adrienne could come to performing on the legitimate stage. So when the junior term ended in September, Adrienne re-enrolled immediately in the senior class. At last, she was at the center of American theater. And conveniently, she was a short train ride from Norris in Philadelphia, but on leave from the university and far away from the terror of Atlanta.

Adrienne boarded at 355 West Fifty-fifth Street, which was very near the academy at Carnegie Hall on Fifty-seventh. For nearly a year, she lived and studied in New York's theater district, attending academy productions at the Empire Theater and the Carnegie Lyceum. She enjoyed play after play on Broadway: "The Girl of the Golden West," a musical with Blanche Bates at the Belasco Theater; a new play, "Her Sister," with Ethel Barrymore at the Hudson; and Hammerstein's "Victoria" at the Theatre of Varieties. She sketched the stage set of "Virginius" at the Lyric and noted in her program of "The Hoyden," a new musical comedy at the Knickerbocker, that Elsie Janis was "a clever little actress in mime and impersonations." On the weekends she visited Norris in Philadelphia.[17]

In the absence of his wife and child, Alonzo took residence in a boardinghouse he apparently owned at 201 Walnut Street, a two-story frame building at the corner of Carter, not far from campus, but in the valley below. Living there also was his cousin Archer and Julia Fambrough, a domestic, whom Alonzo knew from the Fellowship Baptist Church community in Social Circle.[18]

So, the Herndons were divided into three parts. That summer, when Norris was having trouble with his eyes, his parents could attend him only from afar. From New York Adrienne wrote, "Bathe your eyes

in weak salt water real often. Instead of rubbing them with the wash rag fix just a little salt water in the basin and wash them. Don't try to read or write, but play house; play store; play gardening, play on the beach, but keep on your big hat and amber colored glasses." By fall Norris's eyes were better, in time for another year of public school in Philadelphia. A grinning and bespectacled Norris, who had a way of cocking his head to the side, posed that fall for photographs with his Aunt Rachel and cousin Clara on the steps of the brownstone they rented at 1519 Cambridge Street, which was in a White neighborhood. They appeared a loving threesome, content with themselves and the world. In other photographs Norris and Clara are seen amid the neighborhood children, everyone dressed in Sunday finery. With the exception of the moves the Simkinses made, perhaps for more comfortable accommodations, Norris's stay in Philadelphia seemed uneventful.[19] With Adrienne at the Academy, Norris's exile from Atlanta extended for nearly two years. His mother had forsaken Atlanta, not only to escape its violence but also, and perhaps more important, to continue her relentless pursuit of a place on the American stage. Alonzo by then may have lost patience with her efforts. Alone in a boardinghouse in Atlanta, the breakup of his family may have seemed an exorbitant price for her refuge from Southern violence.

For Christmas 1907 the Herndons were together in Philadelphia. It was perhaps then that Adrienne and Norris exchanged the notes that poignantly captured an affection between mother and child, which seemed to deepen with separation. "Mama," Norris wrote in his fourth-grade cursive, "I love you I love you, yes I love you; and I know you love me love me yes love me. Do you knot . . . write Answer." Adrienne responded on the back of his note, "My Darling, Mama loves you more than anything in the world and she prays for your happiness and that God will make you a good boy."[20]

Spending the Christmas holidays in the Northeast, primarily in Philadelphia, the Herndons missed the December 31 inauguration of Atlanta University's third president, Edward Twitchell Ware. "Mr. Herndon and I regret very much," Adrienne wrote to Ware, "that we could not be present on the 31st but our hearts were there and I write now my congratulations to Atlanta University on her good fortune in having another Ware as her third president."[21] The university's founding president was Edward's father, Edmund Asa Ware, a Massachusetts native and a theology graduate of Yale University. After New Year's, Alonzo and Adrienne were in New York City, perhaps celebrating the promise of 1908 as they moved closer to a home.

The Herndons had been planning their house for years. That the design would be Beaux-Arts Classical was probably first suggested by the architecture featured at the Columbian Exposition in Chicago in 1893. The exposition was closed by the time the Herndons married, but they would have seen the exposition buildings when they were in Chicago, either for their honeymoon or on a subsequent trip. They

Alonzo, Adrienne, and Norris reunited briefly in Philadelphia, 1907.

would have seen the work of Richard Morris Hunt, the nation's first architect to be formally trained at the École des Beaux-Arts in Paris. Beaux-Arts spread from Chicago throughout the country. The style was grand and monumental, celebrating the classical world of Greece and Rome. It was appropriate to the Herndons' justified claim to distinction and suited their taste. And it was so different from the design of Bumstead, the solid rambling house that seemed rooted in the earth. Bumstead was a huge, but cozy, cottage; the Herndon house would be a small palace, light, ethereal, as if reaching heavenward.

While studying in Boston, Adrienne would have been familiar with and probably impressed by the summer mansions that Hunt had designed in Newport, Rhode Island, for the Vanderbilts: Marble House and the Breakers. And on her trip to France in 1900 for the Paris Exposition, she had visited several royal estates, such as Versailles and Fountainebleau, the centuries-old chateau complex of the French kings, whose prints Adrienne carefully collected and mounted as souvenirs. Alonzo's inspiration for the new house, however, was closer to home. In Social Circle stood the house of Horance Herndon, Alonzo's White half nephew. Originally built as a log house in 1832, subsequent renovations produced a four-thousand-square-foot structure with a columned front added in 1895 that suggests the classical façade of the Herndons' house. For Alonzo and Adrienne, as for many elite Americans at the turn of the century, the dominant influence in house design was European. It was predictable that the Herndons would bring the Beaux-Arts to their suburban hilltop.[22]

The front of the house with its columns would face University Place, not Walnut, as the building permit had oriented the structure. Rather than look eastward to downtown with a view of the undeveloped area behind the public school, the house would turn south to the privacy of the campus, where terraces had converted an unsightly landscape into a beautiful setting.[23]

The Herndons' house would have its own terraces offering views in all directions from both stories and the flat roof on top that could also serve, according to oral tradition, as an open-air theater for Adrienne's productions.

It would be a large house of nearly six thousand square feet, larger than Bumstead, and symmetrical. Behind the main building would be a two-story carriage house facing Walnut. A side drive would lead under a covered porch to the rear, where the lot extended more than 150 feet to Carter Street. There would be plenty of room for Alonzo's garden and chicken coops.

Adrienne and Alonzo employed no professional architect. They designed their own house, drawing upon their own experience, talent, drive, and financial resources, all of which were considerable. Adrienne was well read and well traveled, and also endowed with an architectural intellect. She had a keen sense of spatial arrangement, and a sharp eye for building detail. Alonzo, whose sole investment for twenty-five years had been real estate, was knowledgeable in building repair and reconstruction. He had grown up familiar with the tradition of the common builder who also served as designer. Architecture at the turn of the century was a young profession in America, barely a generation old. Herndon would have known of early Black architects who had trained in northern White schools and served on the faculty at Tuskegee Institute. But he chose to stick with the older tradition of designer/builder. And although he and Adrienne knew Alexander Hamilton, the leading Black contractor in Atlanta, they chose not to entrust their dream to others. So, Adrienne was the architect and Alonzo the builder/contractor. They hired day laborers and engaged Black craftsmen, like William Campbell, who served as the lead carpenter.[24] Construction of the Herndon home was a huge undertaking with great risk. But this dynamic team created one of the finest houses in Atlanta.

Construction began in 1908. Herndon had applied for a building permit in July. By fall of that year, Atlanta University observers thought that the house was nearing completion, but there was in fact much work still to be done over the next year.[25]

Adrienne and Norris were back in Atlanta before construction began. The Herndons apparently returned to the dormitory on campus, though for some time Alonzo kept his address at 201 Walnut

Building permit. (Courtesy of the Atlanta History Center)

Street. While Norris went back to Mitchell Street School for the last two months of the fourth grade, Adrienne absorbed herself in the design details of the home.

Her domestic project must have been a welcome diversion from the harsh reality of racism at the American Academy. It seems that Adrienne had not been a student in full standing. The president of the academy, Franklin Sargent, had apparently never signed his acceptance of her contract for the junior year; and in senior year Adrienne apparently never appeared in an Academy Stock Company production.[26] She probably sat on the sidelines while the others rehearsed and performed. How had her classmates reacted to her exclusion, or had they been among the ones to oppose her performance on the stage? More important, how had Adrienne managed the humiliation of two school terms as a second-class student? Ironically, upon graduation she was awarded the Belasco silver medal for technical skill, an award usually conferred upon a junior student, but in this instance perhaps offered as a token in substitution for full recognition of her talent and her civil rights. A photograph of her as one of the graduating seniors at the academy appeared in the *New York Morning Telegraph.* Reviews of the academy's performance of the "Choephoroi of Aeschylus," appeared in several publications, but of course with no mention of Adrienne other than her having received the silver medal. Among Adrienne's extensive memorabilia of her dramatic career, there is precious little of her months at the academy. A friend whom she had met apparently during her studies in New York and who had not heard from her in some time, wrote in care of the academy before the senior year ended in March: "Dear Biggy, What has happened to you?"[27] What, indeed. Would Anne Du Bignon have answered that all her illusions about the stage had finally been destroyed? Would she have confided that she was about to return to her real life in Atlanta as Adrienne Herndon? Adrienne apparently did not reveal this situation to even her closest associates. In a letter to President Ware, in which she tried to make final arrangements for Shakespeare's *Twelfth Night,* the senior dramatics program for the 1908 commencement, she led him to believe that she had exciting news to share with him about her months of study. "You will be pleased to learn that I am meeting with *splendid* success in my work here of which I'll speak more fully when I see you."[28] This probably referred to the compromised award of the Belasco Medal. She may have told no one that the New York theater was no escape after all from the Atlanta riot. Northern racism may have been less violent at that time, but no less damaging.

Adrienne and Alonzo took refuge in the preparations for the house. It was to be their "home in the rock," an earthly shelter and a symbol of their spiritual home in Glory. The Herndons had first referred to Bumstead in these terms. "'Worn down to a frazzle' at this juncture," Adrienne once wrote from Paris, "but I am now on the

Plaza St. Louis, thinking of my 'Home in the rock.'" She could have expressed the same sentiment for her future home after her sojourn in New York. There was greater urgency now in proceeding with construction of the house. They broke ground on June 26, 1908, Alonzo's fiftieth birthday. "Wagons are unloading brick on our lot," Adrienne wrote to President Ware, who was spending the summer in Montclair, New Jersey. "Real work will begin Monday." Two weeks later Adrienne gave Ware a progress report: "The stone work is well underway for our basement. It really looks as if we are to have a home."[29]

By the end of 1908, the exterior walls and roof were up. Across the street, the construction of the house of George Towns, Adrienne's colleague at Atlanta University, had just begun. Earlier that year, Towns had asked to purchase from the university the lot across the street from

Herndon residence under construction; photograph featured in Du Bois's Atlanta University Conference publication and identified as: "Residence of a Negro business man, insurance manager and proprietor of barber shops; now building and said to be the finest Negro residence in the South."

Sketch of interior of house in Monmouth, Maine.

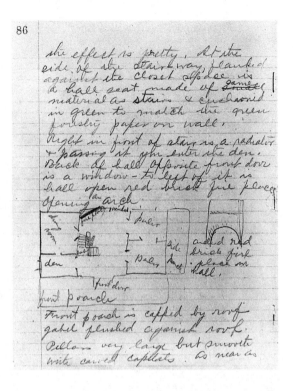

the Herndons. President Ware strongly recommended to the trustees that the lot be sold to Towns with the hope that he would build on it.[30] A small, elite neighborhood was developing around Bumstead and the university's domestic arts house, Furber Cottage. Only for the large parcel west of the Townses' lot was there no scheduled development.

Six white Corinthian columns dominated the front of the Herndon house. Wooden balustrades lined the second-floor terraces and the rooftop. The masonry walls were twelve to eighteen inches thick. The exterior was finished with a richly textured pumpkin-colored brick flecked with rose and purple iron deposits, which came from the superior clay fields around Coshocton, Ohio. Highly fired and impervious to water, the durable brick was laid in extremely fine, thin mortar joints.[31]

The Herndons had chosen an eclectic interior, a mix of styles from many traditions: Italian Renaissance, French Rococo, American Arts and Crafts, and others. Adrienne adapted several ideas from a Colonial house she had visited in Monmouth, Maine, during the summer of 1905, following the trip to Niagara. She made a sketch of its floor plan that was strikingly similar to the arrangement of rooms in her new house. Taking detailed notes on that visit, she recorded that "the hall . . . is the prettiest feature of the house. The stairs begin opposite [the] parlor door[,] . . . run up [a] few steps to [the] landing and then turn and go straight up to [the] upper hall." A similar but more elaborate stair hall with a second, more extended landing would be the centerpiece of the Herndon house. Adrienne also placed the stair hall opposite the front door, so that it would be seen immediately upon entering the house. Just across the reception hall, it looked like a palace courtyard, a pair of lion-headed newel posts standing guard.   *Stair Hall.*

RIGHT: *Music Room.*

BELOW: *Living Room.*

An arcade, airy and light like a Venetian loggia, crowned the stair hall at the second floor. Light filtered through the frosted glass window on the landing. In the house in Monmouth Adrienne noted that "back of [the] hall opposite [the] front door is a window [and] to the left of it is . . . [an] open red brick fire place, [its] opening an arch." Adrienne chose for her house a huge arched fireplace of green-glazed Rookwood tile at the end of the reception hall to the right of the entrance.[32]

The Arts and Crafts informality of the fireplace clashed sharply with the Neoclassical features of the stair hall and reception hall, but such was characteristic of an eclectic interior, where contrasts interplayed within and between rooms.

The parlor off the reception hall, which would become a music room, was an elaborately finished chamber, decorated with a Louis XV–style fireplace and intricate plaster moldings near the ceiling, from which hung a crystal and bronze chandelier. Entering the living room/library through mahogany pocket doors, one saw more Arts and Crafts interior. The large rectangle was liberally furnished with wood: ceiling beams and panels, built-in bookcases, and window seats, all in mahogany. The floors, as in all of the formal rooms on the first floor, were of oak and bordered with parquet of oak, maple, and walnut.

Only in the living room/library would the house have any indication of the Herndon family's racial background and its significance. Pictured on the frieze near the ceiling was a series of murals beginning with the sphinx and pyramids of Giza. Though Egypt was not an unusual subject for such friezes, for the Herndons it clearly represented their African ancestry. Early twentieth-century Black consciousness identified with the great kingdoms of ancient Africa. The next panel depicts slavery. Sophenie, head of the household, is chopping wood; the boy Alonzo carrying it toward their log house on the farm in Social Circle. The skin colors of the figures in the murals are specifically rendered—the African Sphinx a dark brown, Sophenie a medium brown, and Alonzo near white. In showing his origins in slavery Alonzo was

The pyramids and sphinx of Giza. (Courtesy of Van Jones Martin)

Herndon's origin in slavery. (Courtesy of Van Jones Martin)

Alonzo, the farm laborer. (Courtesy of Van Jones Martin)

The mansion, elegant symbol of Herndon's success. (Courtesy of Van Jones Martin)

Herndon's grandfather Carter Herndon passes on the family tradition from generation to generation. (Courtesy of James R. Lockhart)

acknowledging and embracing his lowly beginnings. Unashamed of where he had come from, he was proud of his journey. The central mural shows Herndon as a young farm laborer, a sharecropper, standing in the field with his long-handled hoe and looking up as if with a vision of a better day. The fruits of his labor and the object of his vision are seen next in the picture of the mansion, an elegant symbol of Alonzo's success. The final scene of the family history series could be interpreted as the Herndons passing their tradition from generation to generation. An old, dark-skinned man, presumably Herndon's grandfather, Carter Herndon, is seated before a log house, his index finger pointing in instruction to the young Alonzo, a red-haired boy stretched out on the ground before him. Nearby is Sophenie holding the baby Thomas. How thoughtfully and carefully Adrienne and Alonzo must have been planned the murals, consciously teaching the history of an African people and their inspiring story of achievement in America. The idea of a frieze was probably suggested to Adrienne by an interior decorating manual, but it would have fallen to Alonzo to capture the essence of his life in five images. Significantly, Alonzo chose field labor rather than barbering to depict his critical path to success.[33]

The most elegant room in the house would be the dining room. The Herndons reserved the finest woodwork for it. Like that of the living room, it was mahogany, but more richly detailed. The chimneypiece and the built-in sideboard carried elaborate carvings of architectural elements and animal and floral motifs. The room was a cleaner, simpler, understated version of the dining room in the Harry Payne Whitney residence in Newport.[34]

Alonzo and Adrienne had many details to oversee in the interior. Most of the woodwork, such as the doors, was machined at a planing mill, but sashes and trim were probably made by the carpenters on site. Other elements in the living room/library and the dining room, particularly the mahogany wainscot and panels, which were more elaborate and deeper cut, were also custom work. The Herndons would have given direction to the production of these items, as they

may also have guided final design and assembly of the parquet flooring.[35]

During the first year of construction, the family remained for the most part close to Atlanta. It was a lean year for Atlanta Mutual, which experienced for the first time an excess of expenditures over income. With the young company struggling to survive, and having maintained three separate households the previous year, Alonzo may have been pressed for cash. Surprisingly, he borrowed money from W. E. B. Du Bois, who by December 1909 was forced to ask for repayment: "If it is convenient, I shall have to ask for $50 of the fund which I loaned you. I should like it if possible sometime next week. I hope it will not inconvenience you." In another week Du Bois asked for payment of the full $100 loan.[36] In July there was a short trip to Social Circle. "We are all well and are expecting you next Sunday," Ida Knox wrote.[37] On this trip, unlike the one in early 1904, Adrienne was probably with them, the whole family sharing with Alonzo's homefolk their pride in the progress on the mansion.

Construction on the home continued through 1909. In an Atlanta University conference publication that year, Du Bois featured a photograph of the house under construction with the description: "Residence of a Negro business man, insurance manager and proprietor of barber shops; now building and said to be the finest Negro residence in the South. It will have electric bells and lights, fireplaces, steam-heat, roof-garden, and 15 rooms." In the evolution of the Negro home, Du Bois placed it at the pinnacle. Alonzo modestly estimated the cost of his house at ten thousand dollars.[38]

That same July the Herndons were able to celebrate Adrienne's birthday in Buckroe Beach, Virginia, near Hampton. They stayed at the Bayshore Hotel, a "colored hotel," Alonzo reported in a letter to Edward Ware, "equiped and manned by Black men." The family occupied a room on the second level. "It is very well conducted," he wrote. "Our room [is] named for Booker Washington." Adrienne had penned the letter for Alonzo, the primary purpose of which was to

The home was completed by 1910.

Jennie Olive McNeil Bailey, half sister of Adrienne Herndon, c. 1900. "My sister is already laying her plans to come and visit me next summer and see the new house!"—Adrienne Herndon.

inform Ware that he would make his interest payment presumably on the parcel they had purchased for their house. "I wish I could pay the principle," Adrienne wrote on Alonzo's behalf, "so as to help you wind up the books without a deficiency, but I cannot, so I'll send a check for the interest at once to Dr. Adams; and shall try to get ready for the principle as soon as possible."[39]

In September, just before school started, Adrienne was in Brooklyn visiting her sister and brother-in-law, Jennie and James Bailey, and their children Adrienne Elizabeth, Edward, and John Henry. "You would have a fit over my sister's little children," she wrote to Julia Fambrough. "They are *so cunning*. Maybe you'll get [to] see them next summer for my sister is already laying her plans to come and visit me next summer and see the new house!"[40]

As 1909 drew to a close, Alonzo took sick. Adrienne wrote her sister Jennie just before Christmas: "'Brother' is still sick, but up & walking around still." The holidays passed and Alonzo got well. Soon after the New Year, on January 18, the building inspector declared the house completed.[41] At long last, the Herndons had a home. It seemed that everything was now ready for a new life.

CHAPTER 8

An Untimely Death

Adrienne Herndon.

The Herndons may have moved to their new house as early as Christmas 1909, for by the end of December, the university was forwarding their mail to No. 1 University Place, the first address on the new street. Or perhaps the Herndons moved in January after the final inspection on the building. In any event, Adrienne knew when she moved into the mansion that she had a fatal illness.[1] Probably the first symptom was, ironically, the darkening of her skin. In time she would have felt weak and tired; she may have experienced nausea, lost her appetite, and lost weight. But by then a hormonal deficiency had already run its destructive course. It would have taken several months before the symptoms of Addison's disease first appeared.

Her condition would only get worse. In February, Adrienne was no longer able to teach. In mid-March Alonzo took her to Philadelphia to consult with medical specialists. The trip had probably been arranged by Dr. Loring Palmer, Adrienne's physician, whom she had known since their studies at Atlanta University, and who had received his medical degree from the University of Pennsylvania.

"Dear Mama," Norris wrote to her in Philadelphia at the Hotel Slenton, "I received your card and was glad to hear from you. Grandma is not worring so much since we got your card. Papa please write to grandma so she won't worry." Mattie must have been standing over her grandchild as he wrote. Taking her dictation, he continued: "Tell him to write her a *letter* and tell her how mama is." In anxiety Mattie added her own note: "Tell us all the Dr. says."[2]

The Herndons had left Philadelphia before Norris's card arrived. Apparently, upon their return, they reported that there was some hope concerning Adrienne's condition. Mattie spread the good news. Friends sent Easter messages of relief and best wishes. "I am rejoicing with you," one friend wrote to Mattie, "that Mrs. Herndon is better. I am *so glad* to hear of her improved condition."[3]

But whatever hopes they expressed upon returning to Atlanta, Adrienne and Alonzo knew that their trip to Philadelphia was a desperate one. Before leaving, Adrienne had said to Alice Ware, the wife of Atlanta University's president, "We have only just got ready to live, and now I must die."[4]

Alonzo made arrangements for a trip to Indian Springs in Butts County, not far away. Perhaps the baths there that his brother Thomas had found beneficial would be of some help. "Yes," a hotel owner had

Adrienne with her grandmother Harriet Hankerson, c. 1908.

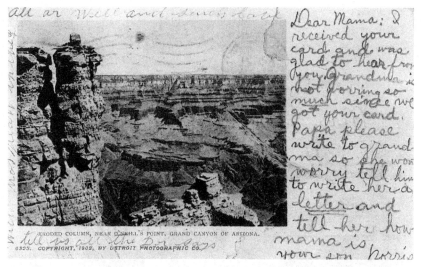

An Easter postcard from a Herndon family friend.

responded to his inquiry, "I can accommodate you and [your] family if you wish to come down for a short stay."[5]

The Herndons never made the trip. Adrienne's condition deteriorated the Sunday after Easter. On Wednesday night, April 6, 1910, she died. Her sudden death shocked everyone. She was only forty years old, and her illness had been brief. Just as it seemed to her family and friends that she would rally, at least for a while, death came quickly. Many may have recalled her last role in the morality play *Everyman*, performed at First Congregational Church, in which her character,

Adrienne lay in state facing east in the mauve-colored music room.

forsaken by everything except the good deeds of life, steps into the grave to meet God alone. How prophetic that last act had been of her death exactly one year later. Some people were confused by the brownish color her complexion had turned and speculated that her death was due to a long-term use of bleaching creams. Curiously, the death certificate recorded the occupation of one of Atlanta's most accomplished professionals as "housewife."[6]

David T. Howard Undertakers prepared the body for burial. Sympathy poured in as Adrienne lay in state facing east in the mauve-colored music room, with floral arrangements stationed around her and a bright light beaming through the terrace doors. This would be the only image the camera would capture of Adrienne in her mansion.[7]

The funeral was held on campus in the chapel of Stone Hall that Sunday. For about a year, Adrienne had been a member there, at the Church of Christ, having been inspired by the faith of her grandmother Harriet and the calm with which she had faced death in 1909. In an eloquent funeral address Edward T. Ware, a minister as well as the university president, recalled the time Adrienne joined the university's church: "In the full maturity of her womanhood and with the thoughtfulness and earnestness which was characteristic of her she took her stand openly among the followers of Christ, little dreaming that so soon she should be called to her heavenly home."[8]

As quickly as the fate that had fallen to Everyman, death came with little warning to Adrienne. But if her stand the year before in the university chapel was any indication of the state of her soul, then she was ready to receive God's grace.

In review of her life, Ware recalled her most recent work: "That home itself is a wonderful evidence of the talent with which our beloved friend was gifted. As in her training and in her teaching she must have the best to be satisfied; so for her home she must have the best and the most beautiful." Ware laid the responsibility for the design of the Herndon house clearly at Adrienne's feet: "No architect drew the plan; no decorator arranged those beautiful rooms. She was architect and decorator. Her power prompted by love, was the master artist who conceived the whole and worked it out to the smallest detail." He concluded poetically: "All beautiful was she, beautiful in spirit, beautiful in body; and beautiful was the setting love had prepared for her and her loved ones, a stately mansion there; but for her soul God had prepared a more stately mansion, and thither has she gone to dwell in her Father's house above."[9]

The funeral procession would have made its way across the city to Southview Cemetery, in which Alonzo was the majority stockholder. Adrienne was the first to be buried in the Herndon family plot.[10] Following Adrienne's burial, relatives and friends may have joined the bereaved family in the mansion, death being the occasion for perhaps its first large gathering of people. A contingent of Adrienne's people would have come: her sister and brother-in-law, Jennie and Joseph Bailey from New York; Joseph Cumming, her uncle, and others of the Hankerson line from Augusta; and Rachael and Clara Simkins from Philadelphia. The Herndons, joined with the Browns, Coopers, and Fambroughs, would have constituted a large contingent from Social

Circle. Tom's widow, Emma, and her adult children, Alonzo II and Carrie, would have arrived from McDonough, as would the Berry clan from Flippen. Alonzo's associates in barbering and life insurance would have been present in full force. But the Atlanta University community would have swelled the ranks: faculty, students, and administrators alike, stunned by this tragic death, and eager to pay their respects to a prominent teacher and a talented performer. But in spite of all the attendants, without Adrienne the house must have seemed a hollow shell. After the guests departed, Alonzo, Norris, and Martha would each have to face alone the emptiness once filled by Adrienne. That night Alonzo would have retired to his bedroom in the northwest corner of the house, finally bowed down by misery and overcome by remorse that their dream home had been realized too late. Just beyond his adjoining study, Norris was in the bedroom at the northeast corner, a grieving boy soon to be thirteen, who had once said, "I had rather not been born if Little Mama couldn't be my mama." Probably in the southeast bedroom was Martha, overwhelmed by the loss of her firstborn. Having centered her world on Adrienne's household for nearly twenty years, she now faced an uncertain future. Southwest in the fourth corner was the largest bedroom, which was adjacent to Alonzo's. This had been Adrienne's place for several weeks—as bedroom, sickroom, and finally as deathbed. Her short life had been a remarkable testament to her talent and strength.

In only one area of struggle had she tragically failed. The theater, whose standard she embraced, indeed so nobly struggled to meet, ultimately rejected her. It was not for lack of talent; she had it in abundance. Nor did she fail for lack of training or persistence. She failed because the goal she set for herself was unattainable. The American stage excluded Blacks. For a while she jockeyed for a position, negotiated with her color, but never came to terms with her race. She had engineered the support of a reluctant family to answer an uncommon calling for a woman of her day. But in the end, it was race that defeated her, no less forcefully than her final struggle with death.

Adrienne lived, nevertheless, her spirit keeping a powerful pres-

"I had rather not been born if Little Mama couldn't be my mama."—Norris Herndon

ence. And through the devotion of her son, she would forever be mistress of the mansion.

Life without Adrienne was perhaps most difficult for Norris. Her death was as abrupt as his weaning had been at fourteen months old. This time, however, her absence was final. There would be no charming postcards, no promised reunions. Left to him now were his father and grandmother. They must have made a devoted trio taking flowers to Adrienne's grave every Sunday.[11]

But the mourning could not last forever. Alonzo was away in New York the following October 31, the seventeenth anniversary of his marriage to Adrienne, and the first since her death. "My dear Son," he wrote to Norris, "Monday will be Mama's and my wedding anniversary. So go up to the shop and get money to get 6 large Cursantha mums and carry out to [the] grave for me. Tell Granma to get something to put them in so they will keep. I can't be there Monday."[12]

Herndon had gone to the Northeast apparently to visit Adrienne's people, her sister Jennie and Jennie's husband, James Bailey. Herndon had the utmost respect for Bailey, a podiatrist from Savannah, who was a self-made man like himself. On that same trip Herndon also traveled to Philadelphia, where he may have visited Rachel, Martha McNeil's sister, who had kept Norris after the riot.

During 1911 Alonzo spent considerable time away. In January he was in Florida visiting Jacksonville and Tampa, most likely for pleasure, a welcome respite from the family sorrow in Atlanta. His travel companion was Loring Palmer, Adrienne's friend and physician, who attended her death. From Florida, Alonzo and Loring left for Cuba and spent a couple of weeks on the island, visiting Havana and the province of Matanzas on the Yumuri River.[13]

Norris was left in Atlanta in the care of Martha and Florence Berry, Alonzo's cousin from Flippen, Georgia, who was the cook. Florence was the younger sister of Archer Berry, a porter in the Peachtree Street barbershop. She would come to assume major responsibility for Norris's care.

About a year after Adrienne's death, Martha took Norris to Philadelphia for an extended visit. It wasn't like the time after the riot, when Adrienne was close by and could visit on the weekends. "Dear Papa," Norris wrote in a homesick note, "I wish for you very much. I don't like the city very much."[14]

Around that same time Martha went to Brooklyn to live with her youngest child, Jennie Bailey. Within a year of his mother's death and for the first time since his birth, Norris was without his grandmother. The past several months had been the most disruptive of his life when he was separated from both Little Mama and Big Mama. Moreover, a big change was afoot in Papa's life.

CHAPTER 9

The Dearest Sweetheart

Jessie Gillespie, c. 1900.

One year before Adrienne's death, Alonzo received a postcard from Theodocia Hall of Chicago. "I want [my husband] to see that beautiful home," she wrote, "meet your most charming wife & son. Then give him some items on [the] insurance business." Her husband was Dr. George Cleveland Hall, Booker T. Washington's personal physician, who would be visiting Atlanta later that April. The Halls were socially prominent in Chicago, having climbed, with some difficulty, to that city's elite "Black 400." Theo, as she was known to her friends, was a tall, red-haired woman who, some said, had a tendency in dress and manner to be loud. One of her best friends was Jessie Gillespie, a hairdresser. It was inevitable that with such assertive friends in high places, Jessie would one day meet one of the most eligible Black bachelors in America.[1]

Herndon may have first known of Jessie through Loring Palmer, a friend of hers who at virtually every stop of his European tour in 1907 sent her a postcard.[2] Jessie would have known of the Herndons' prominence as did Theo Hall, because the Black elite in America was a small group intimately bound by ties of kinship, family, school, church, and social club. These ties extended across state lines and encompassed North and South. The upper crust of Black doctors, lawyers, businessmen, and educators in each city knew their counterparts all over the country.

When Mrs. Hall wrote to Alonzo that spring of 1909, she was

*Theodocia Hall, Jennie Burns,
and Jessie Gillespie, c. 1905.*

*Jessie Gillespie, first row, second
from left, and friends, Chicago,
1897.*

cultivating her social network. Her tie was not to Adrienne but to Alonzo, through her husband as a physician and an associate of Booker Washington. It is unlikely that the Halls would have had any serious interest in industrial sick and accident insurance, which is all Atlanta Mutual offered at the time. Rather, Theo was lining up her social contacts and making sure her husband touched base with one of Atlanta's most prominent families. Such contacts, she knew, paid off, though she would not have known at the time that Alonzo would soon be in circulation for a mate; and that shortly she would place her friend Jessie in line for that position.

Loring Palmer, c. 1900, a friend of Jessie, an associate and physician of Adrienne, and a friend and traveling companion of Alonzo.

About a year and a half following Adrienne's death, Alonzo was engaged to Jessie. After about a year of mourning, Herndon traveled a fair amount, presumably in search of a companion. Significantly, he looked beyond Atlanta, eventually turning to the Midwest, specifically to Chicago, where Jessie, an attractive forty-year-old spinster, was living with her half sisters Emma and Mary Gillespie. About fifty miles across the lake from Chicago was Benton Harbor, Michigan, where George and Theo Hall vacationed in the summer. It is likely that Theo, again through her husband, encouraged Alonzo's visit to their summer cottage. Benton Harbor, which was advertised as the "Atlantic City of the Race," remained for a time the area's leading Black resort, attracting Chicago's elite.[3] Alonzo met Jessie there during the summer of 1911. He would confess later that he was immediately attracted to her. "I love her very much," he wrote to her sisters just before their wedding, "and have [loved her] all most at first sight. I felt that there was something different about her from other ladies that appealed to me in a way that has haunted me every since. And what little knowledge I have of judging human nature, I felt perfectly at home with her and begin thinking of trying to win her affections. And I felt from the very first if I was successful in doing so that she was the woman that could make me happy."[4]

That first meeting for one week of summer in Benton Harbor was the beginning of a short, but heated, courtship mostly by mail. "I know you will tire of all of the stuff I am writing," Alonzo wrote to her just before Thanksgiving, "but when I get to talking to you I never tire. I want to just keep on [indefinitely] to you. Some of thease days I hope to see you face to face again when we won't be so new to each other and we can talk . . . confidentially together. I just had to keep thinking that I must not say too much to you, that I had not known you but a week really. As soon as I saw you and spoke to you [it] seemed as if I had known you long ago."[5]

Jessie was the youngest daughter of Ezekiel Gillespie, a railroad messenger, who, like Alonzo, had had a remarkable rise from slavery. Born in Tennessee in 1818, the son of his White slave master and a slave woman, Gillespie had apparently managed to buy his own freedom and by the 1850s to become one of the earliest Black settlers in Milwaukee. Jessie was born there on September 6, 1871.[6]

Alonzo had again chosen a wife with extremely light skin who could pass for White. Jessie was also a pretty woman, like Adrienne, but there was in Jessie's gaze less tension and in her presence less power. No strong ambition was driving her; Jessie seemed perfectly content to just be. Alonzo was comfortable with her, and their relationship developed quickly.

"My dearest Sweetheart," he wrote her one Sunday morning several months after they first met, "I am thinking of you on this glorious day just as bright and balmy as one could ask and I am all alone except the servants in the back." He explained that Florence had taken Norris home with her to Flippen. "They make so much of his coming," he wrote, "and make him think he is it. I think that is one of the reasons he likes to go, and this being the first Sunday and that is Big Meeting day at Florence's Church and they have baptising."[7]

He wrote in anticipation of his next trip to Chicago, cautioning her not to plan any entertainment for him because he preferred to spend the time with her "going to shows or places of art, as I am not much of a society man." Then he backed down somewhat, knowing that Jessie was more social. "But I shall be governed [entirely] by what suits you and will give you most pleasure even if that is to go straight on to Canada." This may have been a joking reference to a honeymoon destination, but it also suggests that very soon in their relationship they may have seriously discussed marriage.

Within months of their first meeting they were deeply committed, if not engaged. How they should refer to each other was the source of much concern and amusement. Jessie had joked that she was afraid to call him her "Baby." "I might have enjoyed being called your big baby," he answered, "but am glad you was afraid to do so without first consulting my wishes. I thank you for the honor. You may call me your baby provided you don't do it in sarcasm." In closing he wrote, "I must stop talking to my Baby and go to church for I think the [streetcar] is out now.... With much love and many kisses. Remember [me] kindly to Sisters."[8]

Jessie's half sister Mary Gillespie owned and operated a beauty salon and hair goods store on West Madison Street, where Jessie was a hairdresser. The other half sister Emma was an invalid and had been bedridden for years. There had been eleven children in the Gillespie family. Jessie's parents, Ezekiel Gillespie and Catherine Lucas Robinson, brought to their marriage seven children by previous marriages. Jessie was the second youngest of four born to their union.[9] The three separate sets of children, however, were closely knit. When Jessie was only three years old, her mother died. Mary, who was twenty-three years older than Jessie, apparently stepped in as mother for the younger half siblings.

Had Alonzo not come along, Jessie would have continued nevertheless to lead a prosperous life in Chicago supported by and respected for her position in her sister's business. Emma and Mary had never married, but Jessie would have been under the pressure of friends like Theo Hall and may have been concerned about her spinsterhood, particularly since she had passed forty years of age. She had led a very protected life all those years. With the security of her sister's business, she had not had to rely on marriage for financial support. She had developed the independence of a woman obligated to no man.

But Alonzo was not just any man. He was rich, powerful, and

Jessie's father, Ezekiel Gillespie.

Jessie's mother, Catherine Lucas Robinson.

charming. And for twenty years he had loved one of the most independent women of the day. Jessie's less challenging independence was hardly a barrier in their relationship. And it was the source of much teasing during courtship. Jessie and Alonzo had the same middle name: Franklin. He once referred to her as Miss J. Frankly Gillespie. The teasing was in fun, but it sometimes tested the water for a more serious commitment. "If [last night] I had been near the lady that I was at Benton Harber with," he wrote in October 1911, "I should have been with her until time to wash dishes several times . . . even if she was stingy, crankey, mean, and grouchy. I think with clost attention and a great deal of work and care I might get her out of some of that. I guess I shall take the job of taming the schrew."[10]

Jessie admitted to Alonzo that she was somewhat afraid of him. His wealth and personal power were intimidating. But Herndon's down-to-earth manner and good-natured humor must have disarmed his very serious chase. The long-distance courtship worked in favor of an early and brief engagement. Alonzo made his next visit to Chicago, perhaps the third one, that Christmas of 1911, writing from his layover in Cincinnati on the return trip that he had been "royally intertained."[11] Presumably his hosts had been the Halls and the Gillespies. There might have been quite a round of social affairs in his honor. For Theo, Herndon's visits would have been among the highlights of her social career. But there would also have been time for Alonzo and Jessie to be alone with each other. By the time Alonzo left Chicago this trip, he and Jessie had agreed to marry.

There was apparently a fourth trip to Chicago in March. In his April letter to Emma Gillespie, Alonzo expressed his appreciation for their consent to let Jessie marry him. He was the humble fiancé. "Jessie is soon to leave you and Miss Mary," he wrote, "to take up her abode with me in the South. While it will be quite a loss to you, but I am quite sure will be equally as much gain to me, I am not unmindful of the sacrifice that you so cheerfully made for us. I shall never forget

Mary, right, and Emma Gillespie, Jessie's half sisters.

the very kind words of cheer and good wishes when I spoke to you of our intention. The words were to this affect, that you could not reasonably expect for Jessie to all ways stay with you. And I thought how unselfish it was of you and Miss Mary to consent for her to be my wife."[12]

It had all happened so quickly, especially for Norris, who may have had little indication that marriage was coming so soon, until his father returned from Chicago after the new year. Alonzo had conducted a very discreet courtship. Jessie may have had some concern about how Norris would feel about their upcoming marriage. "I told our Boy just what we had planned for ourselves and him," Alonzo wrote to Jessie in January, "and he seemed perfectly delighted and happy. I told him that you had his interest at heart and that you . . . was thinking of his happiness and hoped he would love you as you would him. . . . So all is well along that line."[13]

The wedding was set for Thursday, May 30, in Chicago. This date was the second change in the schedule, a development that must have concerned Jessie's sisters. Alonzo wrote them to explain: "On account of the Titanic disaster . . . we could not sail before the 4th of June [for the honeymoon in Europe]. . . . [Jessie] might change the date [from Monday] to any day of the week she liked." The first change had been to accommodate his son. "As you remember," he continued, "the reason for the change [to Monday] was so Norris could get through with his exams on Friday and we could leave the same day and get there on Saturday afternoon."[14]

In a Monday afternoon rain, father and son left for Chicago by train in a state room. The *Atlanta Constitution* reported on their departure: "A. F. Herndon, one of the best known and most highly respected negroes of Atlanta, left yesterday for New York [*sic*], where Thursday he will be married to Jessie F. Gillespie, taking his bride on a wedding trip that will include the principal countries of Europe." So unusual was this coverage of an event in the Black community, that the *Constitution*'s article itself made news in the *Chicago Defender*. "The *Atlanta Constitution*," the Black paper wrote, "one of the leading daily newspapers of the South, whose love for the Negro is none too great, gives considerable space to Mr. A. F. Herndon. . . . [It is] a splendid story of his life, accompanied by his [photograph] and that of his son and of the interior and exterior of his residence."[15]

Arriving in Chicago the next afternoon, Alonzo and Norris were met by Theo Hall in her brougham. After supper at the Gillespies', they attended a vaudeville performance at the Majestic Theater. The Halls took charge of Norris the next day, touring him through Washington Park, Lincoln Park, and Marshall Fields & Company. But of the wedding day there is only Norris's brief journal entry: "I went downtown with Papa and Mr. [William] Gillespie and we got some candy and flowers. [We] came unto a certain place called Mrs. Hall's. Then we were at the wedding and had a nice time."[16]

William Gillespie, Jessie's half brother.

The Atlanta Constitution *reports on the Herndons' departure.*

A. F. HERNDON, FORTUNE MADE TO TOUR EUROPE WITH BRIDE

Photo by Francis E. Price, Staff Photographer.
A. F. Herndon on the right, and his son on the left.

A. F. Herndon, one of the best-known and most highly respected negroes of Atlanta, left yesterday for New York, where Thursday he will be married to Jessie F. Gillespie, taking his bride on a wedding trip that will include the principal countries of Europe and which will last four months.

Born a slave, commencing life in a community enfeebled by four years of war, handicapped by lack of training and resources, Herndon has achieved in the last forty years a success that is remarkable in the annals of the south, and has placed himself at the head of his race in this city, in a financial way and in all matters of progress.

Steadily Mounts in World.

He numbers his friends among the white people of the city by the score. For many years proprietor of the leading barber shop on Peachtree street, he had for his customers the men who have made history, governors, congressmen, financiers, all of whom liked and respected him. Since going into the insurance and banking business he has steadily mounting in the world, until now, still far from being an old man, he has accumulated a comfortable fortune, built a home that vies in beauty with many show places of the south, and is a force and power for good among his people.

Herndon was born in Walton county, near Social Circle, and took his name from the white family that owned his parents. He was only about 9 years old when set free by the close of the civil war.

At that time he removed to Jonesville, where he grew into early manhood, and it was here that he first practiced his trade. He owned a small barber shop, and by thrift and industry accumulated money. In 1882 he came to Atlanta.

Lays Foundation of Fortune.

It was then that he established the "Herndon's" shop that has been a part of the city for so many years. By successful management and his high self-respect he won the aid and friendship of leading white people, and began to lay the foundations for the fortune which he has accumulated. He was manager of the shop at 66 Peachtree street until a few years ago, when he relinquished that, though still retaining his interest in it, to become president of the Atlanta Mutual Insurance Association, which does a prosperous business among the negroes of the state.

When he came to build his home, near the Atlanta University, it is said Herndon consulted no one but, taking the ideas that he liked best, embodied them in a house that is excellent in taste and proportion. It is built of brick, with a white column entrance, and broad piazzas on each side. The yard is beautifully kept and is surrounded by a substantial stone wall.

"I designed it and built it myself," Herndon says, when you ask him about it.

Accompanying him to New York Monday was his 15-year-old son by a former marriage, who will make the trip abroad with his father. They will return to Atlanta about October 1.

Exterior and interior views of the Herndon residence.

The wedding was apparently a small, private affair at the Hall residence. Theo would have been Jessie's matron of honor, having been her close friend and matchmaker. But who would have been Alonzo's best man? Perhaps Truman Gibson, the secretary of Atlanta Mutual, for whom Alonzo had been best man the previous year.[17] Or perhaps George Hall had stood for Alonzo.

Soon after the ceremony, Alonzo, Jessie, and Norris left Chicago by the Grand Trunk Route to Niagara Falls. In loving sacrifice, Jessie had insisted that Norris join them on the honeymoon. By Saturday they were in Toronto, where Norris wrote his grandmother, "My new mother treats me very nice. She told me she wanted to do for me as my own mother would do."[18]

Continuing to Montreal, they were retracing the Herndons' itinerary during the summer of 1905 when the Niagara movement first

George Cleveland Hall, physician to Booker T. Washington, and possibly Alonzo Herndon's best man.

Norris on board the Carpathia.

*Captain Rostrand
of the* Carpathia.

ABOVE: *Norris's sketch aboard
the* Carpathia.

RIGHT: *The* Carpathia *en route
to Europe after its rescue mission
for the* Titanic.

met. On Monday they were in New York City, where Norris met his grandmother, bringing her a little piece of wedding cake and staying the night.[19]

What did Mattie learn of the new mother from her grandson? Norris would continue to refer to himself as his grandmother's "devoted son," but living so far away from one who was growing up so fast, Mattie surely felt her ties to the Herndons loosening considerably.

The next morning Mattie took Norris to join Alonzo and Jessie on board the *Carpathia*, whose schedule had been delayed by its rescue of *Titanic* victims. It was one of the smaller ships of the Cunard line, but carried nearly one thousand passengers. The Herndons were in first class as "saloon passengers" and had an outside cabin. "Mother and Father didn't stay on deck much," Norris later reported to his grandmother. "They spent all of their time in the cabin."[20]

But Norris was up and about. "There were several children on the boat," he wrote to Mattie, "and we had a fine time. All the people on the boat were very nice and thought we were Italians, some of them did." On his passenger list Norris made a note next to the names of three women: "from Alabama and truly southerners." He also indicated that another was a teacher from Agnes Scott College in Decatur outside Atlanta, but apparently no one on board knew or took issue with their race. "The best thing of all", Norris said, "is to see the Sun set on the water. Oh! it is grand."[21]

Following the southern route, the *Carpathia* reached Gibraltar, where the Herndons went ashore a few hours for a Cook's Tour. The ship continued for the last leg of the two-week voyage, stopping for a while in Genoa and then landing on June 18 at Naples, where the Herndons disembarked to begin a three-month stay in Europe, half of that time in Italy. From Naples and Pompeii, the Herndons went by train to Rome, Florence, and Venice, and ended their Italian journey in Milan. It seemed a strenuous trip—catching trains, finding their way to hotels, making the round of churches, museums, tombs, and ruins, with meals between. But perhaps Alonzo knew how to pace their journey, since it was the same itinerary that he and Adrienne

Norris sketched St. Mark's Basilica and the Bell Tower on the back of an envelope.

had followed in 1900. And though exhausting, travel was a stimulating backdrop for three people getting to know one another.

Norris was most impressed by Venice. "Grandma," he wrote, "Venice actually is a beautiful city surrounded by water, but I thought that you could not walk around any in Venice, but you can walk as much as you like. We stopped at the Grand Hotel which is on the Grand Canal right across from that building with the dome. . . . It certainly was a beautiful location right near the tower. . . . We went up to St. Mark's Square and as we were sitting there all the buildings were lighted up in one second and a beautiful red light was in the tower. It was just grand."[22]

Jessie gave room for father and son to be with each other. "Papa and I went out alone," Norris wrote to his grandmother, "and Papa bought a lot of water color pictures of Venice. After that he and I

Feeding the pigeons in St. Mark's Square, Venice.

LEFT: *Jessie and Alonzo in Naples.*

BELOW: *The three travelers in Pompeii.*

News arrived of the death of Frances Norris. "When [Papa] opened the letter, he wept." Frances Norris, above, on the porch of the Herndon home.

went up in the tower on the 'Lift.' That is what they call elevators over here. They charged 40 cents a piece for us. Wasn't that high! When we reached the top we had a splendid view of the city. We are learning how to speak the language a little, but you know that is a very little."[23]

News from home was slow to reach the travelers. Alonzo had arranged to have the mail sent by Cunard from London. But by the first week of July, they had received only one letter. "When [Papa] opened the letter," wrote Norris, "he wept." Frances Norris had died on June 28 at the age of seventy-four. "[It] was sad," Alonzo said, "but was the best for her. . . . She had been a great care for a long time but had never forgot Norris and I."[24]

From Milan, the Herndons went to Switzerland. "We came through the Alps," Alonzo wrote to Mattie, whom he now called Aunt Martha. "[We came] over the new [railroad,] which has been built since we were here [in 1900,] from Milan, Italy, to Geneva, Switzerland, one of the prettiest and most interesting trips—the Alps [capped] with snow a plenty."[25]

After several weeks away, Norris got homesick. He asked Florence and his Grandmother each for "a nice long newsy letter. I am homesick to see you all." Even Alonzo by the end of July seemed to be counting the days. "We have not turned our head homewards yet," he wrote, "but it won't be long now, just one month and 3 days."[26]

Atlanta's first news of the Herndons since they sailed came July 2 in a postcard to Florence Berry. She immediately informed Mattie. Time in the mansion went slowly that summer, but Florence occupied herself making pickles and jelly and canning peaches, tomatoes, and chow-chow. Will Byers, the servant in the carriage house, apparently kept up the yard and garden, tended the chickens, and did the heavier household work.[27]

Norris celebrated what seemed a quiet and rather lonesome fifteenth birthday on July 15 in Lucerne. His father had been extremely ill for a couple of days, so Jessie spent some of the day with him visiting churches and the old corn market. "I went alone to Glacial Gardens," he told his diary, "and saw the lion [monument] again." Curiously, he made no mention of his birthday, nor of his presents—the coral pin and the faun's head nutcracker from Jessie and the wrist watch from his father. Here was a grieving son who was still struggling with the loss of his mother.[28]

Alonzo was sick the next day but was much improved after taking the medicine Jessie bought at the drugstore. "When I got able, I got up and left for [Baden-Baden, Germany,] . . . this great watering place, one of the greatest in the world," Alonzo wrote from the Grand Hotel de Russie. "I have felt that I have been greatly benefited allready. . . . This is the 4th day here and I think we will stay here at least ten days more."[29] Alonzo progressed from outdoor to indoor springs and to the special baths requiring a physician's referral; Jessie took a Turkish bath. But they stayed only five more days. From Norris's per-

"[We came] over the new [railroad,] which has been built since we were here [in 1900,] from Milan, Italy, to Geneva, Switzerland, one of the prettiest and most interesting trips—the Alps [capped] with snow a plenty."—Alonzo Herndon.

Popular

Motorcar Excursions

round

Berlin

Fare Mk. **2,50** per person

A competent guide will accompany the party paying the necessary admission fees and explaining the various places and objects of interest.

Start from the

Weltreisebureau „Union"

Cook's agency

Unter den Linden 22

(Ecke Passage).

Times of departure 9.00 a. m., 11.15 a. m., 3.45 p. m.

In Berlin, the Herndons were persuaded to take a tour by automobile instead of by carriage. Alonzo in front of the Hotel Victoria in Amsterdam, Holland.

spective, it was a rainy period with not much to do. He read and also took the baths. A master of understatement, Norris declared in his journal that "'Fun' is not a name for the time we had."[30]

His spirit and interests perked up considerably in Heidelberg. "Sailing down the Rhine," he wrote, "is one of the most gorgeous trips there is, I believe. Just beautiful." And in Berlin, they were persuaded to take a tour by automobile instead of by carriage. Their last evening in Germany, the Herndons slowed down and "sat under the Lindens and watched the passers-by."[31]

There were about three more weeks to go in Europe. A nine-hour train ride to Amsterdam, according to Norris, "was a very good one, except in reaching Holland, [they] had the shaky train. It was awful." Norris recorded seeing in Amsterdam "the diamond [boers]. 500 workers," perhaps a reference to South African diamond miners. The canals, the museums with the art of the Dutch masters, the queen's palaces, and the beach made for a full three days in Amsterdam, the Hague, and Rotterdam.[32]

Everyone's shopping seemed to pick up considerably as the trip ended. In Brussels one morning, Jessie bought a lace bertha at the Kaufman Lace Store and returned after dinner to have a dress made. Shopping was also a relief from the constant round of sightseeing. The Herndons spent their first full day in Paris at the Bon Marche, having gone to the department store after breakfast and remained till about five o'clock that evening. They returned almost daily, either to shop or for Jessie's fittings. Staying at the Grand Hotel, they ate most of their meals at the Duval Restaurant nearby.[33]

They had an entire week to see the city. First touring by autobus and then by cab, the Herndons saw most of the major attractions and then focused on their favorite sites. Norris noted that at the Louvre, which they visited at least four times, were "many wonderful pictures and the different kings' household goods such as beds. Crown jewels. Venus De Milo beautiful." They heard the organ in Notre Dame cathedral. When they visited the Cluny Museum, Norris may have recalled the monastery prints his mother had mounted as souvenirs of her visit.

Some nights in Paris, as in other cities they had visited, the Herndons went to the moving pictures before going to bed.[34]

Paris came to an end, as the honeymoon would soon do. On Thursday, August 14, with just ten days more in Europe, the Herndons took a taxi to the train station, the Gare du Nord, and left for Calais. As Norris recorded it, "We took the boat and got sick crossing the channel. Finally we reached the long-looked-for shore of England and took the train right away for London."[35]

They would miss seeing John Hope, who was touring Europe the same summer. "I have heard from Herndon and Jessie," Hope had written to his wife, Lugenia, in mid-July, "[but] I do not think we shall cross each other unless possibly in Scotland or England. They have visited Italy already [and] I shall leave London . . . July 16."[36] Scotland was not in the Herndon itinerary and, unfortunately, England was not

At the House of Parliament in London.

scheduled till late August, when the Herndons were on the last week of the honeymoon. After nearly three months of grueling summer travel abroad, the threesome could wind down in a country where for the first time they spoke the native language. It was easier to become familiar with the streets, and the Herndons ventured as far as Liverpool Street Station and Epping Forest. Twice they went through Westminster Abbey and Parliament. And for more personal business, one morning Norris had a tailor fit him for his first suit with long pants. Jessie's sister Mary had advised against them in a letter to Norris

ABOVE: *One morning Norris had a tailor fit him for his first suit with long pants.*

LEFT: *Norris, upon returning from Europe to spend several days with his grandmother, wears his first long pants to Coney Island.*

Coney Island

earlier that summer. "I like to see you a Boy, as long as you can be one." The same day the travelers went to Shipwright's Barbershop, one of many Alonzo would have visited that summer as he surveyed the best of Europe.[37]

On their last afternoon in London, August 22, the travelers stopped at London Bridge and the Tower of London. The next morning after breakfast, they left for Liverpool, where the train arrived about five o'clock in the evening. Spending that night at the Lime Street Station Hotel, they boarded the *Campania* the next evening for the voyage home.

"Dear Grandma," Norris wrote in his last postcard, "You know we are fixing to sail today at 6 P.M. I hope you will meet us at the boat if you can find out what time our boat comes. About 7 days it makes the passage." He was anxious for Mama to welcome him home. To make sure she would have no difficulty finding him, he gave more specific instructions in a postscript: "You know our boat comes in the pier next to the *Carpathia*'s pier."[38] Surely the *Campania* would have reached New York before his card arrived, but since Norris had kept in touch with home almost daily, it is likely that Martha knew the details of her grandson's arrival. In all probability, she was waiting for him at the pier. He stayed with her for several days while Alonzo and Jessie went on to Atlanta. During the summer, Mattie had moved with Jennie's family from Sutter Avenue to Fulton Street. Though it was a new address, and its accommodations were more modest than the mansion, for the world traveler still grieving for his mother, it had the comforts of home.

CHAPTER 10

To the Top

Alonzo brought his bride back to Atlanta. Energized by his marriage, he continued his climb to the top. The grandeur he had just seen in Europe inspired him to make a palace of his barbershop. With Atlanta Mutual still a small company, he set his sights on the heights of Black insurance.

After an absence of three months on the honeymoon, Herndon would have been anxious to get back to his barbershops. He may have received some of the sales reports while abroad, but mail had been irregular. Charles Faison, his associate, probably managed all three shops that summer, since the partnership with William W. Williams had by then been dissolved. Herndon turned his attention immediately to the flagship barbershop at 66 Peachtree Street. It was a storehouse of three floors and a basement that extended the full block from Peachtree to Broad with access from both streets. Since 1902, Hern-don had leased the building from R. L. and G. D. Warthen and for the last five years had paid the substantial sum of $265 a month.[1] Perhaps the building had never been available for sale. Herndon owned no real estate in Atlanta's central business district.

Having seen the best of Europe, Herndon began the remodeling and refurnishing of the shop, investing thousands of dollars. By spring of 1913, renovations were completed. "This is your barbershop," a newspaper advertisement proclaimed. "It was designed and built to please you. . . . Mr. Herndon's desire to give Atlantans a barbershop unequaled anywhere led him to visit the best shops in the United States and the principal cities of Europe. With the information thus acquired and the experience gained through thirty-one years of service in his profession in Atlanta, he made his plans. Surely no one is better fit to judge of what he offers than himself, and it is but the plain truth when he says that he now offers you the finest barbershop in the world."[2]

Herndon renamed his shop the Crystal Palace. One entered through mahogany and plate-glass doors to a long, elegant parlor lined with French beveled mirrors and lit by crystal chandeliers and wall lamps. Ceiled in white pressed-tin and floored in white ceramic tile, the room accommodated twenty-five custom barber chairs that were outfitted with porcelain, brass, and nickel and upholstered in dark green Spanish leather. "Everything in my shop is the best procurable," Herndon boasted. It was a brilliant display. Even the bootblack stands were of nickel and marble.[3]

Service was unsurpassed. In terms that would appeal to his clientele, yet dignify his men, Alonzo described his barbers as "skilled and courteous[,] . . . cheerful and intelligent men who know their business

Alonzo Herndon in his Apperson Touring Car, c. 1920.

thoroughly and whose service has received the approval of Atlanta's most particular citizens. With this force at command," he claimed, "you are seldom kept waiting."[4]

The barbers were uniformed in white jackets, ready to cut hair, shave, and attend with the most personalized service. "The barber would rub your head," recalled a customer, Albert Daniel, years later "[and] you'd half go to sleep. . . . They were your friends. They were taking care of you. . . . It was a pleasurable thing. You felt like you were elevating yourself." Daniel remembered the fine linens and the red, green, and blue tonic bottles, along with the black bottle of coal tar

The Crystal Palace after its first major renovation, 1913.

for dandruff. "Getting your hair singed was a big thing. The barber had a little taper, a straw, and lit it. After cutting your hair, he would run that taper around it. . . . I guess to seal in the juices."[5]

The eight porters were advertised as "attentive[,] . . . alert and courteous. Some shine shoes; some attend the baths; others keep the floors clean and are at your service generally." In the basement were two large needle showers and sixteen white porcelain bathtubs trimmed in nickel, each in a separate compartment paneled in solid marble.[6]

"Oh, it was a palace! It was beautiful," Daniel recalled. "You went down to this marble room and off of that were private rooms. You could lock the doors; there was a stool and fresh towels. It was a very high class shop." A full-time presser operated in the basement, "ready to sponge and press your suit while you bathe." In the summer, electric fans cooled the shop; a refrigerated ice chest in the basement pumped cold water to the first-floor fountain. Everything was sanitary as well as elegant, metal and marble used in preference to wood wherever possible, and Red Cross sterilizing cabinets with disinfectants placed at each barber's station.[7]

Though the barbershop was significantly upgraded, there was, said the ad, "no advance in prices."[8] A haircut remained a quarter; a shave and a shoeshine one dime each. With a bath that cost a quarter and a pressing that cost forty cents, a patron receiving full service would spend over a dollar, which was about one day's wage for a common laborer. The barber would write down the amount of the charge for the services on a ticket, and the customer would pay the cashier.

In ten years Herndon had doubled the size of the Peachtree Street operation. With his other two shops in the city, he employed a force of about fifty. Perhaps no one in the country had as large a barbering enterprise. But Herndon never forgot how it had all started: "I sometimes in [reminiscence] can see the little one-chair shop in Jonesborough that cost me twenty dollars to furnish, and compare it with the Peachtree shop here that cost twelve thousand to furnish, and I wonder if I have ever felt the pride over this glitter of mirrors and

An advertisement for Herndon's barbershops.

The Largest and Finest Barber Shop in the World

Interior View of Shop (66 Peachtree St., 7 N. Broad St.) Street to Street

25 CHAIRS
20 BATHS
The Finest and Largest BARBER SHOP In the World

A. F. HERNDON
Proprietor of
HERNDON'S
BARBER SHOPS

Interior View of Shop at 7 North Broad Street

Interior View of Shop at 100 North Pryor Street

HERNDON'S BARBER SHOPS

ANYONE who can "pull" a razor without cutting a person's throat can OPEN a barber shop. It is the man who "knows how" to CONDUCT a barber shop that keeps his place open. Herndon's Barber Shops in Atlanta have stood this test.

The conduct of a barber shop is a matter of cleanliness and workmanship.

Unless tools are kept clean and sharp the trade ends. Herndon's shops are conducted on strictly sanitary lines. Every barber changes his white linen suit daily. Every barber sterilizes his hands four times a day in a medicinal solution. Every towel, razor, comb, brush and shaving brush is sterilized before and after using.

Compounds, calculated to kill any possible germ, are used in washing the floors in Herndon's Barber Shops. Porters are required to clean all brass and mirrors twice daily.

These are the reasons why Herndon's Barber Shops are known the country over as the finest establishments of their kind in the universe.

HERNDON'S BARBER SHOPS

66 Peachtree Street   7 North Broad Street   100 North Pryor Street

marble and mahogany as I did over the white-washed board walls with its tiny cheap-looking glass and crude homemade chair."[9]

While Herndon was in Europe, Atlanta Mutual was in the hands of Truman Kella Gibson, the company's first college-trained employee. He had been Adrienne's student at Atlanta University, having performed in and assisted in the management of her dramatic productions. With her death imminent, Adrienne had summoned Gibson to ask for his help in the development of Atlanta Mutual. "My husband has recently acquired a small insurance company," she told him, "and I have persuaded him that you are able, ambitious, and capable of making it a success—helping him to preserve his own investment and creating a name for yourself in a new field of human endeavor." By

The shop after a second renovation in the 1920s.

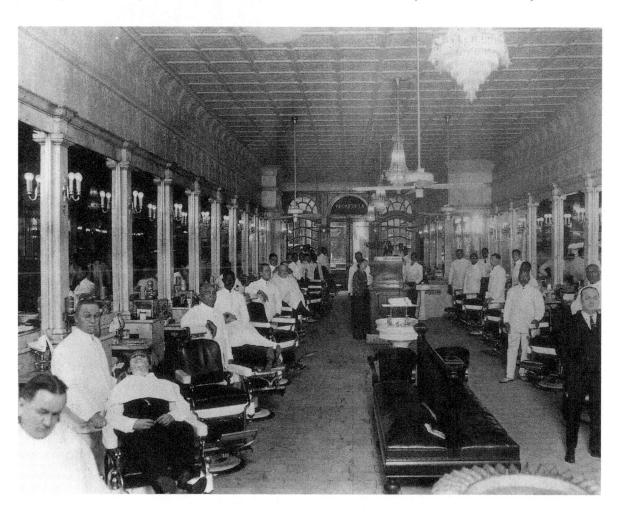

Truman Kella Gibson, vice president and secretary of Atlanta Mutual, and his wife, Alberta.

then, Gibson had completed his studies at Harvard with the intention of going into journalism, but he could not refuse Adrienne. Two months after her death he arrived in Atlanta to fulfill his promise, soon becoming Atlanta Mutual's secretary and Herndon's close friend.[10]

The Atlanta Mutual that Herndon returned to in late summer of 1912 was still a struggling company. It had expanded its operations to Alabama, but was facing the prospect of having to withdraw from Kentucky, where the licensing fee had been raised to $100,000. About that time, an aggressive young businessman was shaking up Black insurance in Georgia, and in the process offered Atlanta Mutual a solution to their problem in Kentucky. Heman Perry, a Texan, sought to operate African American insurance on a scale larger than the penny policies of small industrial companies like Atlanta Mutual. Organizing the Standard Life Insurance Company in Atlanta in 1908, which was just three years after Atlanta Mutual was founded, he proposed to capitalize Standard Life in the amount of $100,000, an unheard-of sum for a Black Georgia company to raise. "Even Alonzo Herndon could not raise that amount of money," some said. Perry's first effort failed, but with the cooperation of Herndon, he succeeded in 1913.[11]

Perry offered to sell Herndon a substantial amount of Standard Life stock. This was an opportunity for Herndon to practice the cooperation that he had always preached. When Atlanta Mutual's board of directors agreed to buy $5,000 of Standard Life stock, it was part of the endorsement Perry needed from Herndon and other associates to secure a $50,000 loan. With the capital he had already amassed, Perry then had the $100,000 required in order to be licensed as the state's first Black legal reserve company offering ordinary insurance with higher benefits at higher premiums. In exchange for the purchase of Standard Life stock, Atlanta Mutual operated its own industrial insurance business in Kentucky under the name of Standard Life, and Herndon became its board director and treasurer.[12]

Herndon was excited about his venture with Perry. "The twentieth century idea is cooperation," he said in a speech at Tuskegee Institute that December. "My aim has been for several years to try to get as many of our people together to cooperate in business and along all

Heman Perry, president of Standard Life Insurance Company.

Herndon and Perry agree to a joint venture that ensures Standard Life's operation as a legal reserve company, 1913. From left to right, unidentified woman, Harry Pace, Heman Perry, and Alonzo Herndon.

Lemuel Haywood, center, with his family. Beginning as an agent and serving in many capacities, including district manager, Heywood eventually became agency director.

OPPOSITE: *"The Million Dollar Team," special agents to open new territory. Lemuel Haywood is seated in the front. Standing behind him are, from left to right, O. H. Lane, Walter Chivers, and Eugene Martin.*

other lines. . . . The great trouble in establishing insurance companies among our people is that it is difficult for our people to understand the advantage of pulling together for the common and for their own good." He cited a White insurance company that employed thousands of people, none of whom were Black, but to whom Blacks paid thousands of dollars in insurance premiums. "Think of what this would mean," Herndon pleaded, "toward supporting a colored company and giving employment to colored men and women."[13]

Herndon saw Standard Life as a shining example of "the perseverance of its President, H. E. Perry, together with the cooperation of its stockholders. . . . We give employment to 150 persons," he boasted, "and the number is growing, and in the office there are 15 persons to take care of the increasing business."[14]

Atlanta Mutual acquired Union Mutual Insurance Association of Alabama in 1915, becoming the largest African American industrial insurance company in the lower South. Company officials of both associations join to formalize the acquisition. Front row, left and right, Lemuel Haywood and Eugene Martin of Atlanta Mutual with unidentified Union Mutual official; second row, left, James T. Harrison, Fred Toomer, and an unidentified official.

It seemed such a promising cooperative undertaking, but it was short-lived. By the end of the next year, Herndon had broken all formal ties with Perry and Standard Life. The arrangement had worked to the disadvantage of Atlanta Mutual. "I was not called into consultation about the affairs of the company," Herndon wrote to Booker Washington's secretary, Emmett Scott. Scott had expressed regret over Alonzo's departure before Standard Life was "well out of the woods" and had wanted to know why Herndon had left. "I could not agree with them" Herndon explained, "when they started to sell all the industrial business . . .[and] after selling all of mine or my company's business, entrusted to their care, and claiming money that had not been earned by them or cost them one penny as theirs, is one of my reasons. Another is, as an inducement for me to help their company do business, they promised, if I with my company would take . . . a $55,000 note, I could write all of the industrial business in all States except Florida. . . . They did break that contract." Herndon resented having to pay 5 percent on all the gross receipts in spite of his dissatisfaction with the arrangement. He turned bitter toward Perry and Standard Life. "They have used me to the 'queen's taste' and I thought it would

In 1920 Atlanta Mutual renovated for its headquarters a two-story building at 132 Auburn Avenue, formerly occupied by the YMCA.

be well to let them catch another sucker." Another difficulty in the Herndon-Perry alliance was the irreconcilable conflict between two men with very different business styles. Perry was the grand schemer, the big deal-maker and risk-taker; Herndon was the conservative and surefooted businessman. Following their break, Standard Life grew phenomenally for a while, outpacing Atlanta Mutual and becoming what appeared to be the most successful Black business in America. Perry's company financed an array of real estate, banking, printing, and drugstore enterprises that would shape the development of Auburn Avenue for decades to come. But in ten years, Standard Life would overextend itself, deplete its assets, and fall into the hands of Whites.[15]

As 1915 dawned, Herndon trudged on alone with Atlanta Mutual, expanding operations gradually. The company had withdrawn from Kentucky but had acquired Georgia's oldest and largest Black insurance company, Union Mutual. In reinsuring Union Mutual, whose operation had been troubled for some time, Atlanta Mutual became

Atlanta Life Branch Office, c. 1925

In back, left to right, Alonzo Herndon, Emmett Scott, and Booker T. Washington, 1914, in a motorcade on Auburn Avenue.

the largest Black industrial insurance company in the lower South. For the first time a Black insurance company was fast on the heels of Industrial Life and Health Insurance Company, a White insurer with mostly Black policyholders. Outgrowing his building at 202 Auburn, and being a loyal Odd Fellow, Herndon moved the company to the new five-story Odd Fellows Building on the adjacent corner where Union Mutual had located its office. With much struggle, but with significant progress, Atlanta Mutual had survived its first decade.[16]

As 1915 came to a close, so did the life of America's most powerful Black leader. Early Sunday morning on November 14, Booker Washington died at his home in Tuskegee after years of ill health. Alonzo was chosen to be one of six honorary pallbearers from Atlanta. He and Jessie Herndon sent a floral tribute and joined the throng of Blacks and Whites, high and low, who paid their respects at a simple, yet moving, funeral in the Tuskegee Chapel that Wednesday.[17]

So what did the next ten years promise? Expanding into other states would be difficult. The Kentucky experience demonstrated that without additional capital the company would not be able to operate in other states. Even in Georgia, increased licensing fees could regulate them out of business. In a sense, Atlanta Mutual was as vulnerable to state legislation in 1915 as had been the little insurance associations

Atlanta Mutual absorbed in 1905. As a mutual assessment agency, however, the company could increase its capital only by assessing its policyholders, most of whom had meager resources. To grow, the company had to reorganize. In September 1916, it filed successfully for incorporation as a stock company with a capitalization of $25,000, 90 percent of the subscription purchased by Herndon. Before the reorganization, the company had begun operations in Arkansas, having obtained a license through Scipio Africanus Jones, a prominent Republican lawyer and friend of Truman Gibson. But once Atlanta Mutual became a stock company, licensing in Arkansas required an authorized capital of $100,000.[18] It was the Kentucky situation all over again. Herndon struggled to hold on to the Arkansas operation. "Don't you know," he wrote Norris, "I have had one of the busiest weeks of my life. . . . I am here [in Arkansas] waiting for the papers from home which is to arrive Monday. And I hope they will be satisfactory so we will go on with the business in Ark. Just as it was going, they wanted me to pull out here and sell out but I have never wanted to do that as we have a good organization and over a $400.00 weekly debit and it is growing."[19]

But Atlanta Mutual was forced to withdraw from Arkansas that spring. Defeated for the time being, Herndon nevertheless resolved to put his company on track for greatness. "If I thought that anything with which I was connected would always be small, I would not want to be in it," he would say.[20]

Within five years, Atlanta Mutual would become Georgia's second Black legal reserve company.

CHAPTER 11

A Home of Her Own

Jessie Gillespie Herndon, new mistress of the mansion.

When Jessie arrived at the mansion to assume her role as Mrs. Herndon, surely she felt the first wife's presence. Adrienne had created the house and endowed it with her spirit. Before she knew she was going to die, Adrienne recorded in her notebook an outline for a story, "The Spiritual Temple." It was about a wife who on her deathbed forbids her husband to remarry. After her death, the husband ignores her request and becomes engaged, but the fiancée dies. Repentant, the man erects a temple to his first wife's memory. Her spirit being satisfied, he succeeds in marrying again.[1] The Herndon mansion was Adrienne's temple. Soon after its construction, Alonzo was free to marry, but the second wife had to live in a monument to the first wife.

Adrienne apparently had had little opportunity to furnish the house during her illness. After her death, Alonzo and Norris probably made do with the furnishings they had had in Bumstead. So Jessie proceeded to put her touch on the mansion.[2] She chose for the living room/library exquisite furnishings: a partners desk and high-back sofa that were simple but elegant and that captured the spirit of the Arts and Crafts interior. The Sheraton-style furniture bought for the music room was of the finest quality and relieved somewhat the ornamentation of the fanciest room in the house. It is unclear whether Jessie or Adrienne chose the bedroom furniture. The seventeenth-century-style English oak suite with elaborate classical features evoked

The mansion, c. 1912.

both wives. Clearly, Jessie had exquisite taste. One can imagine the fine linens that she and her sisters prepared for her bridal trousseau. But the house itself would never fully be hers. Nor would most of the servants develop great fondness for her. Even before she came to live in the mansion, Jessie had misstepped in her relationship to them. Upon his return from Chicago the Christmas before they married, Alonzo had to remind her to make gifts to Florence and Will. "Sweetheart," he wrote, "did you not say in one of your letters before I left [Atlanta] that you had sent Florence and Will a little remembrance? I never told them that you did then, but yesterday Florence seem[ed] so disappointed that you had not sent her something by me, that I told her that you had spoken of sending it before I left, and I was sorry that she had not received it. . . . If you had just thought to send some little thing for her room—a sofa pillow top or just any little thing would have given her the greatest pleasure in the world, and Will a neck tie or anything."[3] Although they were servants whom she had never met, surely she knew by then that Florence was Alonzo's cousin. If Alonzo and Norris had received Christmas gifts from her, then Florence, who lived in the house and was part of the household, would have expected one, too. Perhaps she had forgotten to forward the gifts, or they may have gotten lost in the mail. In either event, it was an unfortunate introduction to the servants of the mansion.

Herndon apparently preferred to employ kinfolk in his house. He perhaps felt an obligation to help his people, and he could more readily entrust them with the care of his property. Alonzo called Florence "Miss Berry," consciously recognizing her in a way she would not have been acknowledged when she was a maid in the household of Frank Inman on Peachtree Street.[4] Florence was not only a cook but also an older companion for Norris and the household's natural link to the Herndons in Walton and Henry counties. She was indeed a servant, but also family.

Jessie would not have been accustomed to this kind of dual relationship. The servant in her family's household in Milwaukee had been a German maid with whom there had probably been little or no personal interaction. But upon arriving in Atlanta she found in service her husband's cousin, a pretty, young woman who may have had as much education as she, and who had a flair for hospitality. Alonzo had once written with such praise of Florence's skill and initiative that it seemed as if he were instructing Jessie on his expectations of her as hostess of the mansion: "You should have seen the table Thanksgiving. Florence decorated it after this fashion: put a large pumpkin in the center and formed a star round it or with it of oranges, bananas and large bunches of . . . grapes. I just tell her I want a nice dinner or tea and she just goes ahead and I don't bother any more and she does the rest." But competent household staff who were family and whose ultimate loyalty was to Alonzo would understandably have been difficult for Jessie to supervise. Jessie would develop a reputation among the

Florence Berry, Alonzo's cousin, was also the cook for the Herndon household.

servants of being bossy.[5] Was there no area where Jessie could comfortably reign?

Atlanta's reception of Alonzo's second wife was probably reserved at first. Few people other than Loring Palmer, the John Hopes, and the Truman Gibsons knew her. To most people she was an outsider. Some may have felt resentful that Alonzo had not selected a wife from Atlanta's elite. And from that group's perspective, Jessie fared poorly in comparisons with Adrienne. She had a better than average education, having attended public grade school in Milwaukee, but that could not have impressed the upper class in a city that was a center for Black higher education.[6]

Atlanta may not have fully appreciated Jessie's profession as a hairdresser. Those who may have turned up their noses at her occupation obviously forgot that Alonzo's wealth and social standing rested on the same trade. Hairdressing for Black women was the same market opportunity that barbering was for Black men, though for Jessie, it had been an occupation rather than a calling. Alonzo had offered before their marriage to "give her a business training," but Jessie declined.[7] A business in service to southern White women would understandably have had little appeal to Jessie. Having lived in the Midwest all her life and having served a White clientele there, she would have had no desire to serve in similar fashion in the deep South. As a woman in her forties, she would have had still less desire to begin anew in a demanding business. She chose, instead, to be Mrs. Alonzo Herndon.

Though Jessie's education and profession did not measure up to Adrienne's, her social-class background nevertheless was higher. The Gillespies had been free Blacks and, moreover, derived status from the father's long-term residence in Milwaukee and from his position as messenger with the Chicago, Milwaukee and St. Paul Railway Company. Ezekiel Gillespie had a white-collar job in mid-nineteenth-century America when most Blacks were slaves. He was one of the leading Black citizens and civil rights advocates in the state, having successfully sued the state board of elections for the right of

Blacks to vote. Unlike the McNeils, who did not belong to Savannah's free Black aristocracy and who lived on the fringes of the Black community, the Gillespies were integral to Milwaukee's Black society and active in its institutional life. Jessie's mother, Catherine Lucas Robin-son, had been a staunch member of St. Paul's African Methodist Episcopal Church in Tiffin, Ohio, her birthplace. She and her husband, Ezekiel, were among the founders of the St. Mark AME Church of Milwaukee.[8]

Jessie may have arrived an outsider, but as the wife of Atlanta's richest Black, she quickly found the inside track to the very top of the Black elite. All doors in the Black community were open to her. The Twelve Club, a small society of women that was perhaps the most exclusive in Atlanta, solicited Jessie's membership. Invitations to Jessie's bridge parties at the mansion became coveted. But for a long time, Jessie would have to confront the memory of Adrienne. Her challenge was

The Twelve Club, Atlanta's most exclusive Black society, welcomed Jessie to its membership. Front row, left to right: Carrie Johnson, Mamie Thomas, Mrs. Clyde Wilkins, Selena Butler, Lugenia Hope, Madeline White; back row, left to right: Mrs. Davage, Nellie Hamilton, Mrs. Thomas Slater, Annie Rucker, and Jessie Penn.

RIGHT: *Jessie Herndon at home on Lake Harris.*

BELOW: *In 1914 Alonzo bought a twenty-acre Florida estate called Moss Hill. The property included a large two-story frame house, which stood in the midst of one of the most profitable orange groves in Lake County.*

to find her own place and speak in her own voice within and without the Herndon household.

About a year and a half into their marriage, Alonzo bought land adjoining Lake Harris in Lane Park near Tavares in central Florida. There on an estate they called Moss Hill in the midst of one of the most profitable orange groves in Lake County, he and Jessie made their winter home. For three thousand dollars, Alonzo bought twenty acres of land on which stood a large two-story frame house.[9] Each winter from December to March, Alonzo and Jessie would retreat there to hunt, fish, and entertain an intimate social circle.

Norris would remain in Atlanta, where he was completing high school at Atlanta University, and boarding on campus. "My darling Son . . . ," Jessie wrote Norris in a newsy letter that first season in Lane Park, "we miss you like everything and talk about you everyday." Their trip to Tavares had had a rough start. "At the Depot in Atlanta," Jessie wrote, "we had more than one hr. to wait. . . . We chatted and had a pleasant time—but bless me, forgot all about having our trunk checked. The result is we have not received our trunk as yet. We have worn these same clothes for one week. 'Nuff sed.' . . . I went to Tavares

Thursday and bought 4 yds [of] brown kaki cloth and had a skirt and waist made, so I look like a farmer right." Jessie was not a country girl, but seemed to adapt easily to Moss Hill. While Alonzo hunted every day, bagging squirrels and ducks, Jessie fished on Lake Harris. But then, Jessie had lived on Lake Michigan and was used to lakefront life. "The fish are not biting at all," she complained to Norris that first season. "Yesterday Davie [a young helper from the area] and I were out fishing and never had one bite. The little Imp said 'Humph, if Mr. Herndon and me was out fishing, we sure would catch us a big mess of fish for supper.'"[10]

The Herndons' orange grove surrounded the house. "Our grove is beautiful," Jessie wrote. "We drove out only once but hope to go again this afternoon. Everybody asks us if we have any bananas out there—so I am going to look out for them. There are only a few snakes at large now." Christmas was approaching when Norris would join his parents in Florida. "My gift for your Grandma," Jessie reminded him, "is in the Xmas box on window seat. Send it for me before Xmas. . . . With much love from Papa and I and a bushel of kisses for my son, Lovingly, Mother."[11] Jessie would never replace Adrienne in Norris's life. Adrienne remained Mama; Jessie became Mother. But there was genuine warmth and affection between them. Jessie identified with one who had lost a mother in childhood as she had. From the honeymoon on, she consciously cultivated their relationship. Norris became the child she had never had. Moreover, she knew that her marriage to Alonzo depended on a good relationship with her stepson. Likewise, Norris was keenly aware that his father expected nothing less of him than love and respect for his stepmother.

As Jessie found her place among the Herndons, Mattie McNeil receded from them. From New York she stayed in touch with Alonzo and Norris with difficulty. "Do you think you will come up this way this summer?" she wrote to Norris that next July after the honeymoon. "If so let me know. I will be so glad to take My Darling in my arms and press kiss after kiss on them dear lips and tell you how much I love you and long for you and to be near you always."[12]

Norris did not make the trip. Nor would a visit have been advisable then, since there had been a major rearrangement among the New York family. Her daughter Jennie had separated from her husband, James Bailey, a podiatrist. Mattie strained to keep the family together, taking care of Jennie's daughter Adrienne. Becoming desperate, she appealed to the Herndons. "My Darling," she wrote to Norris, "I am in need of some money very bad. . . . I am in need of it to get me something to eat." Alonzo had not answered her previous letter, and she feared that he would resent her appeal through the boy, but as she explained, "I have no one to ask for help but your papa." Martha McNeil sought a position as a live-in maid in Greenwich, Connecticut, for thirty dollars a month, but having had no one to keep Adrienne, she was unable to take the job. Moreover, her health by then was in decline.[13] Alonzo was indeed obligated to Mattie, but he expected her immediate family, specifically Jennie, to assume responsibility for her. As a self-made man, Herndon had great difficulty empathizing with those who struggled under better circumstances than he had suffered. No one in Atlanta was more generous to Black children in need. But he had no tolerance for a working adult unwilling to care for her own mother. Alonzo spared no expense for his community children, providing their milk, paying their teachers' salaries, and donating the building for one of the Gate City Free Kindergarten Association nurseries. But he laid the responsibility for Martha's care at the feet of Jennie, who by then was her only living child and who had "a good position." Jennie insisted later that she was helping Martha and Adrienne in the amount of ten dollars per month. "Very good, if true," Alonzo commented skeptically. And in that struggle between the former son-in-law and her daughter, Mattie suffered greatly. Alonzo would send money on occasion, usually through Norris. "Your letter with the money arrived safe," Mattie wrote Alonzo one Christmas, "and we thank you so much for your kind remembrance of us at this time. . . . Oh if you only knew how happy you have made the little ones. . . . Their little faces have all brightened up for the Christmas Day. . . . They all send their thanks to you, Aunt Jessie and Norris."[14]

Jessie and Alonzo were busy that winter season in Florida. Their boat was outfitted with a new engine, and they tried it out on a trip to Eldorado, which was apparently a yacht pier about 150 miles away on the St. John's River at Jacksonville. Though the weather made the return trip a little rough, Alonzo reported to Norris that "the new engine is fine. . . . I am building a boathouse and a little packing house combined. It is 16 x 41 feet. We will finish it up this week and I have nearly worked out the grove and have fertilized it. . . . We are expecting some people from Atlanta next month and we are planing a good time crusing round the lake with our yat. How does that sound to a little country town Jake that I am writing to?"[15]

"Papa is in his element," Jessie wrote to Norris about her husband's oversight of the boathouse. Moreover, Alonzo was beginning to make money on his grove. "The crop sold this year for more than $300," he told Norris. "The grove is looking fine now as if it might bear 1000 boxes."[16]

With the boat and boathouse ready, the Herndons awaited the

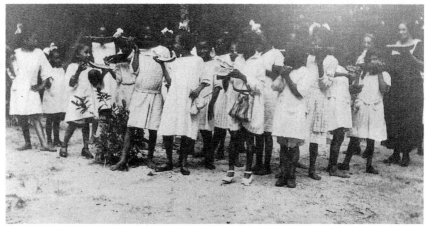

Elizabeth Bowden at Moss Hill.

Eleanor Murphy, Jessie Herndon, and unidentified woman in Tavares, 1916.

delegation from Atlanta. Jessie and Alonzo took their boat to Eldorado to meet Eleanor Murphy, the wife of grocer William Oscar Murphy and the first to arrive. The water was so rough, however, they brought her back on the train. On Sunday night the Herndons and their guests attended a local church service, where a large congregation gathered to hear the presiding elder preach. To Jessie, it was a "typical country service [where] the elders talk back and comment on all the preacher says." Every day the Herndons went boating with Eleanor Murphy; Dr. Moses Amos, the pharmacist/owner of Georgia's first Black drugstore; Dr. C. M. Tanner, an Atlanta minister; and James M. Simmons, a transfer clerk at the Atlanta depot. On Wednesday they went to Eustis and on Friday to Little Ireland, where they caught sixteen fish, which Jessie and Eleanor cleaned themselves. "We are well and happy," Alonzo reported to Norris.[17]

But within days word came of the death of Jessie's sister Emma. Jessie left immediately for Chicago on the train, meeting Norris briefly at the terminal when she passed through Atlanta. Emma had never visited her sister in Georgia, though Alonzo had pleaded with her to

come. "I wish so much that you could get away from your [wheelchair] and run off down here where you could injoy the spring out in the open." Emma had been an invalid for untold years and a heavy responsibility for her sister Mary. Jessie's late marriage may have been due partly to her reluctance to leave Mary with the care of her sister and her salon. But Emma was dead now, and she rushed to Chicago for an extended visit. "Your mother," Alonzo wrote to Norris somewhat regretfully, "spoke as if she would be there for some time yet with her sister Mary." Alonzo was already missing his mate. He ended the season in Florida the next weekend with a big fish fry and barbecue and went back to Atlanta to wait for Jessie.[18]

CHAPTER 12

Alonzo and Norris Herndon,
1907.

The Next Generation

"I love you," Alonzo wrote Norris, "and am allways planning for your . . . welfare and happiness after I am gone." The father was trying to console his son over the death of his grandmother. In the midst of Alonzo's struggles in Arkansas that April of 1918, they learned of Martha's death in New York City.[1]

At about five o'clock one Friday morning, Adrienne, the grand-child who slept with Martha in a brass bed, awoke to discover her grandmother in deep distress, froth having formed in her mouth. She summoned a neighbor to their railroad flat on the far west side of 126th Street. When the neighbor, Caroline Stevens, arrived, she found Mattie seated on the side of the bed crying, "I am dying, I am dying. Don't leave me." Stevens immediately sent the fourteen-year-old Adrienne for the doctor. Adrienne ran the several blocks in the chilly air to the doctor's home on 125th Street, but in half an hour, before she had run back, Mattie was gone. In her last moments Martha McNeil had "appealed to her maker," much as her daughter must have done on her deathbed exactly eight years before. "Mr. Norris," Stevens wrote the boy later, "your grandma was a burden bearer and at that time it was too much for her weak heart. . . . Now, don't worrie to much but bring yourself to feel that grandma is at rest."[2]

Alonzo also sympathized with Norris: "I grieved with you in the loss of your dear Grandma. You have lost one of your dearest and tru-est friends." Norris had in fact lost a mother again, his senior mother.

Mattie's body was brought back to Atlanta and buried next to her daughter in the Herndon plot in Southview Cemetery.[3]

At nearly sixty years of age, and just five years younger than Mattie, Alonzo could see in the near distance his own death. "Of course, [it] is very probably true that I shall go first," Alonzo said to Norris. Nearly forty years separated him from his son, and perhaps for a long time, he had been anxious about his succession. Just the year before, he had written to Norris, "God grant that I may live to see that day when you are twenty-one. . . . I could not help tears coming in to my eyes when I read [your letter] and thought of the promise to take the burden from my shoulders. How glad I am that you begin to see things as a man and not as a child."[4]

It was a heavy burden the son was assuming on behalf of his father and not an easy yoke fulfilling his father's expectations. Norris had come of age, but it was as though a generation were missing between him and his father. At twenty-one, he would begin to take on a career that his father had been building for nearly fifty years. In spite of his youth and inexperience, Norris was the only one to take the reins. Alonzo had long carefully monitored his son's development in the hope that Norris would follow in his footsteps.

"Norris does so well in his studdies," his father had written to Jessie before they married, "and is so thoughtful of his dad, I begin to fear that [I] may get too lax with him." There was really no danger of that. Alonzo was a strict parent who demanded much of his son. As Norris was completing high school, Alonzo assigned him the task of compiling the weekly barbershop reports when he was away in Florida. "You know if you don't get the statements off Sunday," Alonzo reminded Norris, "I won't get them until Wednesday, and you know I am crazy about those statements." Through them he tracked the rise and fall of barbershop sales week to week. "I thank you very much for the Dec. [21] report," he once wrote Norris, "which was a great deal better than December 14 by about $185."[5]

The reports, however, became a source of contention between father and son. Norris often failed to get the statement in the mail on

Norris loved the theater almost as much as his mother did and attended every show his father would allow.

time and sometimes made serious errors in compiling them. Alonzo could be harsh in his disapproval. "Your report was all wrong," he wrote promptly one week. "You only reported $921 when it should have been $1921, so you got the thing all balled up. So you must go with Mr. [Truman] Gibson and get the report together." As for timing, he said, "If you don't write me the report after you get it, what good is there in your taking it for me? I hope you will be more careful in the future."[6]

Jessie was the softer voice of discipline, encouraging Norris's successes, but nevertheless echoing and reinforcing Alonzo's wishes. "I know you would be pleased to see how happy Papa is," she wrote, "when he receives your letter [with the barbershop reports] on Monday A.M. He feels you make an extra effort to get it to him early. I trust you may be able to continue."[7]

But Norris would have extreme difficulty in doing so. His attention and his heart were divided. Beneath his commitment to his father and at times in conflict with it, was his love of the arts. As a child, Norris had demonstrated artistic ability with his colored pencil drawings, but perhaps for want of encouragement, never developed the talent. He studied piano briefly, but apparently had little skill in it. And though he appeared occasionally in college plays, his talent in elocution and stage performance was never developed. Norris had, nevertheless, an avid appreciation of drama and music. He loved the theater almost as much as his mother did and attended every show and performance his father would allow. "You spoke of the shows," his father wrote once from Florida, "but that is not very interesting to me compared with your studdies."[8] Herndon clearly discouraged his son's interest in the arts. Had not the theater been Adrienne's impossible dream? Was not a business career Norris's bird in the hand? Yes, but in Norris's heart, the arts took precedence over barbershop reports.

"You spoke of the shows, but that is not very interesting to me compared with your studdies."
—*Alonzo to his son, Norris.*

In high school Norris's grades began to slip. Cicero and Virgil, algebra and geometry did him in. In college he steered clear of the classics and whenever possible avoided math. But by sophomore year Norris was failing in all of his subjects: organic chemistry, qualitative analysis, psychology, and German. "I am sorry to see," his father wrote after receiving his report card, "instead of geting better as the years go by you are geting worse, not doing as well as last year. I had been warning you about geting too much shows and other frivolities in your head. Now quit everything but something [that] pertains to your lessons and try and get yourself together."[9]

Alonzo regretted that his son was not a sportsman and insisted that physical activity would improve his academic performance. "Your mind is bright enough," Alonzo told him. "It is application you need and a plenty of out-door exercises so you can have a strong body and your vision will be much clearer." Alonzo, after all, had begun backbreaking field labor before he was thirteen years old and believed that physical exertion had shaped his success. "God's plan is for man to work with his hands as well as with his mind," the father instructed, "and you must work or exersis. You can't defeat God's plan."[10]

This was perhaps the most severe rebuke Norris had ever received. Evidently so stunned and shamed by it, he fell silent. For weeks he

In Norris's heart, the arts took precedence over barbershop reports. As a sophomore at Atlanta University, he was failing in all of his subjects.

completely stopped communicating with his family. "What is the matter?" his father asked in a letter the next week, as though he had no clue. "Are you sick? You have not written Florence or your mother a line and they are at a loss to know what has come over you? . . . Today is Sunday again and [I] have no statement from you for last Sunday."[11]

Alonzo's anger had not yet cooled. It seemed as though all of the reservations he had ever held about his son's privileged upbringing suddenly came pouring out with his upset over Norris's grades. "And geting everything you get from . . . [the barbershop. Without] that you would have to get out and hustle just as the other poor boys do, but you can't appretiate it. You will regret someday when things begin to get away from you on account of not taking an interest in and learning to take care of the trust that has been placed in you."[12]

The fear and struggle within Norris must have been mighty. He was afraid of losing his father and his future. If his father disapproved so heartily of him, what did that leave him? Who was he and who should he be? He was certainly not his father. He had not been the impoverished Lonza who sold molasses, peanuts, and axle grease in Walton County to save pennies for his break from home. Norris was a rich man's son, who lived in comfort and would never leave home. At age twenty-one he wasn't the young Alonzo who had just opened his first barbershop in Jonesboro. He was the college student scuffling with his subjects and starting out in the lower ranks of his father's company during summer breaks in Savannah. Moreover, Norris was a young man coming of age and struggling with his homosexual identity. With a father who sternly insisted upon a straight and narrow course and in an early-twentieth-century society that had no tolerance for what it considered deviant, Norris would have to deny himself. He would assume a compromised selfhood, his sexuality arrested, denied, or expressed in secret.[13]

If Norris was not yet sure of who he was, he certainly knew that he wanted to please his father. He did not have his father's entrepreneurial spirit; he took no initiative or pleasure like his father in the steady chase and capture of the dollar. But he wanted nevertheless to do what he thought was honorable and responsible. Wanting to succeed by his father's standards left him little choice but to follow in his father's footsteps. He would devote himself to his father's business. Honor and obedience to his father steered him into adulthood.

Alonzo may have had to wait several days more before he and Jessie returned to Atlanta and the break with his son was healed. But out of that process, Norris emerged with the promise to take the burden off his father's shoulders. Working that summer in the Atlanta Mutual office in Savannah, Norris seemed resigned to the commitment he had made. Ironically, Norris had come to terms with his father shortly before he was to lose Big Mama. "I am quite well and getting along nicely here in Savannah with my work," he wrote his grandmother a few months before she died. But his enthusiasm for the city was reserved for the memories he had of her and the family. "Every time I pass Duffy Street and see the house I think of you and mama and grandpa and Aunt Rachel. . . . I know those were happy old days." Norris longed for a time he had only heard about. One Saturday night, he visited the old city market where his grandfather Archibald McNeil had had a meat stall. "It was in full blast full of people," he wrote his grandmother. "Oh it is fine! . . . Write me about it and Savannah."[14] Norris may have sensed an urgency to record his maternal family history.

Proud of his father's approval of him, he sent to his grandmother the letter his father had just written him in joy over his promise. It was as though he were proudly offering to his mother a certificate of his rite of passage. He asked her to save that letter. "I would like to have it when I am a grown man to always keep."[15] In September, before the start of his junior year, Norris took the train to New York to see his grandmother for the last time. Three months after Martha McNeil's death, Norris reached twenty-one.

The summer before, Atlanta Mutual had surprised Alonzo on his fifty-ninth birthday with an application shower at the Odd Fellows Roof

"I had been warning you about getting too much shows and other frivolities in your head. Now quit everything but something [that] pertains to your lessons and try and get yourself together."
—Alonzo to his son, Norris.

Garden. "[I] was intertained," Alonzo wrote Norris, "with a Banquet and speaches by as many as we had time to hear and they presented me with a beautiful cake and song composed by Mr. Shanks [the secretary-auditor]. . . . They had a beautiful little parasol . . . and showered the [insurance] applications over my head. . . . It was a beautiful tribute to your old Father." Herndon felt justifiably proud of his progress with the company. "I have passed another milestone," he told Norris, referring apparently to the company's plan to add life insurance as a higher benefit alternative to its sick and accident coverage.[16] What Herndon did not realize then was that he would soon be called upon to save the life of his company. The application shower would do little to shield him from the storm that lay ahead for Atlanta Mutual. In the last decade of Herndon's life, his burden was getting heavier.

Norris graduated as one of eleven in Atlanta University's college department in June 1919, having buckled down his junior and senior years to achieve average grades. Probably with little choice in the matter, he enrolled that next fall at Harvard to begin studies for a master's degree in business administration. It became imperative that he prepare to join Atlanta Mutual with as much professional training as soon as possible. The year he graduated from Atlanta University, Truman Gibson, who had served as vice president and secretary, resigned in a dispute with Alonzo on the distribution of stock, leaving Atlanta Mutual with a gaping hole in its top management. Norris was elected to the board of directors, but for the next two years, he would be in Cambridge, Massachusetts, preparing for his father's work.

While Norris was away at Harvard, the company moved to larger quarters, relocating in 1920 from the Odd Fellows Building to 132 Auburn Avenue. With characteristic thrift, Alonzo Herndon had purchased a two-story frame dwelling that he veneered in brick and re-novated extensively for offices, leasing out the second floor. The building had been occupied by the Black YMCA that moved to a new building on Butler Street.

*Honor and obedience to his father
steered Norris into adulthood.
He promised to commit himself
to his father's business.*

*Before the start of his junior year,
Norris took the train to New York
to see his grandmother for the last
time. Three months after Martha
McNeil's death, Norris reached
twenty-one.*

At this time Alonzo was facing the most difficult period of his insurance career. The company had survived the onslaught of claims generated by the influenza of 1918, and Norris had survived the draft of World War I without being called to active duty. Declining collections due to war and migration also plagued the company. But these difficulties were minor compared with Alonzo's management problems. With the first vice president Robert Chamblee in charge of the straight life insurance, and Joseph C. Lindsay, vice president and general manager, directing sick and accident operations, two separate and competing divisions developed, which apparently created discord at every level. In early 1920, the state ordered an independent investigation of Atlanta Mutual that recommended the placement of a single manager over both divisions. Rather than choose between two senior officials, Herndon divided the territories, assigning Chamblee to both operations in Georgia and Lindsay to both in Alabama.[17]

But before the company could implement the arrangement fully and just a few days before Christmas of 1920, Lindsay was arrested in Atlanta on charges of embezzlement of Atlanta Mutual funds and jailed in the Fulton County Tower.[18] Here was a senior official of the company, a trusted associate in whose house Norris had stayed during his summer in Savannah. "Remember us kindly to the Lindsays," Alonzo had written his son. "Tell Mr. Lindsay to take good care of our Baby."[19] But now there were allegations that Lindsay was abusing the money in his care. The shortage uncovered in a routine audit was perhaps the severest blow ever to Herndon's trust in his management team. Moreover, when news of the arrest was reported in the *Atlanta Independent,* it became the strongest challenge yet to the public's confidence in the company. Ben Davis, editor of the *Independent,* ran a series of articles on the crisis, subsequently reporting the involvement of other company officials. "Our information is that . . . the secretary-auditor [Christopher Shanks] has confessed to having embezzled $8,000 of the stolen funds and that the cashier [Marie Anderson] has admitted that she participated in the loot in the sum of approximately $1,000."[20]

"I could not help tears coming in to my eyes when I read [your letter], and thought of the promise to take the burden from my shoulders. How glad I am that you begin to see things as a man and not as a child."—Alonzo to his son, Norris.

Norris pulled up his grades and graduated from Atlanta University in 1919, enrolling that fall in the Harvard University School of Business.

Davis goaded Herndon to make a public statement on the company's internal investigation. This was not the first time that Davis had publicly challenged Herndon. A handsome, dark-skinned man who had become the leading voice in the state's Odd Fellows order, Davis had on occasion expressed his resentment of the power and prestige of Atlanta's light-skinned Black elite. In spite of Davis's taunts, Herndon as usual said nothing to outsiders about his company's internal affairs. While his lawyer and the directors finalized the details of the case, Herndon went into winter retreat in Tavares. Remarkably, nothing in his letters hinted of the crisis. Instead, with the new year he was extolling the beauty of Florida. "Now is the very best time to visit Fla.," he wrote in invitation to his sister-in-law Mary. "[In] Feb. the trees begin putting on the bloom for this year's crop. . . . We have a real good cook and chofer and you can fish if you like it, or just rest."[21] Rest was exactly what he himself needed now more than ever. The turn of events in Atlanta had badly shaken Alonzo, who was then nearly sixty-three years old. Norris's studies in Cambridge could not end too soon.

The schoolwork at Harvard, Norris found, was rigorous. He had been admitted with average grades to graduate study at a school where Atlanta University alumni usually studied an additional two years before receiving the Harvard undergraduate degree. The first year Norris was required to seek tutoring in English from the university, and his quantitative skills would continue to be challenged. He was determined nevertheless to keep his promise to his father, so he dug in to his courses: marketing, insurance, accounting principles, and commercial contracts.

He was one of at least two Black students in his class, and one of a handful in the entire school of about four hundred.[22] In the Boston area Norris may have had difficulty in passing for White, and on campus his Atlanta University background would have made his race widely known. For the first time Norris was in a university community where he was in the minority among Whites. And Harvard Business School students would not have shared the ideals of the New England missionaries he knew from Atlanta University. Moreover, Harvard's racism would be explicit the year following Norris's graduation, when Blacks were denied residence in freshmen dormitories.[23]

During his first year he lived at 1556 Cambridge Street and took his meals at Foxcroft Hall. With so few Blacks in his community and for want of time, Norris's socializing was extremely limited. Radcliffe's graduate society dance for Harvard students offered little or nothing for Blacks. His major social outlet may have been the graduate chapter of Alpha Phi Alpha, the fraternity he had joined at Atlanta University, but he often missed its meetings. Cambridge was simply no match for the full and easy society he had enjoyed in Atlanta. In the Boston area there was not the same rich fabric of family and friends. There were no dinners with Carrie Hennie; no Eloise Murphy or Louise Holmes to escort to campus functions; no rides with Jessie in the Jordan out Peachtree Road; no rallies for the YMCA at the Armory. There was the theater, but he disciplined himself, attending only about once a month. Cambridge may have reminded Norris of his summer in Savannah, when he had complained to his father about being alone. "Go to church and serve the Lord," his father had advised him then, "and you won't get lonesome."[24]

In his second year, Norris had the company of Walter Smith, a first-year student in the program, who had graduated with him at Atlanta University. But for the most part, Norris's studies filled his life in Cambridge. With relief he wrote home in May 1921, "Well our exams come off next week . . . so that by next Saturday I will be through all school work." To prepare himself for his accounting examination, he hired a tutor at a dollar and a half per hour. "I don't want to miss this subject," he wrote his father. Apparently, Norris did not stay to receive his diploma. "The business school men," he said, "don't have any part in the commencement exercises anyway." But more important, Norris was anxious to get home: "I certainly haven't a very strong liking for New England as some people have."[25]

CHAPTER 13

Bearing the Cross

"I am willing to sink everything I have in order to save [Atlanta Mutual] and make it the kind of institution I want it to be."
—*Alonzo Herndon.*

By the time Norris joined Atlanta Mutual in late spring of 1921, the company had for the most part weathered the embezzlement scandal. Norris became a vice president, while Chamblee took on the additional responsibility of Lindsay's function as general manager. Stepping in as secretary and auditor to replace Shanks was Eugene M. Martin, a 1912 graduate of Atlanta University who would become the primary official to oversee Norris's succession to the presidency of the company. The Lindsay-Shanks affair had helped to trigger what would become a still greater crisis for Atlanta Mutual.

The Georgia Insurance Department launched another investigation of the company to determine whether the embezzlement had impaired its financial operations. Atlanta Mutual was given ninety days to prove that it was solvent. In the course of that effort, it appeared to Herndon and his board that the company's consulting actuary and attorney, both White men, wanted to prove Atlanta Mutual's insolvency. They saw virtually within their own ranks a move to wrest control of the company from them. Though advised by friends to sell Atlanta Mutual, Herndon expressed the supreme commitment: "I am willing to sink everything I have in order to save it and make it the kind of institution I want it to be."[1]

That is exactly what Herndon would be required to do. The state investigation found neither impairment nor major irregularities in Atlanta Mutual's operations, but the insurance commissioner William

Wright summoned Herndon to his office. He then ordered the company to comply with the insurance law of 1920, requiring that it increase its deposit immediately from $25,000 to $100,000, surely aware that this order threatened the very existence of the company. How could Atlanta Mutual come up with $75,000 immediately?

Herndon must have stunned the commissioner by responding, "I can't have it before morning."[2] On short notice, Herndon raised the money—a testament to his personal wealth and his unfailing access to capital. From the lion's jaws Atlanta Mutual stepped forth boldly to reorganize as a legal reserve company offering all classes of life insurance, increasing its capital stock to $100,000, and renaming itself Atlanta Life Insurance Company.

Herndon had survived the supreme test because he had kept his own counsel about his business and financial affairs. Unlike Heman Perry, for whom there had been exaggerated claims of wealth, Herndon had apparently told no one how much money he really had.[3] He kept quiet about his earnings and saved in huge amounts. Since his boyhood of saving pennies, Herndon knew how to live on the minimum to save the maximum. As a farm laborer in Coweta County nearly fifty years before, he had held on to fifty of the sixty dollars he earned in six months.[4]

It was a spare lifestyle that he had tried to teach his son. "As to the money," he once responded to Norris's request to buy all new books, "don't spend any more than you have too. I want you to have what you really need but none to waste." That meant buying used books or getting them from the library. It meant for Alonzo salvaging wood from demolished houses to build and repair others, or using a taper again and again down to the nub.[5] The sum total of a life of savings rescued Atlanta Mutual and gave birth to Atlanta Life.

The ordeal of these years, however, had taken a heavy toll on Alonzo. Soon after coming to terms with the state insurance department, Alonzo and Jessie arranged for thorough medical examinations at the Mayo Clinic in Rochester, Minnesota. For some time Alonzo had suffered serious skin eruptions on his arms and had periodically

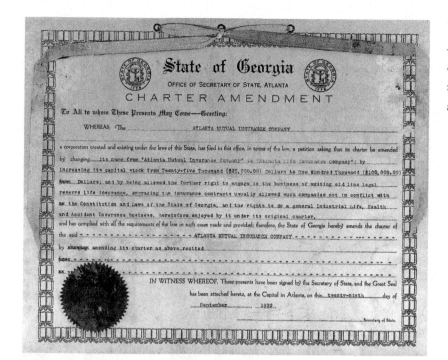

treated them with mineral baths. There was another more serious, but unknown, condition that warranted surgery. Shunning the humiliation of Grady Hospital's segregated and inferior accommodations, Alonzo and Jessie went north, stopping for a day with the Halls in Chicago and finally coming through a heavy snowstorm to Rochester, where they registered at the Kahler Hotel.

"This is a wonderful place," Jessie wrote Norris about the Mayo Clinic. "You can have no conception of its magnitude until you see it. . . . Last Friday they registered 300 patients and it is so every day. They give a most searching examination[,] . . . get your history and the history of the entire family tree." Jessie was found to have a tumor and was scheduled for surgery. "They say it is not a dangerous operation, but I have made your Papa promise not to be operated on until I am out of danger, and should I not recover, to wait awhile before he goes under."[6]

The Herndons were amazed at the absence of Blacks at the clinic. "We have seen only one of your people," Jessie joked to Norris. "Papa says he never saw a place like this for the lack of them [except for]

Atlanta Life officers and board directors. *"Be sure and keep your eye on the business, and don't let them get away with you, as you are to represent me as first vice president. That is me when I am absent."* —Alonzo to his son, Norris.

F.A. TOOMER AUDITOR

CYRUS CAMPFIELD S.S. DIRECTOR

L. M. HILL Med. Director

T. W. HOLMES ATTORNEY

H. W. RUSSELL ASS'T. AGENCY DIREC'

A.F. HERNDON PRES.

R.W. CHAMBLEE VICE PRES. & GEN. MGR.

E.M. MARTIN SEC. & AUDITOR

N.B. HERNDON VICE PRES.

L.H. HAYWOOD AGENCY DIRECTOR

J.T. HARRISON VICE PRES.

S.M. JOHNSON VICE PRES.

ALONZA HERNDON DIRECTOR

C.A. FAISON DIRECTOR

where they are prohibited from letting the sun shine on them." Alonzo was impatient with the clinic process. "You are sent from one desk to another," he said, "and from one Dr. to another until your head fairly buzzes. And a wait at each place from 30 minutes to 6 & 8 hours. . . . I think we will get through with the examinations tomorrow and they will make up their diagnosis in a day or two. And they will tell us what we need to do, and then it will be up to us just what to do." Few persons were aware of the Herndons' mission to the Mayo. Norris's Aunt Jennie complained later that she had not known about Jessie's surgery; she may never have learned of Alonzo's.[7]

That September the charter for Atlanta Life was granted. Avoiding a public sale, Herndon purchased the entire stock issue.[8] With the formation of Atlanta Life, Alonzo reached his greatest milestone in business, and had done so in spite of the pressures and deceits within and without.

Now that Norris was on board, Alonzo could spend still less time at the office. "Be sure and keep your eye on the business," he reminded his son from Tavares, "and don't let them get away with you, as you are to represent me as first vice president. That is me when I am absent."[9]

But Alonzo was back and forth between Atlanta and Tavares, and for the next two years much engaged in the company's expansion into six states. He laid the groundwork with Chamblee, Martin, and Lem-uel Haywood, agency director, for Atlanta Life's entrance into Florida. Norris traveled to the districts in Georgia and Alabama, and was involved with his father in the move into Tennessee that July. But for the most part, Norris was in Atlanta, establishing himself as vice president. He was becoming a faithful steward in his father's business.

But it was obvious that business never took hold of his heart. In his journal entries of 1923, a year of tremendous expansion for Atlanta Life, Norris barely mentioned the forays into other states. In the midst of his entries on the maintenance of his Jordan car and the changes in the weather, Norris noted each meeting he attended on behalf of his father, but seldom stated the substance of the discussions.

He did, however, record with great formality the elder Herndon's going and coming: "Mr. A. F. H. arrives from Florida. . . . A. F. Herndon leaves for Florida with Mr. and Mrs. Vaughn, Lucius, Bessie, etc."[10] Norris served his father with devotion. In fear, in awe, and in adoration, he kept up with his father's every move.

Always having liked the turn of a phrase, Norris tried to capture his father's humor and language on paper. Settling accounts with one of the servants, Alonzo had said "Your time was $4.00, wasn't it? [But] then you killed the dog—that's $5.00." "Lend me your fountain pen," Norris asked after this joke. "Oh go on," Alonzo answered, "you're writing down too much rot."[11]

This "rot," however, was part of the personal detail that colored a remarkable individual. Norris, the theater lover, had a front-row seat for his father's performance—a full and entertaining play of humor and struggle. Norris, the historian, documented some of Alonzo's minutiae for posterity.

As 1923 closed, Atlanta Life entered Kentucky and Missouri. At age sixty-five, Alonzo was still much engaged in Atlanta Life's affairs. "I am trying to get everything straight," he had written to Jessie in late 1923. His hands were full with Atlanta Life expansion. And he was shouldering another heavy load. He had begun the construction of a new office building on Auburn directly across from the Odd Fellows Building. It would be a three-story brick building, the second major office complex on the avenue and in time a prestigious address for Atlanta's physicians, dentists, and other professionals. As he had done for the construction of his house, Alonzo was contractor for the Herndon Building. "I am on the building every day," he told his wife. "I am disappointed that they had not got further with it but they had so much rain that they could not work much. They will get through with the lathing this week and if the weather is still good I hope to get the plaster on next week."[12] After several more days on the building Alonzo went back to Florida to spend Christmas with Jessie.

Norris made the Christmas rounds in Atlanta. With the arrival of Miss Aeolian Bibb from New York, his social group launched a fleet of house parties. Madeline White, a close associate and the daughter of George White, entertained on Houston Street. And Eloise Murphy Milton, who had just married Lorimer Milton that November, gave a supper for Madeline's sister Ruby White Edwards. On Christmas Eve Norris himself threw a whist party. He began Christmas with a breakfast for the Chamblees and ended the day hosting a dinner for the George White family. The Masked Ball by the Collegiate Club at Catholic Hall on Boulevard ended his social year.[13]

Everyone at Atlanta Life geared up for a major sales campaign, which they called the Senatorial Campaign of 1924. That April the company had begun operations in Kansas and by December would enter Texas, later one of its most profitable states. The campaign was an imaginative sales promotion among old and new districts to add thirty thousand dollars of debit and an inspiration for the celebration ahead of Atlanta Life's twentieth anniversary. With the fervor of a political contest, the district managers competed in sales for election to an advisory "Senate." After months of campaigning, the senators would meet in conference in January 1925 at the Herndons' estate in Tavares.

Norris led the motorcade of winners from Atlanta that next Janu-

Alonzo Herndon and Norris (center right) stand with George Lee, second from left, and others at Senatorial Campaign retreat.

ary, stopping at district offices along the way in Macon, Waycross, Jacksonville, and Orlando. His old Jordan gave out a few times, but finally carried them on to Tavares. "Amid flowers of many tints," reported the staff publication *Atlanta Life Bulletin,* "where the air is perfumed with the fragrance of orange blossoms, where many strange and beautiful birds sing tunefully in the trees, surrounded by acres and acres of luscious golden fruit and situated on one of the most picturesque lakes in the beautiful 'Land of Flowers' is the magnificent winter home of President Herndon."[14] It was a rustic setting, but the proceedings were formal, the men meeting in session to discuss their achievement and their plans, and during breaks, strolling in business suits through the orange grove and down by the lake.

This roundup of the company's officers and top salesmen gave Alonzo an opportunity to take a close look at his men as a group. Most of them—Chamblee, Haywood, Johnson, Martin, Russell, and Harrison—had been with him since the company's early years.[15]

They were strong race men—individuals who had preached and lived the uplift of Negroes. Business had been their calling; this trip to Florida, their pilgrimage.

Herndon also looked to family for support: his nephew Alonzo II, Tom's son, whom he considered "a good friend to the whole family" and who would anchor the St. Louis district; and his own son, still young and inexperienced, but nevertheless the one whose competence and commitment he trusted. Alonzo saw Norris and this capable and enthusiastic team of men as the keystone of his enterprise. They were his future.[16]

After the senators ended their conference, after their last boat trip and fish fry, Alonzo prepared to give up most of his Florida estate. That March he sold his big orange grove of thirty acres on Lake Harris for $15,500, earning a huge return on his investment.[17]

Ironically, as Herndon's star reached its height, Heman Perry's fell. Early in 1924, the Georgia Insurance Department ruled that Standard Life was impaired due to the proportion of its assets in real estate. Within a few months, Perry, who was short of cash and unable to borrow from traditional sources, fell victim to a loan that upon default in December forced Standard Life into a merger with two other companies. What everyone had thought was the race's leading enterprise was now in the hands of Whites. After a decade of silence, Herndon could have said, "I told you so." Instead, speaking before his stockholders at the annual meeting in January 1925, he said, "I do not rejoice at their downfall, but I prayed for them and grieved with them." He could well sympathize with a struggling Black insurance company whose operations were under the severest scrutiny and whose capital was short. He had been there just three years before. But as the Black community negotiated to keep Standard Life from going under, Herndon remained hands-off. He was unwilling to revisit the business of Heman Perry.[18]

Alonzo continued his work on the Herndon Building. "My darling," he wrote to Jessie in Tavares, "I hoped to leave here Saturday night, but I find I can't get away then, as the Building is not where I

OPPOSITE: *In celebration of the company's Senatorial Campaign of 1924 (a sales campaign in support of its expansion into six states) and in anticipation of its twentieth anniversary, officers and district sales managers met in retreat at the Herndon estate in Tavares in January 1925. First row, left to right: unidentified man; Lyndon Hill, medical director; Lemuel Haywood, agency director; Norris Herndon, vice president; Robert Chamblee, vice president and general manager; unidentified man; second row, left to right: Alonzo Herndon II, board director; unidentified man; Howard W. Russell, assistant agency director; Eugene Martin, secretary and auditor; James Harrison; unidentified man; and George Lee, district manager.*

can leave it very well. . . . They are putting the roof on the long part." He was suffering from a cold and wanted to put Jessie at ease about his care. "Norris and I are still Batcheloring," he reported, "yet getting our meals on Auburn Avenue."[19]

Construction was taking much longer than scheduled. It was as though Alonzo's life now hung on the completion of the building. The next week he was still at it. "The building has got just about [finished]," he wrote to Jessie again. "I can't afford to leave it. . . . They are cuting the Building up into offices, lathing and plastering and things are quite interesting so much so, I am loth to leave." Finally, in the spring of 1925 the building was completed.[20]

"I want to say that I have done my best." Herndon was speaking at the stockholders annual meeting in January 1926 as though it would be his last. In fact, he had one more annual meeting to go. "I hope that I will leave the world better and a good many people better off because I have lived in it." He could point with pride to hundreds of men and women whom Atlanta Life employed and to the thousands

"I am on the building everyday,"
Alonzo Herndon wrote to Jessie.
The Herndon Building, com-
pleted in 1925, was on Auburn
Avenue across from the Odd
Fellows Building. It became the
more prestigious office location for
Atlanta's Black professionals.

The Atlanta Life office at 132 (later 148) Auburn was given a Beaux Arts style facelift in 1927.

it insured. His barbershops had been the source of a good income for countless men for nearly two generations. He was without question one of the most successful Blacks in American business. But business was not his only concern at the stockholders meeting that January morning. Abruptly, losing no time in getting to what seemed to weigh heaviest on his heart, he said, "You must remember Jesus Christ and watch and pray. Don't let Satan edge in between you and God. . . . When we forget God, our successes will turn to failure." Alonzo was not referring only to reverses in business. "Some successes," he had written to Jessie's sister Mary, years before, "are a failure so far as it relates to happiness." He was consoling Mary for having compromised her business for the sake of her family. "You will really get more real happiness out of doing your whole duty as it comes to you," Alonzo counseled, "than if you had done otherwise and been more successful from a financial standpoint." Herndon was talking about a happiness that money and career could not bring. He was, indeed, invoking God's blessing on his company, but more important, Alonzo was searching his own soul. "There's a cross for everyone," he continued at the meeting, "and I . . . too . . . must bear my own crosses."[21]

Surely, duty to family was one of his crosses. Adrienne's death nearly thirty years before had perhaps been the sharpest rebuke to worldly success. "We have just got ready to live," she had said, "and now I must die." The Herndons learned painfully that a mansion is no preparation for life; that living is a constant readiness, a daily agenda that places love above all else. And only the power of love could help Alonzo bear the cross of a son who would never marry nor have children. The Herndon legacy would be by the third generation in the hands of outsiders, no matter how carefully Alonzo had laid the foundation. But perhaps no cross was more important than the one Alonzo bore on behalf of the larger community, becoming Atlanta's leading Black philanthropist, assuming responsibility for children and youth who, like himself, contended with overwhelming odds. Death, his final cross, was imminent. He accepted this and all his other crosses. Without them there would be no crown.

If Alonzo was ready to die, Norris was unaware of his father's preparations. "Papa has been under the doctor's care ever since he returned from New York," he wrote his Aunt Jennie later that year. "The [heart specialist] keeps him in bed most of the time and says that the main thing he needs is rest. So I do not feel that his condition is really serious." Under the doctor's orders, Alonzo lost considerable weight. "You should see how his clothes hang on," Norris said.[22]

That winter Alonzo and Jessie left Florida for Nassau with George and Theo Hall. "Dr. Hall is a fine fellow to travel with," Alonzo told Norris upon returning to Tavares. "I never wanted for a thing. He spent his money like a drunken sailor." Herndon recalled the banquet where the liquor flowed freely. "Everyone there just helped himself to just what they wanted. No one to say quit." But there were limits to Herndon's health. "I only wished I was well," he complained. "My hands and leg gave me some worry all the time."[23] Moreover, heart disease was taking its toll. This would be Alonzo Herndon's last season in Florida.

The April board meeting in 1927 was one of Alonzo's last visits to the office. But still loath to leave his work, he convened the next three meetings at the mansion. In May, as though he sensed death approaching fast, he nominated Jessie to the board of directors. On a Thursday evening at seven o'clock on July 21, 1927, less than a month after his sixty-ninth birthday and just a few days after his last board meeting, Herndon died at home.

His associates had not expected the end to come so soon. And though his family may have been more aware of his frailty, there was, nevertheless, no way for Jessie and Norris to prepare for their loss. While they nursed their grief privately, they faced an extravagant public mourning befitting Alonzo Herndon's community standing.

The body lay in state in the mansion until the funeral at First Congregational Church on Monday morning. In an extremely long ceremony of tributes, nearly every sector of the community spoke to Alonzo Herndon's worth and character. "The Captain of our army has made his last stand," said George W. Lee, manager of Atlanta Life's

Memphis district and one of the company's most eloquent orators. "God, alone," he said, "compressed into Mr. Herndon enough dynamic power that enabled him to build his towers of work and usefulness higher than the mountains, broader than the expanse of the rivers, deeper than the low lying valleys. . . . No story, no tragedy, no epic poem will be read with greater wonder or followed by mankind with deeper feeling than that which tells the story of his life and death." In his sermon the Reverend J. W. Faulkner, minister of First Congregational, called Herndon "one of God's choicest sons." But perhaps the most touching final tribute was the song of the little girls of the Leonard Street Orphanage. They would have remembered their most generous benefactor, not only because he cared about their sorrows but also because he provided for their joys: oranges in winter and watermelon for his summer picnics. Their presence had said all that needed to be said. Herndon had often remarked, "I never worry about dying or about going to heaven. I will do my part of right living here and leave the rest to God." The service ended, and the barbers bore the coffin to the hearse. Twenty-five funeral cars and three wagons full of flowers followed in procession to Southview Cemetery.[24] The burden, the crosses, were now squarely on Norris's shoulders.

OPPOSITE: *The most touching final tribute: the little girls of the Leonard Street Orphanage. (Courtesy of Atlanta University Center, Robert W. Woodruff Library)*

Epilogue

In 1969, when Norris was seventy-one years old, he received a letter from Cora Herndon. She had cared for him that winter evening in Social Circle when at the age of six he was awaiting his father, who had missed the train. Her memories offered precious details of that boyhood journey. "I have never forgotten," she wrote, "what a nice child you were, so brave with us while knowing that your father would be down here on the next train." In exhausting detail, she updated him on the White Herndons: "My husband lost all the farm lands he inherited from his father." The substantial property that Frank Herndon had given to his son Elisha and that eventually passed to his grandson Emory was gone now—sold to pay the debt from a failing bank. "All our Elisha M. Herndons were very proud of Alonzo," Cora acknowledged, "as he was so kind to them when they went to Atlanta and always went to Herndon Barbershop." The eighty-nine-year-old woman ended her four-page letter in petition for Sardis Baptist Church, the oldest in Walton County. "Give what you would like me to have for this historic church," she wrote.

Norris responded, "I fondly remember my father speaking of your husband, Mr. Emory Herndon. He seemed to have felt that he was kinder to him than the other Herndons and spoke of him many times." He sent Cora one hundred dollars for her church.

The Alonzo Herndons for over a century have quietly and steadily given of their wealth. Since their first gifts to First Congregational Church and to the children of Gate City Free Kindergarten, their philanthropy has totaled more than six million dollars, many times the million dollars estimated in Alonzo's estate in 1927.

Norris had been a faithful steward of the family fortune, leading Atlanta Life through its greatest period of growth following the Depression. He became a multimillionaire, one of the richest Black men in the country, and would ultimately give his wealth away.

In 1933 Norris and Jessie gave the equipment and fixtures of the Peachtree Street shop to the barbers, who eventually moved to Broad Street and operated until 1972 for Whites only—a relic of racism from an earlier stage of Black enterprise.

One winter evening in early 1947, Jessie was returning from Tiffin, Ohio, where she had been visiting family. As the train pulled into the Union Terminal, she suffered a stroke and was taken to the mansion, where on February 1 she died at the age of seventy-five. Norris, who was then fifty years old, unmarried, and childless, proceeded to ensure the family legacy. In his father's name he donated the land and money for the stadium of Morris Brown College. Establishing the Alonzo F. and Norris B. Herndon Foundation in 1950, he formalized the family's philanthropy and sought to protect the future of Atlanta Life and the mansion. By the 1960s he had begun to channel money to civil rights causes: the NAACP, which developed out of the Niagara movement and whose founding he had witnessed as an eight-year-old; and the Student Nonviolent Coordinating Committee, which was in need of bail funds for jailed protesters. Norris was bringing his family's money back full circle to the community from which it had come.

In memory of his mother and father, he dedicated the Herndon mansion as a museum. Collecting the finest of English silver, Venetian glass, Persian carpets, and ancient artifacts, Norris prepared his home to receive the public. The house, its furnishings, and family papers constitute perhaps one of the richest private collections of historical materials documenting an African American family. As a testament to its design, construction, and historical significance, the house has been designated a National Historic Landmark, the country's highest recognition of historic structures.

After nearly fifty years as president of Atlanta Life, Norris relinquished control in 1973 to Jesse Hill Jr., a board director and former company actuary. On a Tuesday morning, June 7, 1977, about a month before his eightieth birthday, Norris, who like his father suffered from heart disease, was discovered dead in his bed, his body turned as though to see his last sunrise.

The Herndon Foundation inherited his wealth—Atlanta Life Insurance Company and the Herndon mansion. The Foundation has become Norris's child and heir to the Herndon legacy. Atlanta Life, which erected a new office building in 1980, remains one of the largest Black financial institutions in the country, still an anchor of Black enterprise at the gateway to the Auburn Avenue commercial district. With the dividends from its Atlanta Life stock, the Foundation continues the family's philanthropy and operates the mansion as a museum, telling new generations the story of an extraordinary family.

APPENDIX

Family Trees

THE HERNDON FAMILY

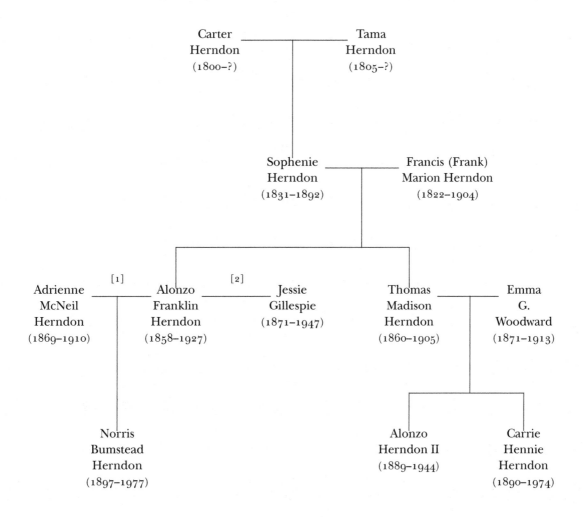

Carter Herndon (1800–?) ——— Tama Herndon (1805–?)

Sophenie Herndon (1831–1892) ——— Francis (Frank) Marion Herndon (1822–1904)

Adrienne McNeil Herndon (1869–1910) —[1]— Alonzo Franklin Herndon (1858–1927) —[2]— Jessie Gillespie (1871–1947)

Thomas Madison Herndon (1860–1905) ——— Emma G. Woodward (1871–1913)

Norris Bumstead Herndon (1897–1977)

Alonzo Herndon II (1889–1944)

Carrie Hennie Herndon (1890–1974)

THE HANKERSON-McNEIL FAMILY

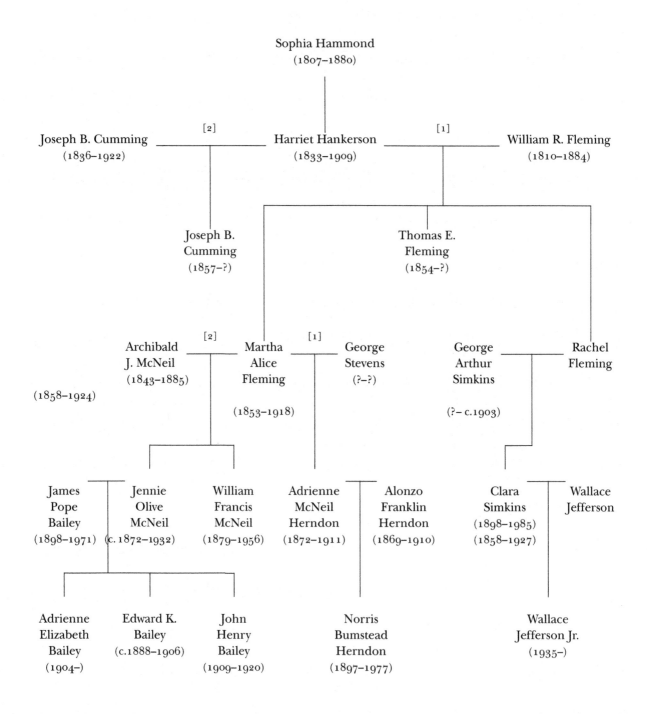

THE GILLESPIE FAMILY

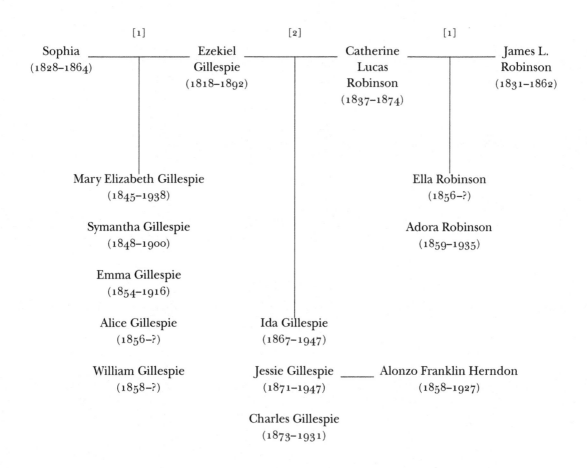

[1]

Sophia
(1828–1864)

Ezekiel
Gillespie
(1818–1892)

[2]

Catherine
Lucas
Robinson
(1837–1874)

[1]

James L.
Robinson
(1831–1862)

Mary Elizabeth Gillespie
(1845–1938)

Ella Robinson
(1856–?)

Symantha Gillespie
(1848–1900)

Adora Robinson
(1859–1935)

Emma Gillespie
(1854–1916)

Alice Gillespie
(1856–?)

Ida Gillespie
(1867–1947)

William Gillespie
(1858–?)

Jessie Gillespie _____ Alonzo Franklin Herndon
(1871–1947)   (1858–1927)

Charles Gillespie
(1873–1931)

Notes

Abbreviations

AHS   Atlanta Historical Society, Atlanta, Georgia

ALCF   Atlanta Life Insurance Company Files, Atlanta, Georgia

AUCA   Atlanta University Center Archives and Special Collections, Robert W. Woodruff Library, Atlanta, Georgia

HFP   Herndon Family Papers, Herndon Home, Atlanta, Georgia

FBCR   Fellowship Baptist Church Records, in possession of
        Lena Williams of Atlanta, Georgia

GDAH   Georgia Department of Archives and History, Atlanta, Georgia

GHS   Georgia Historical Society, Savannah, Georgia

1. Homecoming

1. Cora Upshaw Herndon to Norris B. Herndon, 30 March 1969, HFP.

2. Ibid.

3. Ibid.

4. Interview with Girtha Cooper Patrick, Atlanta, 22 August 1985; interview with Tommie Johnson, Atlanta, 8 May 1995.

5. Alonzo Herndon, autobiographical statement, HFP.

6. Ibid.

7. See Eugene M. Martin, "Characters and Conditions That Created the Herndon Foundation," in *Atlanta Life Insurance Company Manual of Instructions,* undated, HFP, for the story of Herndon's beatings during slavery; also Herndon, autobiographical statement for his mother's work and earnings, HFP.

8. The identification of Frank Herndon as Alonzo Herndon's father was

determined in interviews with Homer Perry, Atlanta, 28 August 1983, and 15 September 1983, and confirmed in a telephone interview with Perry on 12 June 1987. Elizabeth M. Protsman also confirmed by telephone on 30 September 1988 and in an interview on 13 May 1999, Atlanta, that her great-great-grandfather Frank Herndon was the father of Alonzo Herndon. For Frank Herndon's economic status, see the Walton County, Georgia, Tax Digest for the Social Circle District, 1859, p. 50, GDAH. The genealogy of the White Herndons is compiled in Ruth Herndon Shields, *The Descendants of William and Sarah (Poe) Herndon of Caroline County, Va., and Chatham County, N.C.* (Privately printed, 1956), 126, 127.

9. Interview with Bessie Vaughn Rodd, Cincinnati, 26 December 1983.

10. Patrick, interviews, 22 and 27 August 1985.

11. Ibid.

12. Ibid.; Rodd, interview; interview with Magnolia Sleet, Cincinnati, 26 December 1983; interview with Lena Williams, Atlanta, 18 January 2000.

13. Interview with Annie Lou Reeves, Social Circle, Georgia, 16 December 1983; interview by telephone with Lessie Herndon Hill, Atlanta, 9 April 1996; family history statement written in the 1950s by Florence Herndon Lynch, in the possession of Florence McGehee of Detroit, Michigan.

14. Interview by telephone with Mamie Knox Davis, Cincinnati, 12 May 1995.

15. On 29 November 1873, a few years after Fellowship Baptist Church was built, Merriman Herndon sold to the church for ten dollars a half acre of land on Rocky Fork Creek with the stipulation that the land and premises be used only for a church. See Walton County, Georgia, Superior Court Deed Records, Book V, p. 315, GDAH. See Walton County, Georgia, Superior Court Deed Records, Book E, p. 287, GDAH, for the sale of the adjoining half acre for fifteen dollars by Frank Herndon on 18 October 1897.

16. Protsman, interview; photograph of Sophenie, Alonzo, and Thomas Herndon; Herndon, autobiographical statement, HFP.

17. U.S. Census, Population Schedule 1, 1870, Walton County, Georgia, Social Circle District, p. 2, microfilm, GDAH. See Herbert Gutman, *The Black Family in Slavery and Freedom, 1750–1925* (New York: Pantheon, 1976), 230–56, for a discussion of slave surnames; see 207–9 and 402–12 for the practice of apprenticeship of children following Emancipation.

18. "Fellowship Community Club Bulletin," 1978, HFP, contains a brief history of the church. See also the Fellowship Baptist Church minutes and membership roster for 1904, FBCR.

19. Membership roll and minutes, 27 January 1900, FBCR.

20. See Shields, The Descendants, 128. See also the will of Frank M. Herndon, Walton County, Georgia Ordinary Court Estate Records, 20 July 1903, Book A, p. 114, microfilm, GDAH. The comparison of the wealth of Frank and Alonzo Herndon is based on the Walton County, Georgia, Tax Digest for the Social Circle District, 1905, p. 102, GDAH, and the Fulton County, Georgia, Tax Digest Colored Returns, 1905, p. 22, GDAH.

2. Adrienne's Debut

1. Interview of Helen Martin by Alexa Henderson, Atlanta, 27 May 1981.

2. "Life Work Opens for Southern Woman," *Boston Traveler,* 25 January 1904.

3. Henry Austin Clapp to David Belasco, Boston, 16 December 1903, HFP; David Belasco to Anne Du Bignon, New York, 8 January 1904, HFP.

4. *Boston Evening Transcript,* 29 January 1904; *Boston Globe,* 29 January 1904.

5. "Miss Du Bignon Reads Cleopatra," *Boston Herald,* 29 January 1904.

6. "Antony and Cleopatra," *Boston Daily Advertiser,* 29 January 1904.

7. *Boston Courier, Boston Daily Advertiser, Boston Evening Transcript, Boston Globe, Boston Herald, Boston Journal, Boston Post, Boston Times, Boston Transcript, Cambridge Press,* and the *Dorchester Beacon.*

8. "Music and Drama," *Boston Transcript,* 23 January 1904.

9. *Boston Herald,* 29 January 1904; "Recites the Difficult 'Antony and Cleopatra,'" *Beacon Journal,* 30 January 1904.

10. *Boston Traveler,* 25 January 1904.

11. U.S. Census, Population Schedule I, 1870, Richmond County, Georgia, Ward 4, p. 72, microfilm, GDAH; McNeil family Bible, HFP; *Augusta City Directory,* 1877, Augusta College, Augusta, Georgia; copy of death certificate for Harriet Hankerson, 8 February 1909, HFP; photograph of Thomas Fleming, HFP.

12. Interview by telephone with Kathy Belcher Beckwith, Washington, D.C., summer 1988. George Stevens had a sister, Jane, whose family maintained ties with Martha McNeil and the Herndons.

13. U.S. Census, Population Schedule I, 1880, Chatham County, Georgia, Savannah, p. 19, microfilm, GDAH.

14. Barbershop ledger, January 1904, HFP; *Boston Evening Transcript,* 29 January 1904.

15. Minutes of Board of Directors, Atlanta Life, 28 October 1925, ALCF.

16. Horace Bumstead to Adrienne Herndon, Boston, 20 January 1904, HFP.

17. Anna Curry to Alonzo Herndon, Boston, 8 September 1901, HFP.

18. Invitation of Samuel and Anna Curry to Adrienne Herndon, Boston, 29 December 1903, HFP.

19. George Britt to Anne Du Bignon, Boston, 9 February 1904, HFP.

20. Receipts of B. J. Stetson & Company, 19, 22, 30 January 1904, and 16 February 1904, HFP.

21. Annual Catalogue, School of Expression, 1901–2, p. 31, HFP.

22. Invoice of Steinert Hall, 3 February 1904, HFP; notebook of Adrienne Herndon, HFP.

23. W. E. B. Du Bois, ed., *The Negro American Family*, Atlanta University Publications, no. 13 (Atlanta: Atlanta University Press, 1908), 114.

24. *Boston Traveler,* 25 January 1904.

25. Notes Adrienne had prepared apparently for an interview with the *Boston Traveler,* c. 1904, HFP.

26. *Atlanta Journal,* 16 May 1922.

27. *Boston Traveler,* 25 January 1904.

28. Ibid.

29. Janet Owen to Adrienne Herndon, Boston, 9 July 1904, HFP; List of Organizations, HFP.

30. Percy Jordan to Anne Du Bignon, New York, 22 January 1904 and 27 December 1904, HFP.

31. Program of *The Merchant of Venice,* Atlanta University, 29 May 1905, HFP; playbill, 5 May 1905, HFP.

32. David Belasco to Anne Du Bignon, New York, 20 January 1905, HFP.

3. Alonzo's Debut

1. U.S. Census, Population Schedule, 1880, Clayton County, Georgia, Table 3, (Washington, D.C.: Government Printing Office, 1880), p. 121; U.S. Census, Population Schedule, 1880, Walton County, Georgia, Table 3 (Washington, D.C.: Government Printing Office, 1880), p. 128.

2. The information on Anthony Battle was contained in an unidentified and undated publication reproduced for the Old Jail House Museum in Jonesboro, Georgia. Nelson Smith, the barber, was identified in Doris F. Curry, *Abstracts of Clayton County, Georgia, 1870 Census* (N.p., 1978), 126–28;

Herndon, autobiographical statement, HFP; Imperial Council of the Ancient Arabic Order, Nobles of the Mystic Shrine for North America, *Official Souvenir Guide,* Atlanta, Georgia, 1914, 135, HFP.

3. Minutes of Board of Directors, Atlanta Life, 18 October 1925, ALCF.

4. Herndon, autobiographical statement, HFP; see also Herndon's testimony about his arrival date in Atlanta in *Atlanta Loan and Trust Company v. Alonzo Herndon,* Fulton County Superior Court, no. 11, 154, volume 2, 441, HFP; U.S. Census, Population Schedule, 1880, Fulton County, Georgia, Table 3 (Washington, D.C.: Government Printing Office, 1880), p. 123.

5. Herndon, autobiographical statement, HFP; *Atlanta City Directory,* 1859, AHS.

6. *Atlanta City Directory,* 1882, AHS.

7. Herndon, autobiographical statement, HFP.

8. Ibid.; *Atlanta City Directory,* 1883, 1884, 1885, AHS.

9. *Atlanta City Directory,* 1885, AHS.

10. Fulton County, Georgia, Tax Digest, 1890, GDAH; *Atlanta City Directory,* 1886, 1887, AHS. Tate, an ex-slave, was Atlanta's first Black businessman, whose grocery catered mostly to Whites. In 1865 he and Gradison B. Daniels (also an ex-slave) founded the city's first Black school, the Jenkins Street School.

11. *Atlanta City Directory,* 1886, AHS. James R. Steele was the son of Carrie Steele, a stewardess at the Atlanta train depot. In 1888 she founded the Carrie Steele Orphanage, which Herndon generously supported.

12. *Atlanta City Directory,* 1888, AHS.

13. *Atlanta City Directory,* 1885–90, AHS.

14. Herndon, autobiographical statement, HFP.

15. Advertisement, *Kennesaw Route Gazette,* December 1875, AHS.

16. *Atlanta City Directory,* 1859–60, p. 65, AHS; address by Joe Crocy, *Southern Hotel Journal,* June 1946, AHS.

17. Sanborn Fire Insurance Map, c. 1895, AHS; photograph of Markham House, c. 1895, AHS; photograph of Markham House Barbershop, c. 1895, HFP.

18. *Atlanta Constitution,* 19 May 1896; leases between Charles Beerman and Company and Alonzo Herndon, 22 August 1889 and 15 May 1891, HFP.

19. Photograph of Markham House Barbershop, c. 1895, HFP.

20. Interview with Albert Edwards, Atlanta, 21 May 1985.

21. Charles A. Faison, "My Friend and Business Associate," *The Vision,* July 1928, 11, ALCF.

22. Photograph of Markham House Barbershop, c. 1895, HFP.

23. Sanborn Fire Insurance Map, c. 1895, AHS; Edward R. Carter, *The Black Side: A Partial History of the Business, Religious, and Educational Side of the Negro in Atlanta, Ga.* (Atlanta, 1894), 27.

24. Herndon, autobiographical statement, HFP.

25. First Congregational Church Directory, First Congregational Church Records, Auburn Avenue Research Library on African-American Culture and History (Atlanta–Fulton County Public Library System), Atlanta, Georgia.

26. Martin, interview; see also "The First Congregational Church of Atlanta," n.p., n.d., p. 19, HFP.

27. For a discussion of the American Missionary Association and the teachers that served the freedmen, see Jacqueline Jones, *Soldiers of Light and Love: Northern Teachers and Georgia Blacks, 1865–1873* (Chapel Hill: University of North Carolina Press, 1980), 14–48.

28. Herndon, autobiographical statement, HFP; Faison, "My Friend."

29. Fulton County, Georgia, Tax Digest, Colored Returns, 1890, GDAH.

30. Rodd, interview.

31. Interview with Rose Martin Palmer, Atlanta, 12 September 1997.

32. *Atlanta City Directory*, 1886–92, AHS; rental property account, Sharp-Boylston and Day, 9 February 1915, HFP.

33. *Atlanta Constitution*, 18 May 1996.

34. Ibid.

35. *Atlanta City Directory*, 1898, AHS; lease with Robert Dohme, 19 May 1897, HFP.

36. Barbershop ledger, 1902, HFP.

37. Telephone interview with Albert Daniel, Atlanta, 8 August 1990.

38. Barbershop ledger, 1902, HFP.

39. Fulton County, Georgia, Tax Digest, Colored Returns, 1910, GDAH.

40. *Atlanta Constitution*, 10 and 13 December 1902; barbershop ledger, 1902, HFP.

4. Diamond Hill

1. See the *Atlanta City Directory*, 1878, 1884, 1895, AHS. With money from her father, Norris entered Oberlin College in Ohio as a slave in 1859, but was forced to make it on her own after the outbreak of the Civil War. She graduated a free woman in the college class of 1864. See copies of selected pages from the *Catalogue of Oberlin College*, 1863–64, HFP; Alumni File, 1899,

1911–12, 1936, HFP; copy of letter from M. B. Lukens to Mr. Harkness, 15 October 1912, Oberlin College Archives, HFP; see Myron W. Adams, *A History of Atlanta University* (Atlanta: Atlanta University Press, 1930), 84. The 1900 Fulton County Tax Digest assessed Norris's real and personal property at $6,000. For a detailed discussion of the founding of Storrs School and Atlanta University see Adams, *A History*, 1–9, and Clarence A. Bacote, *The Story of Atlanta University: A Century of Service, 1865–1965* (Atlanta: Atlanta University Press, 1969), 3–45. Alonzo may have first met Norris through Page Norris, apparently her brother, who had barbered with him in the Hutchins and Betts partnerships. Norris would have known Adrienne's family through her half sister Alice Miller, an early graduate of Atlanta University, who had taught Adrienne at the West Broad Street Public School in Savannah. See *Atlanta City Directory*, 1884, 1888, AHS, for information on Page Norris.

2. Sanborn Fire Insurance Map, 1892, AHS; *Atlanta City Directory*, 1893, AHS; *Savannah City Directory*, 1886, 1889, 1890, 1894, GHS.

3. See Willard P. Gatewood, *Aristocrats of Color: The Black Elite, 1880–1920* (Bloomington: Indiana University Press, 1990), chapter 6, for a review of the literature and a discussion of the significance of color among the Black upper class.

4. Adams, *A History*, 11, 12.

5. *Georgia House Journal*, 422, cited in Adams, *A History*, 26. The $8,000 was a voluntary contribution of the state treasury in place of any claim by Blacks to Georgia's federal allocation for agricultural education as provided by the Morrill Act of 1861.

6. Interview with Kathleen Adams, Atlanta, 29 July 1983.

7. Adams, *A History*, 14. The Bumstead Cottage was built by 1885. President Edmund Asa Ware died there that year on September 25, having collapsed nearby on Vine Street.

8. The information on Norris's kinship with Miller was obtained in interviews with Adams, 27 and 29 July 1983.

9. *Savannah City Directory*, 1879, GHS; burial register, Laurel Grove Cemetery, 26 June 1885, Savannah, Georgia; James H. C. Butler to Horace Bumstead, Savannah, 8 November 1886, Series 1, 1863–1961, Box 20, Folder 6, Addie [Adrienne] McNeil, AUCA; James H. C. Butler to Thomas Chase, Savannah, 7 December 1886, AUCA.

10. Adrienne McNeil to Horace Bumstead, Greensboro, Georgia, 13 September 1889, Series 2, 1836–1966, Correspondence Routine, Box 22, Folder 1, AUCA.

11. William H. Crogman, *Progress of a Race* (Atlanta: J. L. Nichols and Co., 1898), 392–93.

12. *Bulletin of Atlanta University,* no. 199, April 1910, 2, AUCA.

13. Adams, interview, 27 July 1983.

14. *Baby's Book,* illustrated by Frances Brundage, c. 1898, HFP; *Atlanta City Directory,* 1897, AHS.

15. *Baby's Book,* HFP; Adams, interview, 27 July 1983.

16. Photograph, HFP; *Baby's Book,* HFP.

17. *Baby's Book,* HFP.

18. Adrienne Herndon to Norris Herndon, Paris, 1900, HFP; S. Johnson to Norris Herndon, Jersey City, New Jersey, 5 February 1911, HFP; note of Jennie Bailey to Norris Herndon, New York City, c. 1950, HFP.

19. Adams, interview, 29 July 1983.

20. Adrienne Herndon to Norris Herndon, Boston, date unknown, HFP; Adrienne Herndon to Norris Herndon, Venice, 15 July 1900, HFP.

21. *Baby's Book,* HFP.

22. Adams, interview, 29 July 1983.

23. *Baby's Book,* HFP; Promotion Record of Oglethorpe School, 1906, HFP; report cards of Mitchell Street School, 1908–12, HFP.

24. The house occupied a portion of the northeast lot, originally a nine-acre parcel purchased in 1870 for $2,700 from John Collier by Edmund Asa Ware, the first president of Atlanta University, and by Erastus M. Cravath, one of the first trustees who became president of Fisk University. The lot eventually came under Atlanta University ownership. See Adams, *A History,* 79–81. Square footage was estimated from the 1911 Sanborn Fire Insurance Map, AHS.

25. Photographs of the Bumstead Cottage interior, c. 1900, HFP; piano receipt, 1893, HFP.

26. U.S. Census, Population Schedule 1, 1900, Fulton County, Georgia, Atlanta City Division, p. 99, microfilm, GDAH; interview with Bazoline Usher, Atlanta, 5 March 1986.

27. Leroy Davis, *A Clashing of the Soul: John Hope and the Dilemma of African American Leadership and Black Higher Education* (Athens: University of Georgia Press, 1998), 174.

28. Interview with Grace Hamilton, Atlanta, 16 March 1987; Edward T. Ware to Alonzo F. Herndon, Atlanta, 25 October 1916, HFP; Alonzo Herndon to E. T. Ware, Atlanta, 24 October 1919, HFP.

29. Speech of Alonzo Herndon at Atlanta Life managers conference, Atlanta, January 1924, ALCF.

30. *Atlanta City Directory,* 1907, AHS; Patrick, interview, 22 August 1985; Rodd, interview; interview with Julius Cooper, Monroe, Georgia, 31 August 1985; Martha McNeil to Norris Herndon, Augusta, 1 April 1914, HFP; interview with Norris Connally, Atlanta, summer 1998.

31. Rental income report of Sharp-Boylston and Day, 9 February 1915, HFP.

5. *Unity in Division*

1. O. E. Carter, *The Trolley Titans: A Mobile History of Atlanta* (Glendale, Calif.: Interurban Press, 1981), 60; Adams, *A History,* 78, 84; Alonzo Herndon to Jessie Gillespie, Atlanta, December 1911, HFP.

2. *Atlanta City Directory,* 1899, AHS.

3. *Atlanta Journal,* 14 May 1905.

4. See John Hammond Moore, "Jim Crow in Georgia," *South Atlantic Quarterly,* 66 (fall 1967), 554–65. By the end of the nineteenth century, most Blacks had been effectively disfranchised by the cumulative poll tax, which required payment of all back poll taxes before voting. For many Black men, however, in cities like Atlanta, where they had voted regularly, the Democratic party's exclusion of Blacks from the primary effectively nullified voting power in the general election. White Democratic candidates generally had no opponents. Nevertheless, political conflict increasingly focused on race and the issue of Black disfranchisement. In 1908, in spite of petitions to the Georgia legislature in opposition to disfranchisement, a constitutional amendment was ratified, establishing additional voting qualifications that further ensured Black disfranchisement. Alonzo Herndon had been among those who petitioned the state legislature unsuccessfully to defeat the proposed amendment. See also the chapter on racial politics in John Dittmer, *Black Georgia in the Progressive Era, 1900–1920* (Urbana: University of Illinois Press, 1977), 90–104.

5. *Atlanta Constitution,* 4–6 February 1905; barbershop ledger, February 1905, HFP.

6. Photograph, 1905, HFP; Thomas Herndon to Alonzo Herndon, March 1905, HFP; *Henry County, Georgia, Obituaries, 1900–1907,* extracted from the *Henry County Weekly,* microfilmed newspapers, 1900–1907 (Roswell, Ga.: W. H. Wolfe Associates, 1994), 229.

7. For a discussion of the founding of the Niagara Movement and its participants, see David Levering Lewis, *W. E. B. Du Bois: Autobiography of a Race, 1868–1919* (New York: Henry Holt and Co., 1993), 315–22.

8. Louis Harlan, ed., *The Booker T. Washington Papers: Vol. 4, 1895–98* (Urbana: University of Illinois Press, 1979), 26.

9. Herndon, autobiographical statement, HFP.

10. Flyer, 5 May 1905, HFP.

11. Lewis, *W. E. B. Du Bois,* 84, 97, 320.

12. Alonzo Herndon to Martha McNeil, Niagara Falls, Canada, 14 July 1905, HFP; Adrienne Herndon to Martha McNeil, Toronto, Canada, 18 July 1905, HFP.

13. Alexa Henderson, *Atlanta Life Insurance Company: Guardian of Black Economic Dignity* (Tuscaloosa: University of Alabama Press, 1990), 3–5, 13.

14. Ibid., 17, 44.

15. W. E. B. Du Bois, "Postscript by W. E. B. Du Bois," *Crisis* 34 (September 1927): 239.

16. Henderson, *Atlanta Life,* 17.

17. *Atlanta Age,* 30 September 1905, HFP.

18. Melville J. Herskovits, *The Myth of the Negro Past* (New York: Harper and Bros., 1941), 162–67.

19. Henderson, *Atlanta Life,* 19.

20. Some White insurance providers, however, like the Industrial Life and Health Insurance Company, had mostly Black policyholders. Its cofounder and first president, John N. MacEachern, had shaped much of Georgia's insurance regulations. His support of the 1905 law suggested that his motive in part may have been to eliminate Black competition. See Henderson, *Atlanta Life,* 12, 14.

21. Minutes of Board of Directors, Atlanta Life, 4 April 1927, p. 248, ALCF.

22. "The NAACP Organized," *Atlanta Independent,* 10 February 1917; application for charter, Atlanta Branch Papers of the NAACP, Correspondence Series A, Library of Congress, microfilm.

23. *Atlanta Age,* 30 September 1906, HFP; Herndon, autobiographical statement, HFP.

24. Henry A. Rucker was President William McKinley's appointee as Collector of Internal Revenue and had substantial real estate. See "History of the Company," *The Vision,* July 1928, ALCF.

25. See *Atlanta Loan and Trust Company and Others v. Alonzo F. Herndon,* Fulton County Superior Court, no. 11, 154, volumes 1 and 2, Georgia, 1910.

26. Henderson, *Atlanta Life,* 51–52.

27. Interview of Robert Chamblee by Alexa Henderson, Atlanta, 13 August 1974; minutes of Board of Directors, Atlanta Life, 3 May 1927, p. 249, ALCF.

28. Chamblee, interview; minutes of Board of Directors, Atlanta Life, 3 May 1927, p. 252, ALCF.

29. Henderson, *Atlanta Life,* 46.

30. Chamblee, interview; Henderson, *Atlanta Life,* 46; minutes of annual meeting, Atlanta Life, 27 January 1926, 214–15, ALCF.

6. All Hell

1. News article "The Atlanta Massacre," from the *Independent,* undated, in 1906 Atlanta Riot files, AHS; *Atlanta Constitution,* 23 September 1906; *Atlanta Evening News,* 22 September 1906.

2. *Atlanta Constitution,* 23 September 1906.

3. Barbershop ledger, September 1906, HFP; Walter White, *A Man Called White: The Autobiography of Walter White* (New York: Viking, 1948), 9; Mary White Ovington, *The Walls Come Tumbling Down* (New York: Harcourt, Brace, 1947), 65; *Atlanta Evening News,* 25 September 1906; Max Barber, "The Atlanta Tragedy," *The Voice* 3 (November 1906): 473.

4. *Atlanta Evening News,* 22 September 1906.

5. *Atlanta Journal,* 23 September 1906.

6. *Atlanta Constitution,* 23 September 1906; Charles Crowe, "Racial Massacre in Atlanta, September 22, 1906," *Journal of Negro History* 54 (April 1969): 155.

7. For recollections of the difficulty Blacks had in obtaining weapons prior to the riot, see Jacqueline Anne Rouse's *Lugenia Burns Hope: Black Southern Reformer* (Athens: University of Georgia Press, 1989), 42, 43. See also information from the interview of Mrs. M. G. Wartman, March 19, 1974, cited in Dittmer, *Black Georgia,* 126. For news accounts of alleged racial assaults before the riot, see *Atlanta Journal,* 1 August 1906; *Atlanta Constitution,* 22 September 1906.

8. *Atlanta Constitution,* 23 September 1906.

9. Crowe, "Racial Massacre," 158; *Atlanta Constitution,* 23 September 1906.

10. *Atlanta Constitution,* 23 September 1906.

11. Ibid.

12. Crowe, "Racial Massacre," 168.

13. Gregory Lamont Mixon, "The Atlanta Riot of 1906" (Ph.D. diss., University of Cincinnati, 1989), 561.

14. *Atlanta Constitution,* 23 September 1906.

15. White, *A Man Called White,* 11.

16. William H. Crogman quoted in Ovington's *The Walls Come Tumbling Down,* 65.

17. Barbershop ledger, 22–30 September 1906, HFP.

18. Barbershop ledger, September 1906, HFP.

19. For an account of the Brownsville incidents, see Mixon, "Atlanta Riot," 607–16.

20. *Atlanta Constitution,* 25 September 1906.

21. Ibid.; Mixon, "Atlanta Riot," 607.

22. *Atlanta Constitution,* 25 September 1906.

23. Ibid.

24. *Atlanta Journal,* 25 September 1906.

25. Ibid.

26. "The Dives Must Go," *Atlanta Constitution,* 17 September 1906.

27. *Atlanta Journal,* 25 September 1906.

28. *Atlanta Constitution,* 23 September 1906.

29. *Atlanta Journal,* 25 September 1906.

30. *Atlanta Constitution,* 23 September 1906.

31. *Atlanta Journal,* 25 September 1906.

7. *A New Home in the Rock*

1. Adrienne Herndon to Booker T. Washington, Atlanta, 12 February 1907, in Louis R. Harlan and Raymond W. Smock, eds., *The Booker T. Washington Papers: Vol. 9, 1906–1908* (Urbana: University of Illinois Press, 1979–80), 216–17.

2. Ibid., 217.

3. *Atlanta City Directory,* 1907, AHS.

4. Jennie Bailey to Norris Herndon, New York, 29 September 1906, HFP; Martha McNeil to Norris Herndon, New York, 1 April 1907, HFP.

5. Warranty deed, Horace Bumstead to Atlanta University, 1 October 1906, AUCA.

6. Barbershop ledger, 1906, HFP; *Atlanta City Directory,* 1906, AHS.

7. Program, "Alumni Prize Speaking," 14 December 1906, HFP.

8. Usher, interview, 5 March 1986.

9. Program, "Dramatic Reading by Adrienne McNeil Herndon," Savannah, 5 April 1907, HFP; program, "The Shadow," Atlanta, 4 May 1903, HFP. "The Shadow" was a tale of a tragic mulatto, someone like Adrienne, caught between

the races. Nambok, an Indian of the Pacific Northwest who has been lost at sea, returns home after a long sojourn among Whites. He is a marginal person, rejected by his tribe for his encounter with Whites, and yet is excluded by the alien race.

10. Unidentified Savannah newspaper, April 1907, HFP; program, "The Herndon Recitation," Chattanooga, 22 April 1907, HFP.

11. Program, 17 March 1906, HFP; *Dorchester Beacon*, 30 January 1904.

12. Playbills, "As You Like It," 5 May 1906, 27 May 1907, HFP.

13. Usher, interview, 10 April 1986.

14. Bond for title, Atlanta University to Alonzo Herndon, 30 May 1907, Atlanta University Presidential Papers, Financial Records, Box 1, Folder 14, AUCA. Herndon made the first payment of $560, leaving the remainder to be paid in four equal installments over the next four years at 6 percent annual interest. The lot was originally part of a nine-and-a-half-acre tract purchased from John Collier in 1870 by Edmund Asa Ware and Erastus Cravath, Atlanta University's founders, and ultimately acquired by the university.

15. Adams, *A History*, 72, 73.

16. Catalog of American Academy of Dramatic Arts, 1907–8, pp. 8, 14, HFP.

17. Envelope of unidentified person to Anne Du Bignon, 9 March 1908, HFP; *Catalogue of the American Academy of the Dramatic Arts, 1907–8*, HFP; programs, "The Girl of the Golden West," "Her Sister," c. October 21, 1907, HFP; "Virginius," "The Hoyden," undated, HFP.

18. *Atlanta City Directory*, 1907, AHS; Sanborn Fire Insurance Map, 1911, AHS.

19. Adrienne Herndon to Norris Herndon, New York City, summer 1907, HFP; Jennie McNeil Bailey to Mattie McNeil, New York City, 10 August 1907, HFP; photographs of Norris in Philadelphia, HFP.

20. Norris Herndon to Adrienne Herndon, Philadelphia, c. 1907, HFP.

21. Adrienne Herndon to Edward T. Ware, Philadelphia, 1908, AUCA.

22. See Antoinette F. Downing and Vincent J. Scully Jr., *The Architectural Heritage of Newport, Rhode Island, 1640–1915*, 2d ed. (New York: American Legacy Press, 1982), 171–75, for an assessment of the impact of the Beaux-Arts style on late-nineteenth-century American architecture. I am grateful to Knox Herndon and his mother, Helen, and to the current owners, Dena Johnston and Bob Bailes, for showing me the Social Circle house and sharing its history.

23. Adams, *A History*, 84.

24. See Michael Leroy Porter, "Black Atlanta: An Interdisciplinary Study of

Blacks on the East Side of Atlanta, 1890–1930" (Ph.D. diss., Emory University, 1974), 244–45. Porter interviewed Cliff Nelms, who had helped to build the main staircase of the home. Nelms confirmed that the carpenter, William Campbell, was a Black man, and that all of the subcontractors for the house were Black, except those for the electrical and plumbing systems. A carpenter named William Campbell was listed in the *Atlanta City Directory* in 1905, 1906, and 1910, but not in 1908 or 1909, when the house was being constructed. He was living in White neighborhoods and was not designated as colored but is presumed to have been a light-skinned Black.

25. Building permit, Atlanta, 1908, AHS; *Bulletin of Atlanta University* (fall 1908): 2, AUCA.

26. Contract with American Academy of the Dramatic Arts, 3 June 1907, HFP.

27. *Morning Telegraph,* 12 March 1908; E. K. Curlee to Anne Du Bignon, Paris, 8 February 1908, HFP.

28. Adrienne Herndon to E. T. Ware, New York, 15 March 1908, AUCA.

29. Adrienne Herndon to Mattie McNeil, Paris, August 1900, HFP; Adrienne Herndon to E. T. Ware, Atlanta, 25 June 1908 and 16 July 1908, AUCA.

30. *Bulletin of Atlanta University* (fall 1908): 2, AUCA; building permit, 12 October 1908, AHS; Atlanta University Trustees Report, 18 June 1908, AUCA.

31. See Ann DeRosa Byrne, "Herndon Mansion Historic Structures Report," c. 1981, HFP, for a description of the style and construction of the house. The bricks were manufactured by Coshocton, a company located in Coshocton, Ohio. I am grateful to Linda Yoder of the Coshocton Library for providing information on the brick company from the Coshocton City Directory and for sharing information on the soils of the area from the *Centennial History of Coshocton County, Ohio,* vol. 1 by William J. Bahmer, 1909. The masonry was done by Black men, who were numerically dominant in Georgia and elsewhere in the South. Black men were similarly dominant in plastering, cement finishing, and painting and were prevalent in carpentry. See the U.S. Census, Population Schedule, vol. 4, 1910, Atlanta, Table 8 (Washington, D.C.: Government Printing Office, 1910), 536.

32. Adrienne's notes from 1905 identified the Monmouth house as the property of Mr. Chamberlain and Miss Maybel Wutherall, HFP.

33. Maxwell Keith, *Beautiful Interiors,* c. 1905, HFP.

34. A clipping titled "The Whitney Residence at Newport," by B. F. Thurston, from an unidentified and undated magazine, HFP.

35. Interview with Jan Jennings, Atlanta, 16 February 1989. See also Jennings's essay "The Aesthetics of Everyday Interiors" in *The Interiors Handbook for Historic Buildings,* ed. Charles E. Fisher, Michael Auer, and Anne Grimmer (Washington, D.C.: Historic Preservation Education Foundation, 1988).

36. W. E. B. Du Bois to Alonzo Herndon, Atlanta, 17 and 20 December 1909, W. E. B. Du Bois Papers, University of Massachusetts, Amherst, microfilm.

37. Ida Knox to Alonzo Herndon, Social Circle, Georgia, 15 July 1908, HFP.

38. Du Bois, *The Negro American Family,* 81, 96; building permit, Atlanta, 16 July 1908, AHS.

39. Alonzo Herndon to E. T. Ware, 24 July 1909, AUCA.

40. Adrienne Herndon to Julia Fambro, New York, 24 September 1909, HFP.

41. Adrienne Herndon to Jennie Bailey, Atlanta, 22 December 1909, HFP; building permit, 18 January 1910, AHS.

8. An Untimely Death

1. Henry Bailey to Norris Herndon, New York, 31 December 1909, HFP; speech of Truman Gibson, Atlanta, June 1960, HFP.

2. Norris Herndon to Adrienne Herndon, 16 March 1910, HFP.

3. Annadel to Mattie McNeil, Jacksonville, Florida, 25 March 1910, HFP.

4. *Bulletin of Atlanta University,* April 1910.

5. John Stewart to Alonzo Herndon, Indian Springs, Georgia, 29 March 1910, HFP.

6. Playbill, "Everyman," 5 April 1909, HFP; Patrick, interview, 22 August 1985; death certificate, Atlanta, 7 April 1910, HFP.

7. Photograph, April 1910, HFP.

8. Alonzo Herndon to Jessie Gillespie, Atlanta, 6 November 1911, HFP; *Bulletin of Atlanta University,* April 1910, p. 2.

9. *Bulletin of Atlanta University,* April 1910, p. 3.

10. Interview with Albert Watts, Atlanta, 19 June 1998.

11. Norris Herndon to Martha McNeil, Atlanta, 16 March 1911, HFP.

12. Alonzo Herndon to Norris Herndon, New York City, 27 October 1910, HFP.

13. Alonzo Herndon to Martha McNeil, Mantazas, Cuba, 21 January 1911, HFP; Alonzo Herndon to Norris Herndon, Havana, 25 January 1911, HFP.

14. Norris Herndon to Alonzo Herndon, Philadelphia, 1 April 1911, HFP.

9. The Dearest Sweetheart

1. Theodosia Hall to Alonzo Herndon, April 1909, HFP; Gatewood, *Aristocrats of Color*, 122.

2. Loring Palmer to Jessie Gillespie, Glasgow, Berlin, Dresden, and Versailles, 1 July to 10 August 1907, HFP.

3. *Indianapolis Freeman*, 30 July 1910 and 20 August 1910, cited in Gatewood, *Aristocrats of Color*, 201.

4. Alonzo Herndon to Mary and Emma Gillespie, Atlanta, 25 April 1912, HFP.

5. Alonzo Herndon to Jessie Gillespie, Atlanta, 20 November 1911, HFP.

6. Ezekiel Gillespie had begun in business, first peddling small goods in Indiana and then selling groceries on the corner of Mason and Main streets in Milwaukee. By the 1850s he had become a railroad messenger for the Milwaukee and St. Paul Railway Company. Gillespie was refused registration and the ballot for a governor's election in 1865. With the support of the *Evening Wisconsin,* a Milwaukee paper, and others, he brought suit against the board of elections in *Gillespie v. Palmer.* The state supreme court decided unanimously that based on an 1849 referendum Blacks had the right to register and vote. For information on Gillespie's background and his civil rights activities, see John O. Holzhueter, "Ezekiel Gillespie, Lost and Found," *Wisconsin Magazine of History* 60 (spring 1977): 179–84.

7. Alonzo Herndon to Jessie Gillespie, Atlanta, c. December 1911, HFP.

8. Ibid.

9. Anita Burden to the Herndon Home, Lima, Ohio, 6 April 1995, HFP; Holzhueter, "Ezekiel Gillespie," 181. Five children were born to Ezekiel and his first wife, Sophia, who died in 1864, and two children were from Catherine Lucas's marriage to James Robinson, who died in 1862.

10. Alonzo Herndon to Jessie Gillespie, Atlanta, 25 October 1911, HFP.

11. Alonzo Herndon to Jessie Gillespie, Atlanta, 20 November 1911, HFP; Alonzo Herndon to Norris Herndon, Cincinnati, 2 January 1912, HFP.

12. Alonzo Herndon to Emma Gillespie, Atlanta, 10 April 1912, HFP.

13. Alonzo Herndon to Jessie Gillespie, 12 January 1912, HFP.

14. Alonzo Herndon to Mary Gillespie, Atlanta, 25 April, 1912, HFP.

15. Journal of Norris Herndon, 27 May 1912, HFP; *Atlanta Constitution*, 28 May 1912; *Chicago Defender*, 8 June 1912.

16. Journal of Norris Herndon, 30 May 1912, HFP.

17. Alonzo Herndon to Jessie Gillespie, Atlanta, 20 November 1911, HFP.

18. Norris Herndon to Martha McNeil, Toronto, 1 June 1912, HFP.

19. Norris Herndon to Martha McNeil, Chicago, 31 May 1912, HFP.

20. Norris Herndon to Martha McNeil, Milan, 9 July 1912, HFP.

21. Ibid.

22. Ibid.

23. Ibid.

24. Ibid.; Alonzo Herndon to Martha McNeil, Baden-Baden, Germany, 21 July 1912, HFP.

25. Norris Herndon to Martha McNeil, Milan, 9 July 1912, HFP; Alonzo Herndon to Martha McNeil, Baden-Baden, Germany, 21 July 1912, HFP.

26. Alonzo Herndon to Martha McNeil, Baden-Baden, Germany, 21 July 1912, HFP.

27. Florence Berry to Martha McNeil, Atlanta, 9 July 1912, HFP.

28. Journal of Norris Herndon, 15 July 1912, HFP. The sandstone carving of a dying lion memorializes the Swiss guards killed in Paris in 1792 as they fought to protect Marie Antoinette.

29. Alonzo Herndon to Martha McNeil, Baden-Baden, Germany, 21 July 1912, HFP.

30. Journal of Norris Herndon, 25 July 1912, HFP.

31. Journal of Norris Herndon, 31 July 1912, HFP.

32. Journal of Norris Herndon, 1–4 August 1912, HFP.

33. Journal of Norris Herndon, 8 August 1912, HFP.

34. Journal of Norris Herndon, 10–14 August 1912, HFP.

35. Journal of Norris Herndon, 15 August 1912, HFP.

36. John Hope to Lugenia Hope, Leeds, England, 10 July 1912, John Hope Papers, AUCA, microfilm.

37. Journal of Norris Herndon, 20 August 1912, HFP.

38. Norris Herndon to Martha McNeil, Liverpool, England, 24 August 1912, HFP.

10. To the Top

1. Lease for 66 Peachtree Street, 25 March 1907, HFP.

2. *Atlanta Constitution*, 25 May 1913.

3. Ibid.

4. Ibid.

5. Daniel, interview.

6. *Atlanta Constitution,* 25 May 1913.

7. Daniel, interview; *Atlanta Constitution,* 25 May 1913.

8. *Atlanta Constitution,* 25 May 1913.

9. Herndon, autobiographical statement, HFP.

10. In a speech to Atlanta University alumni in June 1960, Gibson described Adrienne's influence on his life. He recalled that she had first wanted him upon his graduation to join her in the development of "a chain of theaters in Savannah, Atlanta and Nashville for the creative growth and cultural development of our people."

11. Henderson, *Atlanta Life,* 58.

12. Ibid., 58–60.

13. *Atlanta Independent,* 20 December 1913.

14. Ibid.

15. Emmett Scott to Alonzo Herndon, Tuskegee, 11 January 1915, Booker T. Washington Papers, Library of Congress, Washington, D.C. (hereafter cited as BTWP); Alonzo Herndon to Emmett Scott, Lane Park, Florida, 18 January 1915, BTWP. For an account of Perry's decline, see Henderson, *Atlanta Life,* 101–2.

16. Henderson, *Atlanta Life,* 60–61, 71.

17. "Floral Design for Booker T. Washington," list of honorary pallbearers, BTWP, microfilm.

18. Henderson, *Atlanta Life,* 66, 67.

19. Alonzo Herndon to Norris Herndon, Hot Springs, Arkansas, 20 April 1918, HFP.

20. Speech of Alonzo Herndon, Atlanta, January 1924, HFP.

11. A Home of Her Own

1. Notebook of Adrienne Herndon, 1905, HFP.

2. Fulton County, Georgia, Tax Digest, Colored Returns, 1912, GDAH.

3. Alonzo Herndon to Jessie Gillespie, Atlanta, 12 January 1912, HFP.

4. Alonzo Herndon to Florence Berry, Boston, 15 December 1910, HFP; *Atlanta City Directory,* 1910, AHS.

5. Holzhueter, "Ezekiel Gillespie," 181; Alonzo Herndon to Jessie Gillespie, Atlanta, December 1911, HFP; Rodd, interview.

6. Milwaukee County Historical Society to the Herndon Home, Milwaukee, Wisconsin, 21 January 1992, HFP.

7. Alonzo Herndon to Emma Gillespie, Atlanta, 10 April 1912, HFP.

8. Holzhueter, "Ezekiel Gillespie," 181, 183.

9. Deed, Lake County, Florida, 4 February 1914, HFP; interview with Rodd, telephone, 30 April 1987.

10. Jessie Herndon to Norris Herndon, Lane Park, Florida, 4 December 1914, HFP.

11. Ibid.

12. Martha McNeil to Norris Herndon, New York City, 11 July 1913, HFP.

13. Ibid.; Martha McNeil to Norris Herndon, New York City, 18 January 1915, HFP.

14. Martha McNeil to Alonzo Herndon, New York City, 22 December 1915, HFP.

15. Alonzo Herndon to Norris Herndon, Lane Park, Florida, 24 January 1916, HFP.

16. Jessie Herndon to Norris Herndon, Lane Park, Florida, 20 January 1916, HFP; Alonzo Herndon to Norris Herndon, Lane Park, Florida, 24 January 1916, HFP.

17. Jessie Herndon to Norris Herndon, Lane Park, Florida, 14 February 1916, HFP; Alonzo Herndon to Norris Herndon, Lane Park, Florida, 18 February 1916, HFP.

18. Alonzo Herndon to Emma Gillespie, Atlanta, 10 April 1912, HFP; Alonzo Herndon to Norris Herndon, Lane Park, Florida, 23 February and 2 March 1916, HFP.

12. The Next Generation

1. Alonzo Herndon to Norris Herndon, Little Rock, Arkansas, 13 April 1918, HFP.

2. Caroline M. Stevens to Norris Herndon, New York City, 23 April 1918, HFP.

3. Alonzo Herndon to Norris Herndon, Little Rock, Arkansas, 13 April 1918, HFP.

4. Ibid.; Alonzo Herndon to Norris Herndon, Atlanta, 1 July 1917, HFP.

5. Alonzo Herndon to Jessie Gillespie, Atlanta, December 1911, HFP; Alonzo Herndon to Norris Herndon, Lane Park, Florida, 14 January 1916, HFP; Alonzo Herndon to Norris Herndon, Lane Park, Florida, 5 January 1916, HFP.

6. Alonzo Herndon to Norris Herndon, Lane Park, Florida, 11 December 1914, HFP.

7. Jessie Herndon to Norris Herndon, Lane Park, Florida, 1 February 1916, HFP.

8. Alonzo Herndon to Norris Herndon, Hot Springs, Arkansas, 25 April 1918, HFP; Alonzo Herndon to Norris Herndon, Lane Park, Florida, 13 January 1916, HFP.

9. Report card, Atlanta University, 1917, HFP; Alonzo Herndon to Norris Herndon, Lane Park, Florida, 27 February 1917, HFP.

10. Alonzo Herndon to Norris Herndon, Lane Park, Florida, 27 February 1917, HFP.

11. Alonzo Herndon to Norris Herndon, Lane Park, Florida, 5 March 1917, HFP. Florence was apparently in Florida cooking for the Herndons. About one year later and less than two months after Martha's death, Florence died. Girtha Patrick in an interview of 22 August 1985, stated that the cause of her death was peritonitis.

12. Alonzo Herndon to Norris Herndon, Lane Park, Florida, 5 March 1917, HFP.

13. It was common knowledge among Norris's circle of friends and business associates that he was homosexual.

14. Norris Herndon to Martha McNeil, Savannah, 2 July 1917, HFP.

15. Ibid.

16. Alonzo Herndon to Norris Herndon, Atlanta, 1 July 1917, HFP.

17. Henderson, *Atlanta Life,* 77.

18. *Atlanta Independent,* 6 January 1921.

19. Alonzo Herndon to Norris Herndon, Atlanta, 1 July 1917, HFP.

20. *Atlanta Independent,* 30 December 1920.

21. Alonzo Herndon to Mary Gillespie, Tavares, Florida, 7 January 1921, HFP.

22. Another Black student was Benjamin Tanner Johnson of Philadelphia, who had graduated from Howard University. See the *Harvard Directory,* 1921–22, HFP.

23. For a dicussion of Harvard's exclusion of Blacks from freshmen dormitories, see Werner Sollors, Caldwell Titcomb, and Thomas A. Underwood, eds., *Blacks at Harvard: A Documentary History of African-American Experience at Harvard and Radcliffe* (New York: New York University Press, 1993), 195–227.

24. Journal of Norris Herndon, 1917, HFP; Alonzo Herndon to Norris Herndon, Atlanta, 1 July 1917, HFP.

25. Norris Herndon to Alonzo Herndon, Cambridge, Massachusetts, 17 May 1921, HFP.

13. Bearing the Cross

1. George Washington Lee, "Hail to the Memory of the Founder," an address in Atlanta, June 1970, cited in Henderson, *Atlanta Life,* 79.

2. Interview of J. D. Bansley Jr. by Alexa Henderson, January 1975, cited in Henderson, *Atlanta Life,* 79.

3. Henderson, *Atlanta Life,* 80–81.

4. Herndon, autobiographical statement, HFP.

5. Alonzo Herndon to Norris Herndon, Lane Park, Florida, 13 January 1916, HFP; Chamblee, interview; speech of Edwin Thomas at the natal day service of Atlanta Life Insurance Company, 24 June 1988.

6. Jessie Herndon to Norris Herndon, Rochester, Minnesota, 23 April 1922, HFP.

7. Ibid.; Alonzo Herndon to Norris Herndon, Rochester, Minnesota, 23 April 1922, HFP.

8. See Henderson, *Atlanta Life,* 79, 80, for an account of the capitalization of Atlanta Life. Herndon offered a thirty-day stock option for the stockholders to obtain a portion of the new issue.

9. Alonzo Herndon to Norris Herndon, Tavares, Florida, 7 December 1921, HFP.

10. Journal of Norris Herndon, 10 December 1923, 4 July 1923, HFP.

11. Journal of Norris Herndon, January 1921, HFP.

12. Alonzo Herndon to Jessie Herndon, Atlanta, 13 December 1923, HFP.

13. Journal of Norris Herndon, 16–28 December 1923, HFP.

14. George W. Lee, "A Profile of Mrs. Alonzo Franklin Herndon," *The Vision,* March 1969, ALCF; *Atlanta Life Bulletin,* ALCF, 15 November 1924.

15. Howard Walter Russell was the assistant agency director, and James T. Harrison was district manager in Birmingham.

16. Note of Alonzo Herndon attached to his letter from Alonzo Herndon II from New Orleans, 29 April 1916, HFP.

17. A. F. Herndon to O. O. Hamilton, Atlanta, 3 March 1925, HFP.

18. Henderson, *Atlanta Life,* 102; Alonzo Herndon at stockholders meeting, 28 January 1925, ALCF.

19. Alonzo Herndon to Jessie Gillespie, Atlanta, 29 January 1925, HFP.

20. Alonzo Herndon to Jessie Gillespie, Atlanta, 8 February 1925, HFP.

21. Minutes of the Atlanta Life Stockholders Meeting, 27 January 1926, ALCF.

22. Norris Herndon to Jennie Bailey, Atlanta, 4 October 1926, HFP.

23. Alonzo Herndon to Norris Herndon, Tavares, Florida, 16 March 1927, HFP.

24. The funeral, a costly affair at $1,031, was conducted by James C. Chandler and featured more than twenty-four items of songs, remarks, Scripture, prayers, tributes, and resolutions that may have extended beyond two hours.

Selected Bibliography

MANUSCRIPT COLLECTIONS

Atlanta Historical Society, Atlanta, Georgia: *Atlanta City Directory;* Sanborn
  Fire Insurance Maps; Subject Files

Atlanta Life Insurance Company Files, Atlanta, Georgia: *Atlanta Life Bulletin;* Minutes of Board of Directors Meetings; Minutes of Stockholders
  Meetings

Atlanta University Center Archives and Special Collections, Robert W.
  Woodruff Library, Atlanta, Georgia: Atlanta University Papers; *Bulletin of
  Atlanta University;* John Hope Papers

Auburn Avenue Research Library on African-American Culture and History (Atlanta–Fulton County Public Library System), Atlanta, Georgia:
  First Congregational Church Records

Augusta College, Augusta, Georgia: *Augusta City Directory*

Fellowship Baptist Church Records, in the possession of Lena Williams,
  Atlanta, Georgia: Fellowship Baptist Church Minutes and Membership
  Lists; Fellowship Community Club Bulletin

Georgia Department of Archives and History, Atlanta, Georgia: Tax Digests
  for Fulton County and Walton County, Georgia; Superior Court Deeds of
  Fulton County and Walton County, Georgia; Ordinary Court Records of
  Fulton County and Walton County, Georgia; U.S. Bureau of the Census.
  Population Schedules (Microfilm) for Chatham County, Clayton County,
  Fulton County, Richmond County, and Walton County, Georgia

Georgia Historical Society, Savannah, Georgia: *Savannah City Directory*

Herndon Home, Atlanta, Georgia: Atlanta Life Insurance Company Papers;
  Atlanta Loan and Trust Papers; Herndon Family Papers; Rose Martin
  Palmer Family Papers; Fred and Juanita Toomer Papers

Library of Congress, Washington, D.C.: Booker T. Washington Papers;
  NAACP Papers. Microfilm
University of Massachusetts, Amherst, Massachusetts: W. E. B. Du Bois
  Papers. Microfilm

NEWSPAPERS

Atlanta Age, 30 September 1906

Atlanta Constitution, 1896–1927

Atlanta Evening News, 1906

Atlanta Independent

Atlanta Journal

Boston Courier, 1904

Boston Daily Advertiser, 1904

Boston Evening Transcript, 1904

Boston Globe, 1904

Boston Herald, 1904

Boston Journal, 1904

Boston Post, 1904

Boston Times, 1904

Boston Transcript, 1904

Boston Traveler, 1904

Cambridge Press

Chicago Defender, 1912

Crisis, 1920–27

Dorchester Beacon, 1904

(New York City) Morning Telegraph, 1908

INTERVIEWS

Adams, Kathleen. July 1983

Aiken, Lucy Rucker. August 1983. Atlanta, Ga.

Allen, Elsie. April 1993. Atlanta, Ga.

Beavers, Marcus and Vivian. July 1984. Atlanta, Ga.

Beckwith, Kathy Belcher. Summer 1988, Washington, D.C.; July 1992,
  Atlanta, Ga.

Bell, John. May 1985. Atlanta, Ga.

Brown, Henry. November 1944. Atlanta, Ga.

Byrne, Anne. October 1983. Atlanta, Ga.

Collins, Helen. October 1987. Atlanta, Ga.

Cooper, Ann Nixon. September 1992; June 1998; March 1999.
  Atlanta, Ga.

Cooper, Julius. August 1985. Monroe, Ga.

Conn, Helen. February 1987. Atlanta, Ga.

Connally, Norris. October 1992; October 1993; May 1998. Atlanta, Ga.

Cox, Fred Allen. March 1989. Atlanta, Ga.

Daniel, Albert. August 1990. Atlanta, Ga.

Davis, Alpha Allen. August 1988. Atlanta, Ga.

Davis, Mamie Knox. May 1995. Cincinnati, Ohio

Delorme, Grace. May 1985. Atlanta, Ga.

Edwards, Adrienne Bailey. April 1999. Atlanta, Ga.

Edwards, Albert. May 1985. Atlanta, Ga.

Edwards, Norris. April 1999. Atlanta, Ga.

Greer, Josephine. May 1995. Cincinnati, Ohio

Hamilton, Grace. March 1987; July 1988; Atlanta, Ga.

Hannon, Virginia Rose. March 1993. Atlanta, Ga.

Herndon, Helen. September 1995, Atlanta, Ga.; July 1998, Social
    Circle, Ga.

Herndon, Knox. July 1998. Atlanta, Ga.

Hill, Frank. June 1990. Atlanta, Ga.

Hill, Lessie Herndon. April 1996. Atlanta, Ga.

Holmes, Hamilton. August 1994; November 1994. Atlanta, Ga.

Jefferson, Clara. February 1984. New York, N.Y.

Jefferson, Wallace and Serena. January 1991; May 1999. Atlanta, Ga.

Jennings, Jan. February 1989. Atlanta, Ga.

Johnson, Tommie. May 1995. Atlanta, Ga.

Long, Birdie Cox. March 1989. Atlanta, Ga.

Love, Josephine Harreld. April 1984. Atlanta, Ga.

Mapp, Frederick. June 1984. Atlanta, Ga.

McGehee, Florence. July 2000. Atlanta, Ga.

Milton, Eloise. July–December 1983; November 1992. Atlanta, Ga.

Palmer, Rose Martin. January 1991; September 1997. Atlanta, Ga.

Patrick, Girtha Cooper. August 1985. Atlanta, Ga.

Perry, Homer. August 1983; September 1983. Atlanta, Ga.

Porter, Marion. June 1983–October 1987. Atlanta, Ga.

Protsman, Elizabeth. September 1988; May 1999. Atlanta, Ga.

Reeves, Annie Lou. December 1983. Social Circle, Ga.

Robinson, Henry. May 1985. Atlanta, Ga.

Rodd, Bessie Vaughn. December 1983; April 1987. Cincinnati, Ohio

Roddy, Nora Lee Madison. October 1984. Tiffin, Ohio

Simon, Edward L.. September 1983. Atlanta, Ga.

Sleet, Magnolia. December 1983. Cincinnati, Ohio

Sutton, Roswell O. February 2000. Atlanta, Ga.

Usher, Bazoline. March 1986; April 1986. Atlanta, Ga.

Wardlaw, Albert. February 1989. Atlanta, Ga.

Washington, Alice. June 1994. Atlanta, Ga.

Watts, Albert. June 1998. Atlanta, Ga.

Whitlock, Gussie. August 1988. Atlanta, Ga.

Williams, Lena. January 2000. Atlanta, Ga.

Williams, Roberta. May 1995. Atlanta, Ga.

PUBLISHED WORKS

Adams, Myron W. *A History of Atlanta University*. Atlanta: Atlanta University
  Press, 1930.

Alexander, Adele Logan. *Ambiguous Lives: Free Women of Color in Rural Georgia, 1789–1879*. Fayetteville: University of Arkansas Press, 1991.

———. *Homelands and Waterways: The American Journey of the Bond Family,
  1846-1926*. New York: Pantheon Books, 1999.

Bacote, Clarence A. *The Story of Atlanta University: A Century of Service,
  1865–1965*. Atlanta: Atlanta University Press, 1969.

Baker, Ray Stannard. *Following the Color Line: An Account of Negro Citizenship
  in the American Democracy*. New York: Doubleday, Page and Co., 1908.

Ball, Edward. *Slaves in the Family*. New York: Farrar, Straus and Giroux,
  1998.

Barber, Max. "The Atlanta Tragedy." *The Voice* 3 (November 1906):
  473–79.

Bleser, Carol. *The Hammonds of Redcliffe*. New York: Oxford University Press,
  1981.

Buckley, Gail Lumet. *The Hornes: An American Family*. New York: Alfred
  Knopf, 1986.

Bundles, A'Lelia. *Madam C. J. Walker*. New York: Chelsea House Publishers,
  1991.

———. *On Her Own Ground: The Life and Times of Madam C. J. Walker*. New
  York: Scribners, 2000.

Burton, Orville Vernon. *In My Father's House Are Many Mansions: Family and
  Community in Edgefield, South Carolina*. Chapel Hill: University of North
  Carolina Press, 1985.

Carter, Edward R. *The Black Side: A Partial History of the Business, Religious,
  and Educational Side of the Negro in Atlanta, Ga*. Atlanta, 1894.

Carter, O. E. *The Trolley Titans: A Mobile History of Atlanta*. Glendale, Calif.:
  Interurban Press, 1981.

Cashin, Edward J. *The Story of Augusta*. Augusta, Ga.: Richmond County
  Board of Education, 1980.

Church, Annette, and Roberta Church. *The Robert R. Churches of Memphis: A
  Father and Son Who Achieved in Spite of Race*. Ann Arbor: Edwards Brothers,

1974.

Crimmins, Timothy James. "The Crystal Stair: A Study of the Effects of Class, Race, and Ethnicity on Secondary Education in Atlanta, 1872–1925." Ph.D. diss., Emory University, 1971.

Crogman, William H. *Progress of a Race*. Atlanta: J. L. Nichols and Co., 1898.

Cromwell, Adelaide M. *The Other Brahmins: Boston's Black Upper Class, 1750–1950*. Fayetteville: University of Arkansas Press, 1994.

Crowe, Charles. "Racial Massacre in Atlanta, September 22, 1906." *Journal of Negro History* 54 (April 1969): 155.

Curry, Doris F. *Abstracts of Clayton County, Georgia, 1870 Census*. N.p., 1978.

Davis, Edwin, and William Ransom Hogan. *The Barber of Natchez*. Baton Rouge: Louisiana State University Press, 1954.

Davis, Leroy. *A Clashing of the Soul: John Hope and the Dilemma of African American Leadership and Black Higher Education*. Athens: University of Georgia Press, 1998.

Day, Caroline Bond. *A Study of Some Negro-White Families in the United States*. Cambridge: Harvard University Press, 1932.

Dittmer, John. *Black Georgia in the Progressive Era, 1900–1920*. Urbana: University of Illinois Press, 1977.

Downing, Antoinette F., and Vincent J. Scully Jr. *The Architectural Heritage of Newport, Rhode Island, 1640–1915*. 2d ed. New York: American Legacy Press, 1982.

Doyle, Don H. *New Men, New Cities, New South: Atlanta, Nashville, Charleston, Mobile, 1860–1910*. Chapel Hill: University of North Carolina Press, 1990.

Drago, Edmund L. *Black Politicians and Reconstruction in Georgia: A Splendid Failure*. Baton Rouge: Louisiana State University Press, 1982.

Du Bois, W. E. B. *Souls of Black Folk: Essays and Sketches*. Chicago: A. C. McClurg & Co., 1903.

———, ed. *Economic Co-operation among Negro Americans*. Atlanta University Publications, no. 12. Atlanta: Atlanta University Press, 1907.

———, ed. *The Negro American Family*. Atlanta University Publications, no. 13. Atlanta: Atlanta University Press, 1908.

———, ed. *The Negro in Business*. Atlanta University Publications, no. 4. Atlanta: Atlanta University Press, 1899.

Flynn, Charles L., Jr. *White Land, Black Labor: Caste and Class in Late Nineteenth-Century Georgia*. Baton Rouge: Louisiana State University Press, 1983.

Fox-Genovese, Elizabeth. *Within the Plantation Household: Black and White Women of the Old South.* Chapel Hill: University of North Carolina Press, 1988.

Franklin, John Hope. *From Slavery to Freedom: A History of Negro Americans.* 3d ed. New York: Vintage, 1969.

Garrett, Franklin M. *Atlanta and Environs: A Chronicle of Its People and Events.* Vol. 2. Athens: University of Georgia Press, 1954.

Gatewood, Willard P. *Aristocrats of Color: The Black Elite, 1880–1920.* Bloomington: Indiana University Press, 1990.

Greenwood, Janette Thomas. *Bittersweet Legacy: The Black and White "Better Classes" in Charlotte, 1850–1910.* Chapel Hill: University of North Carolina Press, 1994.

Gutman, Herbert. *The Black Family in Slavery and Freedom, 1750–1925.* New York: Pantheon, 1976.

Guy-Sheftall, Beverly. *Finding a Way: The Black Family's Struggle for an Education at the Atlanta University Center.* Atlanta: African American Family History Association, 1983.

Harlan, Louis. *Booker T. Washington: The Wizard of Tuskegee, 1901–1915.* New York: Oxford University Press, 1983.

———, ed. *The Booker T. Washington Papers: Vol. 4, 1895–1898.* Urbana: University of Illinois Press, 1979.

———, and Raymond W. Smock, eds. *The Booker T. Washington Papers: Vol. 9, 1906–1908.* Urbana: University of Illinois Press, 1979–80.

Henderson, Alexa. *Atlanta Life Insurance Company: Guardian of Black Economic Dignity.* Tuscaloosa: University of Alabama Press, 1990.

Henry County, Georgia, Obituaries, 1900–1907. Roswell, Ga.: W. H. Wolfe Associates, 1994.

Herskovits, Melville J. *The Myth of the Negro Past.* New York: Harper and Bros., 1941.

Holzhueter, John O. "Ezekiel Gillespie, Lost and Found." *Wisconsin Magazine of History* 60 (spring 1977): 179–84.

Jennings, Jan. "The Aesthetics of Everyday Interiors." In *The Interiors Handbook for Historic Buildings,* ed. Charles E. Fisher, Michael Auer, and Anne Grimmer. Washington, D.C.: Historic Preservation Education Foundation, 1988.

Kennedy, William J., Jr. *The North Carolina Mutual Story: A Symbol of Progress, 1898–1970.* Durham: North Carolina Mutual Life Insurance Company, 1970.

Kuhn, Clifford M., Harlon E. Joye, and E. Bernard West. *Living Atlanta: An Oral History of the City, 1914–1948*. Athens: University of Georgia Press, 1990.

Leslie, Kent Anderson. *Woman of Color, Daughter of Privilege: Amanda America Dickson, 1849–1893*. Athens: University of Georgia Press, 1995.

Lewis, David Levering. *W. E. B. Du Bois: Autobiography of a Race, 1868–1919*. New York: Henry Holt and Co., 1993.

Mason, Herman "Skip," Jr. *Going Against the Wind: A Pictorial History of African-Americans in Atlanta*. Atlanta: Longstreet, 1992.

Meier, August, and David Lewis. "History of the Negro Upper Class in Atlanta, Georgia, 1890–1958." *Journal of Negro Education* 28 (spring 1959): 128–39.

———. "Negro Class Structure and Ideology in the Age of Booker T. Washington." *Phylon* 23 (fall 1962): 258–66.

Merritt, Carole. *Homecoming: African American Family History in Georgia*. Atlanta: African American Family History Association, 1982.

Mixon, Gregory Lamont. "The Atlanta Riot of 1906." Ph.D. diss., University of Cincinnati, 1989.

Ovington, Mary White. *The Walls Come Tumbling Down*. New York: Harcourt, Brace, 1947.

Perdue, Robert E. *The Negro in Savannah, 1865–1900*. New York: Exposition Press, 1973.

Plante, Ellen M. *The Victorian Home: The Grandeur and Comforts of the Victorian Era, in Households Past and Present*. Philadelphia: Running Press, 1995.

Pomerantz, Gary M. *Where Peachtree Meets Sweet Auburn: The Saga of Two Families and the Making of Atlanta*. New York: Scribner, 1996.

Porter, Michael Leroy. "Black Atlanta: An Interdisciplinary Study of Blacks on the East Side of Atlanta, 1890–1930." Ph.D. diss., Emory University, 1974.

"Postscript by W. E. B. Du Bois." *Crisis* 34 (September 1927): 239.

Powers, Bernard E., Jr. *Black Charlestonians: A Social History, 1822–1885*. Fayetteville: University of Arkansas Press, 1994.

Rabinowitz, Howard N. *Race Relations in the Urban South, 1865–1890*. New York: Oxford University Press, 1978.

Rouse, Jacqueline Anne. *Lugenia Burns Hope: Black Southern Reformer*. Athens: University of Georgia Press, 1989.

Seale, William. *The Tasteful Interlude: American Interiors through the Camera's*

Eye, 1860–1917. 2d ed. Nashville: American Association for State and Local History, 1981.

Shapiro, Herbert. *White Violence and Black Response: From Reconstruction to Montgomery.* Amherst: University of Massachusetts Press, 1988.

Shields, Ruth Herndon. *The Descendants of William and Sarah (Poe) Herndon of Caroline County, Va., and Chatham County, N.C.* Privately printed, 1956.

Sollors, Werner, Caldwell Titcomb, and Thomas A. Underwood, eds. *Blacks at Harvard: A Documentary History of African-American Experience at Harvard and Radcliffe.* New York: New York University Press, 1993.

Spritzer, Lorraine Nelson, and Jean B. Bergmark. *Grace Towns Hamilton and the Politics of Southern Change.* Athens: University of Georgia Press, 1997.

Stickley, Gustav. *Craftsman Homes: Architecture and Furnishings of the American Arts and Crafts Movement.* 1909. Reprint, New York: Dover Publications, 1979.

Tagger, Barbara. "The Atlanta Race Riot of 1906 and the Black Community." Master's thesis, Atlanta University, 1977.

Thornberry, Jerry J. "The Development of Black Atlanta, 1865–1885." Ph.D. diss., University of Maryland, 1977.

Thurmond, Michael L. *A Story Untold: Black Men and Women in Athens History.* Athens: Clarke County School District, 1978.

Vlach, John Michael. *Back of the Big House: The Architecture of Plantation Slavery.* Chapel Hill: University of North Carolina Press, 1993.

Walker, Juliet E. K. *The History of Black Business in America: Capitalism, Race, Entrepreneurship.* New York: Twayne Publishers, 1998.

Walrond, Eric D. "The Largest Negro Commercial Enterprise in the World," *Forbes,* 2 February 1924.

Weare, Walter B. *Black Business in the New South: A Social History of the North Carolina Mutual Life Insurance Company.* Urbana: University of Illinois Press, 1973.

White, Walter. *A Man Called White: The Autobiography of Walter White.* New York: Viking, 1948.

Index

References to illustrations are printed in boldface type. The abbreviation AFH refers to Alonzo Franklin Herndon.

Academy Stock Company, 107, 113–14
Adams, Kathleen Redding, comments of, about Herndon family, 54, 58
Addison's disease, 125
Allen, Peyton, and NAACP, **82**
American Academy of Dramatic Arts, 105-7, **106**, 113–14
American Missionary Association, and Atlanta University, 40, 49
Antony and Cleopatra, Adrienne's recital of, 16–18, **18**, 21
apprenticeship, AFH's, 11–12
As You Like It, Adrienne's production of, 104
Atlanta: AFH's arrival in, 33–35; Black colleges in, 48–50, 54, 62–63 (*see also* Atlanta University). *See also* race riots
Atlanta Age (publication), 77, 80, **81**
Atlanta Benevolent and Protective Association: AFH's purchase of, 75–76; first office of, in Rucker Building, 80
Atlanta Life Insurance Company, **207**; employees of, **168, 200, 203–4,** 203–6; establishment of, 198, 201, 241 (n. 8); expansion of, 201–2; Norris's involvement with, 201–5, **203–4,** 213–14; precursor of (*see* Atlanta

Mutual Insurance Association); Senatorial Campaign (sales campaign), **203–4,** 203–5
Atlanta Loan and Trust Company, suit filed by, against AFH, 81–82
Atlanta Mutual Insurance Association, 122; competitors of, 83–84; employees of, 80–84, **81,** 161–62, **162, 164–66,** 204–5; establishment of, 77–84; expansion of, 161–70; investigation of, by state, 192, 197–98; management problems at, 190, 192, 195; Norris's involvement with, 189–90, 197; precursors of, 70, 75–77; relocation of, **167,** 169, 190; and Standard Life, 162–68, 205. *See also* Atlanta Life Insurance Company
Atlanta University, **48**; AFH's affiliation with, 64; and "co-education of the races," 49–50, 227 (n. 5); establishment of, 40, 48–50; faculty and staff, **50,** 61–63, **62–63,** 109 (*see also* Herndon, Adrienne McNeil [AFH's first wife], as teacher); protection of, during race riots, 95; students, **30, 31,** 40, **49, 52–53,** 54
Aunt Alice (Alice Newsome), and Norris, 2, 13

Badger, Roderick (wealthy Black Atlantan), 41, 54

Bailey, James (Adrienne's brother-in-law), 124, 131, 179

Bailey, Jennie McNeil (Mrs. James) (Adrienne's half sister), 21, **22**, 46, 124, **124,** 132; relationship of, with AFH, 179–80, 201

Bailey, John Henry (Jennie's son), **70**

Barber, Max, and Niagara Movement, **74,** 75

barbershops, **160,** 208; AFH's early days in, 4–5, 32–35, 159, 161; attacked during race riots, 85–86, 89–90, 92, 94–95; fires at, 41–43, 45; Markham House (Loyd Street), 25, 35–39, **36–37,** 41–43, **42,** 64; Norcross Building (Marietta Street), **42,** 43–45; Norris's involvement with, 185–86; 100 Pryor Street (Candler Building annex), **69,** 70; and racism (*see* racism, in service industries); 34 North Forsyth, 101. *See also* 66 Peachtree Street (barbershop)

Battle, Anthony (Jonesboro barber), 32

Beall, Noble P. (barbershop owner), 35

Belasco, David (theater manager), 16, **18,** 28–31, 105

Belasco Medal, Adrienne awarded, 114

Ben Greet Company, 104

Benton Harbor, Mich., Black resort, 135

Bernhardt, Sarah, Adrienne's idol, 104

Berry, Archer (AFH's cousin), 65, 102, 107, 132

Berry, Florence (AFH's cousin), 65, 132, 136, 148, 172–73, **173,** 188, 240 (n. 11)

Betts, William R., partnership of, with AFH, 35

Boston, Adrienne's debut in, 16–18, **18,** 21–23, 27–30

Boston School of Expression, Adrienne's studies at, 16, 23, 30, 55

Bowden, Elizabeth, **182**

Bowen, James W. E., response of, to race riots, 96, **96**

Brown, McHenry (Mack) (friend of

AFH), 2, 13

Brownsville, race riots in, 96, 99

Bryant, Rev. Peter James: and Atlanta Benevolent and Protective Association, 75–76; response of, to race riots, **99,** 100

Bumstead, Horace (president of Atlanta University), 23, 50, **50**

Bumstead Cottage, 50, 59, **60, 61,** 227 (n. 7), 228 (n. 24); sale of, to Atlanta University, 102

Burns, Jennie, **134**

Campania (ship), 154

Campbell, William (Herndon residence carpenter), 112, 233 (n. 24)

Carpathia (ship), **144,** 145

Chamblee, Robert (Atlanta Mutual/Atlanta Life employee), 83, 192, 197, 201, **204,** 204–5

Chivers, Walter (Atlanta Mutual employee), **165**

Cobb, Erasmus (free Black barber), 36

Connally, Carrie Hennie Herndon (Mrs. Herbert) (AFH's niece), 65, **70,** 72, **72**

Crogman, William, response of, to race riots, 94, **94,** 97

Crystal Palace (Peachtree Street barbershop). *See* 66 Peachtree Street (barbershop), renovations of

Cumming, Joseph Bryan (Adrienne's relative), 27, **27**

Cumming, Maj. Joseph B. (Adrienne's relative), 27

Curry, Anna, founder of the School of Expression, 23, 25

Curry, Samuel, founder of the School of Expression, 23, **23,** 25

Daniel, Albert, comments of, on Crystal Palace, 157–59

Darktown, race riots in, 94–95

Davis, Benjamin (newspaper editor): and Atlanta Mutual embezzlement, 192, 195; and NAACP, **82;** response of, to race riots, 98, **98**

Decatur Street (Atlanta), 86–87, **87**

Diamond Hill, 48–49, 64–65

Dohme, Robert, business relationship of, with AFH, 43

Du Bignon, Anne (Adrienne's stage name), **24, 29**; at American Academy of Dramatic Arts, 105–7, 113–14; Boston debut of, 16–18, **18**, 21–23, 27–30; at School of Expression, 16, 23, 30, 55. *See also* Herndon, Adrienne McNeil (AFH's first wife)

Du Bois, Nina Gomer, **63**

Du Bois, William E. B.: at Atlanta University, 61–62, **62–63**; and Herndon residence, 122–23; and Niagara Movement, 73–75, **74**, 77; response of, to race riots, 97, 99, **100,** 102

education, Black, 48–50, 54, 62–64, 195–96, 225 (n. 10), 227 (n. 5). *See also* Atlanta University

embezzlement, at Atlanta Mutual, 192, 195, 197

Faison, Charles (Markham House barber), **37,** 39, 70, 155

Fambrough, Julia (Social Circle native), 65, 107

Fellowship Baptist Church (Social Circle, Ga.), 2, 8–10, 13–14, **14,** 222 (n. 15)

fires, at barbershops, 41–43, 45

First Congregational Church (Atlanta), 14, 39–40, 97, 209, 211, 212

Fleming, Martha (Mattie). *See* McNeil, Martha (Mattie) Fleming (Adrienne's mother)

Fleming, Thomas (Adrienne's maternal uncle), 20, **21**

Fleming, William R. (Adrienne's maternal grandfather), 19–20

Florida estate. *See* Moss Hill (AFH's Florida estate)

free Blacks, 36, 136, 174–75

Gate City Free Kindergarten Association, 180, **181,** 212

George Britt Company, 23

Gibson, Alberta (Mrs. Truman), **162**

Gibson, Truman Kella (Atlanta Mutual employee), 161–62, **162,** 190, 238 (n. 10)

Gillespie, Catherine Lucas Robinson (Jessie's mother), 137, **138,** 175, 236 (n. 9)

Gillespie, Charles (Jessie's brother), **139**

Gillespie, Emma (Jessie's half sister), 137, 139–40, **140**; death of, 182–83

Gillespie, Ezekiel (Jessie's father), 136–37, **138,** 174–75, 236 (nn. 6, 9)

Gillespie, Ida (Jessie's sister), **139**

Gillespie, Jessie. *See* Herndon, Jessie Gillespie (AFH's second wife)

Gillespie, Mary (Jessie's half sister), 137, 139–40, **140,** 183, 208

Gillespie, William (Jessie's half brother), **141**

Gillette, William (theater manager), 31, 105

Hall, George Cleveland (friend of Jessie), 133, 135, **143,** 209

Hall, Theodocia (Theo) (friend of Jessie), 133–35, **134,** 209

Hankerson, Harriet (Adrienne's maternal grandmother), **19,** 19–20, **21,** 27, 54, **126,** 128

Harrison, James T. (Atlanta Mutual/Atlanta Life employee), **166,** 204–5

Harvard University, Norris at, 190, 195–96

Haywood, Lemuel (Atlanta Mutual/Atlanta Life employee), **164–66,** 201, **204,** 204–5

Heard, James, killed in race riot, 96

Herndon, Adrienne McNeil (AFH's first wife), 6, **16, 54, 125**; chain of theaters proposed by, 238 (n. 10); courtship of, 39–41; death of, 125–28; dramatic readings by, 103, 232 (n. 9); education of, 25, 39–40, 51–

Herndon, Adrienne McNeil (cont'd)
55, **52–53**; family of, 17–21, 27,
46–47, 51, 102, 218 (see also names of
individual family members); in family
photographs, **19, 22, 70, 101, 110,
126**; funeral of, **128**, 128–30; and the
Niagara Movement, 75; and Norris,
54–58, 107–9; oratorical skills of,
27–28; prenuptial agreement of, 16,
25; response of, to race riots, 101–2;
Shakespearean productions by,
16–19, **18**, 21, **30**, 31, 104–5; "Spiritual Temple" (story), 171; as teacher,
25, 31, 52–55, **53**, 61–63, **63**, 102–5,
161–62, 238
(n. 10); wedding of, 25, **26**. See also
Du Bignon, Anne (Adrienne's stage
name); Herndon residence
Herndon, Alonzo Franklin ("Lonza"),
229 (n. 4); and Adrienne's death,
125–26, 130–32; and Adrienne's
drama pursuits, 16, 21–28, 31, 107;
arrival of, in Atlanta, 33–35; and
Atlanta Loan and Trust Company,
81–82; and Atlanta University, 64;
courtship of, Adrienne, 39–41; —,
Jessie, 135–41; death of, 209, 211,
242 (n. 24); educational background
of, 40–41, 63–64; entrepreneurial
spirit of, 4–6, 40–41, 47, 78; family of,
6–15, 65, 102, 119–21, 173,
205, 217 (see also names of individual
family members); at Herndon Cemetery, 10–11, **12**, 15; in Jonesboro,
Ga., 4, 11, 32–33, 159, 161; at Mayo
Clinic, 198–99, 201; at Moss Hill,
177–78, 180–83, 195; and NAACP,
78–79; and National Negro Business
League, 79; and the Niagara Movement, 72–75, **74**, 77; philanthropy of,
64, 78, 180, **181**, 208, **210**, 211;
photographs of, **1**, 6–7, **9**, **32**, **43**, **46**,
61, **67**, **81**, 155–56, **187**, **189**, **207**;
—, with family, **4**, **70**, **110**, **184**, **193**;
—, with groups, **63**, **74**, **163**, **169**,

203–4; —, on second honeymoon,
142, **146–47**, **151–52**; in Social
Circle, Ga., **4–5**, **12**; real estate holdings of, 45, 65–66, 202, 205–6, **206**
(see also barbershops; Moss Hill
[AFH's Florida estate]); relationship
of, with Jennie, 179–80; —, with
Norris, 184–89, 201–2; response
of, to race riots, 92, 94–95, 97–98,
100–102; on second honeymoon,
143–54; and sharecropping, 2–4, **5**,
6–7, 11–12, 121; and slavery, 2, 6–9,
119–21;
and Social Circle, Ga., connections,
1–4, 6–15, 65; wedding of, to Adrienne, 25; —, to Jessie, 140–43. See
also Atlanta Life Insurance Com-pany;
Atlanta Mutual Insurance Association;
barbershops; Herndon residence
Herndon, Alonzo Franklin, II (AFH's
nephew), 72, **72**, 205
Herndon, Carrie Hennie (Mrs. Herbert
Connally; AFH's niece), 65, **70**, 72, **72**
Herndon, Carter (AFH's maternal grandfather), 11–12, 121
Herndon, Charles T. (AFH's half
brother), **8**, 9
Herndon, Cora (Emory's wife), 1–2, 13,
212
Herndon, Elisha (AFH's half brother),
2, 13
Herndon, Emory (AFH's half nephew),
1–2, 13
Herndon, Frank (AFH's father), 6–15,
221 (n. 8), 222 (n. 15); will of, ex-
cludes Black children, 14
Herndon, Harriet (AFH's maternal
aunt), 9
Herndon, Jessie Gillespie (AFH's second
wife), **133–34**, 133–35, **139**, **171**;
and Atlanta Life, 209; and Black
society, 133–35, 174–75; courtship
of, 135–41; death of, 213; family of,
136–40, **138–41**, 174–75, 182–83,
208, 219, 236 (nn. 6, 9); at Herndon

residence, 171–74; on honeymoon, 143–54, **146–47, 152**; at Mayo Clinic, 198–99, 201; at Moss Hill, **176,** 177–78, 180–83, **182**; relationship of, with household staff, 172–74; —, with Norris, 177–78, 186; wedding of, 140–43

Herndon, Merriman (AFH's paternal grandfather), 10, 222 (n. 15)

Herndon, Norris Bumstead (AFH's son), **131, 188, 191;** and Adrienne's death, 125, 130–32; and art appreciation, **186,** 187; and Atlanta Mutual/Atlanta Life, 189–90, 197, 201–5, **203–4,** 213–14; death of, 214; early childhood of, 54–58, **55–57, 59, 63;** in family photographs, **19, 70, 101, 108, 110, 153, 184, 191, 193;** on father's second honeymoon, **142–43,** 143–54, **147;** at father's second wedding, 140–41; at Harvard, 190, 195–96; at Niagara Falls, **74,** 75; in Philadelphia after race riots, 101–2, 107–9; philanthropy of, 212–14; relationship of, with father, 184–89, 201–2; —, with Jessie, 177–78, 186; —, with Mattie, 56–57, 102, 154, 178–79; sexual orientation of, 188, 240 (n. 13); in Social Circle, Ga., 1–2, 12–13; social group of, 196, 202–3

Herndon, Sophenie (AFH's mother), 3–4, **4,** 6–11, 119–21

Herndon, Thomas (AFH's brother), **4,** 9, 13, **70–71,** 71–72, 121

Herndon Building (Auburn Street), 202, 205–6, **206**

Herndon Cemetery (Herndonville, Ga.), 10–11, **12**

Herndon residence, 129; architectural influences on, 109, 111, 116–19, 121; construction of, 112, 114–16, 123–24, 233 (n. 24), 234 (n. 31); exterior, **115,** 116, **123, 172,** 234 (n. 31); furnishings for, 171–72, 213; household staff of, 172–74; interior,

116–22, **117–18, 120, 122;** lot for, purchased, 105, 233 (n. 14); murals, 119–21, **120;** as National Historic Landmark, 213

Hill, Lyndon (Atlanta Life employee), **204**

honeymoon, AFH's second, 143–54

Hope, John: and Black colleges, **62,** 62–63; in Europe, 151; exclusion of, from meetings after race riots, 97; and Jessie, 174; and NAACP, **82**

Hope, Lugenia, at Morehouse College, 62

Hunt, Richard Morris, influence of, on Herndon residence, 111

Hutchins, William Dougherty, partnership of, with AFH, 34–35

Industrial Life and Health Insurance Company, 83, 169, 230 (n. 20)

insurance industry: racism in, 78, 197–98; regulations affecting, 76–77, 162, 169–70, 205, 230 (n. 20). *See also* Atlanta Life Insurance Company; Atlanta Mutual Insurance Association; Industrial Life and Health Insurance Company

Jim Crow. *See* racism

Johnson, Charles H., and NAACP, **82**

Johnson, Henry Lincoln (AFH's attorney), 82; response of, to race riots, 98

Johnson, Solomon (Atlanta Mutual/Atlanta Life employee), 80, 83, 204–5

Jones, Scipio Africanus (attorney), 170

Jonesboro, Ga., AFH in, 4, 11, 32–33, 159, 161

King, Rev. L. H., and NAACP, **82**

Knights and Daughters of Tabor, mutual-aid society, 77

Knox, Bill (friend of AFH), 9, **10**

Lane, O. H. (Atlanta Mutual employee), **165**

Laney, Lucy, founder of Haines Institute, 104, **104**

Lee, George (Atlanta Life employee), **203–4**, 209, 211

Leonard Street Orphanage, **181, 210,** 211

Lindsay, Joseph C. (Atlanta Mutual employee), embezzlement by, 192

lynchings. *See* race riots

mansion, Herndon. *See* Herndon residence

Markham House (Loyd Street). *See under* barbershops

Martin, Eugene (Atlanta Mutual/Atlanta Life employee), **165–66,** 197, 201, **204,** 204–5

Mayo, Febe (slave), 9

Mayo Clinic, AFH and Jessie at, 198–99, 201

McGhee, Frederick L., and Niagara Movement, **74,** 75

McNeil, Adrienne. *See* Herndon, Adrienne McNeil (AFH's first wife)

McNeil, Archibald (Adrienne's stepfather), 21, 46, 51

McNeil, Jennie Olive. *See* Bailey, Jennie McNeil (Mrs. James) (Adrienne's half sister)

McNeil, Martha (Mattie) Fleming (Adrienne's mother), **20, 56, 179;** and Adrienne's death, 125–26, 130, 132; and Adrienne's education, 51; death of, 184–85, 189; family of, **19,** 19–21, 27, 46–47, 51, 218; relationship of, with Jennie, 132, 179–80; —, with Norris, 56–57, 102, **153,** 154, 178–79, **191**

McNeil, Willie (Adrienne's half brother), 21, **22**

Merchant of Venice, The, Adrienne's direction of, **30,** 31

militia, state, response of, to race riots, 90, 92–96, **93**

Miller, Alice (Adrienne's teacher), 51, 226 (n. 1)

"Million Dollar Team" (Atlanta Mutual employees), **165**

miscegenation, 47–48; in Adrienne's family, 17–21, 27, 47; in AFH's family, 6–15

Mitchell Street Public School, Norris at, 58, **59**

mob violence. *See* race riots

Morehouse College, 62–63

Morgan, Clement, and Niagara Movement, **74,** 75

Morris Brown College, 62, 213

Moss Hill (AFH's Florida estate), **176–77,** 177–78, 180–83, **182,** 195; sale of, 205; as Senatorial Campaign retreat, **203–4,** 203–5

Murphy, Eleanor (Mrs. William Oscar), 182, **182**

mutual-aid groups, Black: Good Samaritans, 39; Knights and Daughters of Tabor, 77; transformation of, 68–70, 75–78

National Association for the Advancement of Colored People (NAACP), 78–79, **82**

National Negro Business League, 79

Newsome, Alice (Aunt Alice), and Norris, 2, 13

New York City, Adrienne's studies in, 105–7, 113–14

Niagara Movement, 72–75, **74,** 77, 213

Norris, Frances (Auntie Nor), 46–47, **47,** 54, 102, **148,** 226 (n. 1); death of, 148

Odd Fellows Building, 169, 189, 190

Pace, Harry, and NAACP, **82**

Palmer, Loring: as friend of AFH, 54, 132–33, **135**; as friend of Jessie, 133

Penn, William F., and NAACP, **82**

Perry, Heman (Black businessman), 162–68, **163**, 198, 205

Philadelphia, Norris in, after race riots, 101–2, 107–9

philanthropy: AFH's, 64, 78, 180, **181**, 208, **210**, 211; Norris's, 212–14

Pitts, Ammina, at Bumstead Cottage, 59, 61, **61**

Proctor, Rev. Hugh, comments of, on racial unrest, **97**, 98

race riots, **88, 91**; barbershops attacked during, 85–86, 89–90, 92, 94–95; and Black retaliation, 90, 92, 94–96; in Brownsville, 96; casualties of, 86, 89–90, 95–96, 99–100; in Darktown, 94–95; on Decatur Street, 86–87; impact of rumors on, 86, 89, 92, 99–100; response to, 86, 94, **95**; —, by Adrienne, 101–2; —, by AFH, 92, 94–95, 97–98, 100–102; —, by Black leaders, 94, **95**, 96–100; —, by Du Bois, 97, 99, 102; —, by police, 87, 96; —, by state militia, 90, 92–96, **93**; —, by White leaders, 86–87, 90, 96–98, 100

racism: in Black community, 48, 195; in education, 49–50, 62–63, 195–96, 227 (n. 5); in insurance industry, 78, 197–98; in newspaper coverage, 141; and passing for White, 20–21, 46–47, 61, 195 (see also racism, in the theater); in service industries, 34, 43–44, 65, 67–68, 73, 213; in the theater, 17–21, 30–31, 113–14, 130; and voting rights, 68, 174–75, 229 (n. 4), 236 (n. 6). See also miscegenation; race riots

Rucker, Henry A. (Black businessman), 80, 230 (n. 24)

rumors, impact of, on racial unrest, 86, 89, 92, 99–100

Russell, Howard Walter (Atlanta Life employee), **204**, 204–5

Sargent, Franklin, at American Academy, 113

School of Expression, Adrienne's studies at, 16, 23, 30, 55

Scott, Emmett (Washington's secretary), 166, **169**

Senatorial Campaign, Atlanta Life sales campaign, **203–4**, 203–5

Shakespeare's plays, Adrienne's productions of, 16–19, **18**, 21, **30**, **31**, 104–5

Shanks, Christopher (Atlanta Mutual employee), 190; embezzlement by, 192

sharecropping, and AFH's family, 2–4, **5**, 6–7, 11–12, 121

Silvey, John, business relationship of, with AFH, 36–37

Simkins, Clara (Adrienne's cousin), **70**, 108, **108**

Simkins, Rachel (Adrienne's maternal aunt), 102, 108, **108**

Sims, David H., and NAACP, **82**

66 Peachtree Street (barbershop), 32, **33, 44**, 45, **157**, 213; renovations of, 155–61, **158, 160–61**

slavery, and AFH's family, 2, 6–9, 119–21

Smith, Nelson (Jonesboro barber), 32

Social Circle, Ga.: AFH's beginnings in, 1–15; architectural influence from, on Herndon residence, 111; residents from, in Atlanta, 65

society, Black, 133–35, 174–75, **175**, 202–3

Southview Cemetery, Herndon family plot in, 129, 185, 211

"Spiritual Temple" (story by Adrienne), 171

Standard Life Insurance Company, 162–68, 205

Steele, Carrie (founder of orphanage), 225 (n. 11)

Steele, James (barber), 35, 225 (n. 11)

Stephens, Elizabeth A. ("Addie"), 19.

Stephens, Elizabeth A. *(cont'd)*
  See also Herndon, Adrienne McNeil
  (AFH's first wife)
Stephens, George (Adrienne's father),
  21, 223 (n. 12)
Stevens, Caroline, and Mattie's death,
  184

Tate, James (wealthy Black Atlantan),
  35, 225 (n. 10)
Tavares, Fla. *See* Moss Hill (AFH's Florida
  estate)
Terrell, Joseph (Georgia governor),
  response of, to race riots, 90, 96
theater: Adrienne's productions for,
  16–19, **18**, 21, **30**, 31, 104–5; racism
  in, 17–21, 30–31, 113–14, 130. *See
  also* Du Bignon, Anne (Adrienne's
  stage name)
Titanic (ship), 141, 145
Towns, George: at Atlanta University,
  61–62, **62–63**, 115–16; and NAACP, **82**
Towns, Nellie, **63**
Twelve Club (exclusive Black society),
  175

Union Mutual, 82–83; acquired by
  Atlanta Mutual, 168–69
Usher, Bazoline, comments of, about
  Adrienne, 59, 61

Vine City, **64**, 64–66

Walton, Fred, killed in race riot, 86, 95
Ware, Edmund Asa, 62–63, 109, 227
  (n. 7)
Ware, Edward Twitchell, 109; Adri-
  enne's eulogy given by, 128–29
Washington, Booker T., 73, 79, **79**, 101,
  169; death of, 169
West Broad Street School (Savannah,
  Ga.), 51, **51**
White, George: Adrienne boards with,
  40–41; response of, to race riots, 94,
  95
White, Walter F.: and NAACP, **82**, 94;
  response of, to race riots, **85**, 86, 94
Whitney, Ga., 9–10, **11**
William Gillette Theater Company,
  31
Williams, William W., partnership of,
  with AFH, 101, 155
Woodward, James (Atlanta mayor), re-
  sponse of, to race riots, 86–87, **88**, 97
Wright, Louis T., and NAACP, **82**
Wright, William, insurance commis-
  sioner, 197–98

Zachary, Gilbert, killed in fire, 43

CPSIA information can be obtained
at www.ICGtesting.com
Printed in the USA
LVOW02s1508230517
535558LV00018B/285/P